THE MAGIC OF HOLOGRAPHY

THE MAGIC OF HOLOGRAPHY

Philip Heckman

ILLUSTRATED WITH DIAGRAMS
BY THE AUTHOR & PHOTOGRAPHS

Atheneum 1986   New York

To Nancy,
with love and thanks

Library of Congress Cataloging-in-Publication Data

Heckman, Philip M.
The magic of holography.

Bibliography: p. 275
Includes index.
SUMMARY: Presents a history of the developments in
holography from early discoveries in optics to the first
hologram of Denis Gabor. Also discusses possible
future applications of holography.
1. Holography—Juvenile literature.   [1. Holography]
I. Title.
TA1540.H43   1986   621.36′75   85-27489
ISBN 0-689-31168-0

Published simultaneously in Canada by
Collier Macmillan Canada, Inc.
Composition by P & M Typesetters, Waterbury, Connecticut
Printed and bound by Fairfield Graphics,
Fairfield, Pennsylvania
Designed by Rueith Ottiger/Levavi & Levavi
First Edition

CONTENTS

PREFACE

"The best way to learn about holography is to make a hologram. It's very easy," says Dr. Tung H. Jeong, pioneering holographer and professor of physics at Lake Forest College in Illinois.

In his summer workshops, Dr. Jeong has made holographers out of children as young as ten. In fact, he finds them better students than adults. "Older people worry too much; they're afraid they're going to do something wrong. Young people almost always make the best holograms."

This book won't put a hologram in your hands, but it will do the next best thing: It'll tell you how the next hologram you see works.

In the Introduction, you'll meet holograms and read about some of their amazing properties. A hologram is like a photograph in some ways. But in many more ways the two are very different.

The rest of the book progresses from the most familiar aspects of light and its behavior to the strangest. The journey will have four stages.

Part I describes a hologram as a device for changing image information from one form to another. "A hologram is a program that tells a beam of light what to do," is how Dr. Jeong puts it. And the light beam's job is to form an amazingly realistic image—an image that makes it difficult to tell whether the objects it shows are present.

Part II takes a look at the way light behaves in general. Most of the properties that go into making and viewing a hologram are behaviors you've seen at work elsewhere. Like Dennis Gabor, the inventor of holography, you'll learn to look at these behaviors from the point of view of light itself.

Part III tells how light, acting as described in Part II, makes a hologram and then, using the hologram, recreates an image identical to the original object.

Part IV is a survey of the jobs holograms do and possibly will do. The future of holography is wide open at this point. Dr. Jeong says when he talks to young people about holography, "They ask about things too outlandish for me to think about. But I never say no. I say not yet, maybe you'll have something to do with making it work."

ACKNOWLEDGMENTS

This book is the product of conversations with and contributions from dozens of people, without whom I would've been hopelessly lost. Above all, I must thank André Gabor, whose prompt and patient responses to my numerous requests for information about his brother were as generous as they were invaluable.

I'd like to thank Dr. Tung H. Jeong, Lake Forest College, who inspired this book, for finding the time to talk with me about the state of the art, and allowing me to photograph holograms from his private collection.

For critical readings of portions of the manuscript, I thank Professor Bahaa Saleh (electrical engineering); Professor David Lindberg and Associate Professor Daniel Siegel (history of science); and post-doctoral student Ron Reynolds and Professor Emeritus Ragnor Rollefson (physics) of the University of Wisconsin/Madison. I also thank Ronald R. Erickson for his detailed notes and remarks in a pre-publication review and his enthusiastic guidance. I take full responsibility for any factual errors this book might contain despite the excellent comments of these authorities.

I am indebted to the individuals and organizations listed in the photo credits for their information as well as the illustrations they provided. I am especially grateful to L.S. Bartell, University of Michigan; David Casasent, Carnegie-Mellon University; Gordon W. Ellis, University of Pennsylvania; John A. Gilbert, University of Wisconsin/Milwaukee; to Toni Sue Bowins, research associate, and Maurice Halioua, director, Center for Optics, Lasers, and Technology, New York Institute of Technology; B. Michael Donahoe, NASA Ames Research Center; Dr.

Ralph F. Wuerker, TRW Energy Development Group; and Dr. George W. Stroke for correspondence above and beyond the call of duty.

I also am grateful to the staff of the Museum of Holography, New York City, for their hospitality and the use of their library and files; and to New York artists and holographers Rudie Berkhout, Sam Moree, Jason Sapan, and Dan Schweitzer for their insight and vision. Special thanks go to Matt Hansen and Bob Lopez for showing me how to make a hologram, to Franklynn Peterson and Judi K-Turkel for showing me how to sell a book, and to my editor, Marcia Marshall, for showing me how to make this tale of light more coherent.

Finally, I thank my wife, Nancy, for her patience and support, and my daughter, Cass, for her sense of wonder.

Philip Heckman

PART 1

THE IDEA OF HOLOGRAPHY

WHAT'S SO SPECIAL ABOUT A HOLOGRAM?

The museum is mostly dark, with spots of light centered on the various displays. Holding hands, a father and his two-year-old daughter enter and begin to tour the room. The man wants to pause at every exhibit, first peering at it closely, then stepping back and moving from side to side for a better look. The little girl wants to run.

Soon a display catches her eye and the girl hurries to grab her father's fingers and pull him toward it. He follows, slightly off balance, to a face on the wall. The man hoists his daughter to his hip so she's even with the figure's gaping mouth.

"What is it?" he asks.

"A lion," she answers, delighted to be both scared and safe.

"Want to pet him on the nose?"

She reaches out eagerly, then giggles as her hand passes back and forth through empty air.

First Sight

Eighteen years earlier, holographic images of such realism were
new to almost everyone. The first seemingly solid image made
of nothing but light was only a few months old when it made
its first public appearance at a scientific conference. Emmett
Leith, one of its inventors, describes how experienced scientists
behaved when they got their first sight of a hologram:

> We presented a paper, and we also brought holograms
> along to show. Spectra-Physics at that time was a new com-
> pany, trying to sell lasers. They had rented a suite in the ho-
> tel where the meeting was held, and they invited us to show
> holograms using their facilities. This was a perfect match. Af-
> ter the talk it was mentioned that the holograms of which we
> spoke would be on display in the Spectra-Physics suite.
> There was a general exodus from the meeting room, no doubt
> to the consternation of the following speakers, who then
> were left with an audience of reduced size. The suite was
> filled to capacity, and there was a long line reaching through
> the door and far down the corridor. Although these viewers
> were optical scientists, they nevertheless reacted much as
> novices, continually inquiring where the object (a toy train)
> was hidden.[1] (Fig. 1–1)

FIG. 1–1 The train that wasn't there amazed some of the world's most
respected scientists in 1964.

Your first impression of a good hologram is likely to be the same. Whether the image you see appears to be hiding behind the hologram as the toy train did or sticking out in front like the lion's face, its realism will surprise you. A holographic image copies an object in almost every characteristic except physical substance.

Changing View

No single photograph can show how closely a holographic image resembles a solid object. Holographic realism is the product of everyday sights you probably take for granted. But you've never seen these sights in an ordinary photo.

Objects in real life have sides. If a photograph shows one side of an object but not the other, it will never show more. If a hologram shows one side and not the other, however, you can often see the other side just by moving your head.

The two photographs in Figures 1–2 a and b show how different viewing positions reveal the sides of an object seen in a hologram. The same effect is even more pronounced when one object that has been holographed stands in front of another. Moving your head then hides or reveals what's in the background.

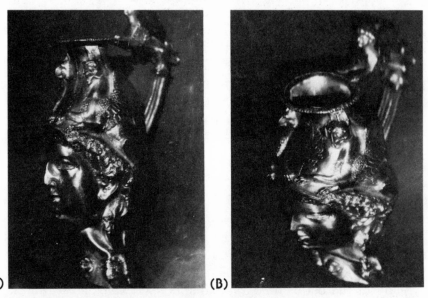

(A) (B)

FIG. 1–2a, 1–2b This amphora, a vase for carrying wine or oil, dates from the fourth or third century B.C. The camera shows how its holographic image allows you to see both side and inside.

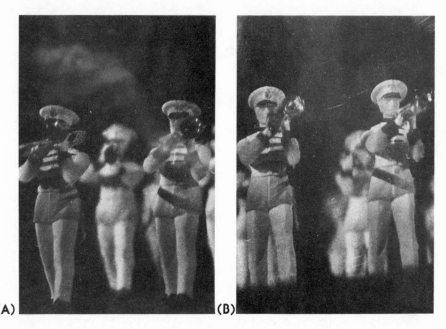

(A)   (B)

FIG. 1–3a, 1–3b Notice the shift in position of the band members and the difference in the highlights on their trombones as the photographer's point of view changes.

The changes in a holographic image as you shift your viewing position sometimes are quite detailed. For example, you expect highlights and shadows to look different from different sides of an object. And so they do in its holographic image. The members of the marching band in Figure 1–3 *a* and *b* show different profiles to the camera, depending on its position. They also peek from behind their instruments. And to top off the performance, the reflections from their trombones change as well.

Neat trick, you say? Well, there's more, because a good hologram mimics an actual object in other ways, too.

"Special Effects"

What you see in a good hologram seems real because it is. Your eyes are not being fooled when you watch the holographic scene change as you move. The hologram is actually showing you a different view.

Many of the better holograms display scenes of great depth. Holographed objects seem to extend a noticeable distance from front to back. This is not an optical illusion. A camera detects the same effect and proves your eyes are not being deceived.

For example, to bring the band members in the second row into sharp focus for Figure 1–4, the camera had to be adjusted. This made the front row blurry. Your eyes have to make a similar adjustment to focus for actual objects or their holographic images.

Holograms reproduce scenes faithfully. If it's a quality hologram, you'll be able to see whatever changes would occur in the appearance of the actual objects. In other words, the holographic image behaves exactly as the actual object would appear under the same circumstances. This is most obvious when a holographic scene contains a lens.

Notice how the lens in Figure 1–5 *a* and *b* magnified different parts of the phone behind it, according to the camera's point of view. Hold a real lens over a real phone and you'll see the same effect.

The properties of holograms described so far are nothing out of the ordinary in themselves. In each case, they copy everyday effects you're already familiar with from the world around you. But because these effects are impossible in a photograph, they're a big surprise at first.

FIG. 1–4 The photographer had to adjust the camera to focus a deeper part of the holographic image than that shown in Figures 1–3a and b.

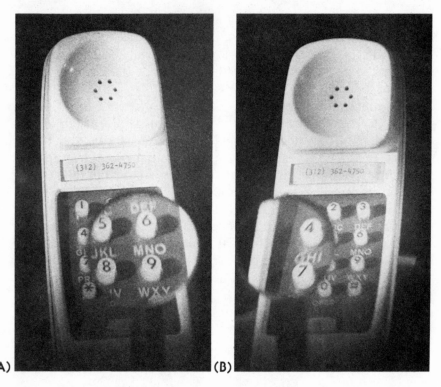

(A) (B)

FIG. 1–5a, 1–5b A hologram of a lens acts just like a lens.

The Holographic Window

Looking at a hologram is a lot like looking through a window. What you see depends on where you're standing. Your view from the the right side is different from your view from the left, the top, or the bottom. A photograph can't begin to give you this viewing freedom.

The advantage holograms have in this regard becomes more dramatic when you consider the view through only part of the window. Let's say your shade is drawn, but it has a hole in the center. From a distance you can see little through the hole. But at close range, almost everything visible from the whole window is also visible through the hole.

Cut a photograph in half and you have half an image, no matter how you look at it. But half a hologram presents more than half a view. In some cases, you'll still be able to see practically the entire original image (Fig. 1–6 a,b).

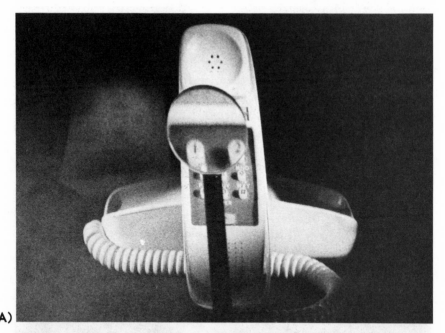

FIG. 1–6a, 1–6b One of the most startling properties of holography is the hologram's ability to produce a full image from a part of itself. The intact hologram (6a) shows one telephone. After it was cut in two, each half retains the ability to show an entire phone, but from a slightly different angle. If these two pieces were cut in half again and again, the total number of images would double and redouble. Soon, however, each fragment would become such a small window that viewing the entire image would be difficult. Even so, each piece of the hologram would continue to carry a record of a full image, no matter how faint it became!

Color and Motion

Some holograms show colors far more brilliant than those in a photograph. The hologram photographed for the dust jacket of this book is one of these. Not only does its image change with point of view, but its colors also change. This kind of hologram produces scenes in all the colors of the rainbow from the white light of an ordinary lamp.

The holograms mentioned so far make still-life images, that is, images of objects that are motionless. Other holograms, however, display scenes that change in a way suggesting movement. These holograms aren't movies, but their effects are somewhat similar (Fig. 1–7 a,b).

These are a few of the wonders holography has to offer. Other effects and properties need further explanation, which will come later in the book.

(A)

FIG. 1–7a, 1–7b A viewer who walks around this hologram sees changing images of a man sticking his hand farther and farther into the movie audience. The overall effect of the images coming into view one after the other is similar to the effect of consecutive movie frames—appearance of motion.

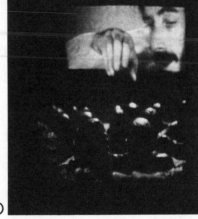

(B)

The Magic of Holography

You can look at an actual object from many positions and see many slightly different views of it. Holography is a way of using laser light to make a single recording of the way an object looks from many different positions. This recording, the hologram, has the ability to change the light shining on it into the same multiple views as if the actual object were still in front of you.

Holograms come in many forms, with many properties. Some seem to do the impossible. Even Dennis Gabor, who made the first hologram in 1947, would have been surprised if he'd been able to look ahead to see what became of his invention. By the time he stood beside his own holographic portrait (Fig. 1–8), holography had proved itself as entertainment and tool. And the magic seems far from exhausted.

A hologram is one bit of evidence of the magical machinery of the universe. Its beauty and mystery are products of universal laws of physics. As a sign of how well those laws mesh, a hologram is no more remarkable than the sun or the surface of a pond or the workings of your eye. Their complexities are equally intricate.

And that's the real magic.

FIG. 1–8 Dennis Gabor, the inventor of holography, was in his seventies when he finally met his holographic self.

LET THERE BE SIGHT

Got a penny?

Take a look at the man on the front—the sixteenth president of the United States. Abraham Lincoln unknowingly posed for the coin just a year before his assassination.

The artist who designed the mold for the first Lincoln penny needed a model to work from. He might have chosen any of a number of drawings, engravings, or sculptures of this famous statesman. Instead he selected the most accurate record available from 1864, the state of the art at the time. He chose a photograph.

Holography and photography are closely related in some respects: Both use film and both are visual recordings. So it's tempting to describe holography as "three-dimensional photography." But that's a poor description because a hologram and a photograph are more dissimilar than similar.

That's why it's helpful to explain holography by showing how it differs from photography. The best place to begin understanding these differences is with the subject of sight.

A Look at the Eye

Figure 2–1 shows how the structures of the eye form a pathway for light from your surroundings. Simply put, this light enters your eye through a clear cover called the *cornea*, which bends the light to pass through an adjustable membrane called the *iris*. The iris delicately controls the amount of light allowed into your eye through a hole called the *pupil*. The pupil dilates, or expands, to admit more dim light and constricts to limit brightness and glare.

Just behind the iris, a flexible lens directs light onto the *retina*, which is a light-sensitive area on the back wall of your eyeball. Some special cells there, the cones, react to brightly lit colors. The remaining cells, the rods, provide low-light, black-and-white vision. Under the right conditions, the rods are sensitive enough to detect a candle flame thirty or more kilometers away.

Your eye's lens is adjustable—tiny muscle fibers change its shape, depending on whether the object in view is near or far away. The lens brings the light the cornea focused from every

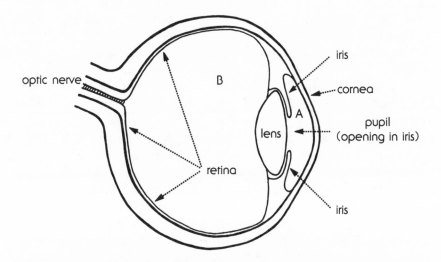

FIG. 2–1 Main structures of the eye: *Cornea,* clear tissue that helps focus light entering the eye; *iris,* colored tissue that expands and contracts to regulate the amount of light allowed through an opening called the *pupil; lens,* a mass of clear fibers that changes shape to bring the images of objects both near and far into focus on the *retina,* a layer of light-sensitive cells connected to the *optic nerve.* Chamber **A** is filled with a pressurized clear fluid that keeps the cornea hard and brings nutrients to it and the lens. Chamber **B** contains a clear jelly that keeps the retina pressed against the back of the eyeball.

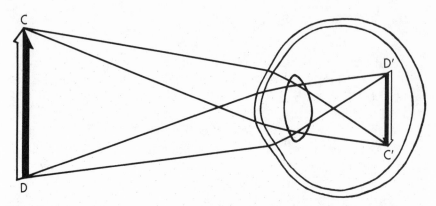

FIG. 2–2 Light from every point on an object reaches the eye's entire cornea. Here you see two of the many possible routes light takes from point **C** to the retina. No matter where light from C enters the cornea, the lens will focus it on the corresponding point **C¹.** Light from every other point on the object produces its own corresponding image point on the retina, just as light from **D** ends up at **D¹.**

unobstructed point on the object to a corresponding point on your eye's retina. The focusing power of the cornea and lens produces an upside-down, reversed image of the object inside your eye (Fig. 2–2).

The eye is often compared to a camera in the way it works to gather, focus, and detect light. This analogy is unfortunate not only because it's backward—the eye came first, of course—but also because the comparison suggests the eye is all there is to seeing.

The eye is known as the organ of sight, but it's not the only structure in the body that contributes to vision. Just as important are the brain and the nerves that link it with the eye. Damage to any of these parts can change the ability to see.

Actually, what happens after the light strikes the retina is even more impressive than what happened before. Up to that point, the light is a mass of information. After it's been processed by the brain, it can be taken as evidence of an object's existence.

A Look at the Brain

Your eye's retina is an extension of your brain. Here the information carried in an image is translated into a language your brain can "read." The image helps your brain construct a view of the world.

Those light-sensitive retinal cells, perhaps as many as 130 million of them, are connected to the brain by way of a bundle of fibers known collectively as the optic nerve. Light falling on each cell produces a chemical change that causes a tiny electrical signal to flow along the nerve. Each cell is able to send several signals a second.

The electrical messages from cells throughout the retina tell your brain a great deal about the image your eye has detected. But your brain has quite a bit of work of its own to do. After all, the image on the retina is made up of many millions of signals that need to be analyzed.

Seeing calls for some thought (largely unconscious) and some experience. It's the brain that makes sense of the image information entering the eye. It's the brain that reads the eye's messages and interprets them to identify what is visible. In a sense, your life determines much of what you see. What a newborn infant may know only as a colorful jumble of shapes, a toddler recognizes as his parents.

Consider the optical illusion in Figure 2–3. From a single image, your brain can reach at least two different conclusions about what it sees. The eye is an important organ of sight, certainly. But properly speaking, the eye doesn't see—the brain does.

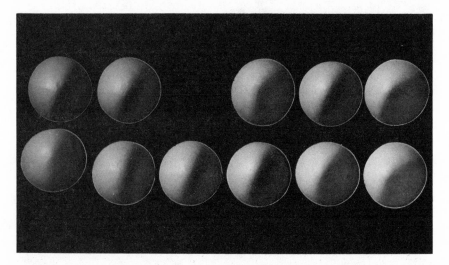

FIG. 2–3 Eggs or eggshells? Your brain receives the same information about this photo whether you interpret it as a view of bulging eggs or hollow eggshells. You can even switch from one interpretation to the other. It's impossible, however, to see both at the same time.

2–D Plus 2–D Equals 3–D

From front to back, your organs of sight operate with remarkable precision. Demands on their powers can be extreme, from catching a ball to reading a book, for instance, but visual tasks of all kinds are possible because of the way eye and nervous system work together.

The lens of your eye directs incoming light onto the retina, which has the shape of the inside of the eyeball. The image formed on it is two-dimensional; it has height and length but no depth. It's as thin as a photograph cupped in your hand.

The eye's two-dimensional image is the raw material from which the brain senses a three-dimensional world. Even though the image on your retina has no depth of its own, it contains some information that suggests depth to an observer.

These "one-eyed" depth clues work best when the object viewed is familiar. By now you can distinguish a round ball from a flat disk by its shading alone, for example, and you realize that a human being who appears to be smaller than your hand is actually of normal size but far away.

Artists take advantage of your sense of the "correct" size of familiar objects when they paint them different sizes in different parts of the canvas to suggest they're nearer or farther away. Other clues of perspective come from overlapping objects or objects shaded to indicate roundness. These visual tips are similar to those that enable an experienced driver who has the use of only one eye to accurately judge distances between cars on the highway.

Most of us receive extra information for sensing depth, however. This information about the third dimension comes from another source—the other eye. The information from each eye is not merely duplication. The 2-D images from your two eyes are decidedly different. The following demonstration shows this clearly:

Close your left eye. Raise one finger at arm's length and hold it so that it covers some small object on the far side of the room.

Now, without moving your finger or your arm, open your left eye while closing your right. Notice that your finger no longer covers the object. It appears to have shifted, even though you didn't move at all.

Remember this second position as you close your left eye and open your right. Your finger now covers the object again. By alternately opening and closing your eyes in this way, you can make your finger seem to jump back and forth.

This effect is known as *parallax*. The one-eyed observer has to shift his head to get a new point of view. This causes objects nearby to appear to move sideways in relation to distant ones. But the two-eyed observer doesn't have to move because his eyes automatically record a scene from positions about six-and-a-half centimeters apart. As a result, the left eye detects more of the left sides of objects while the right eye detects more of the right sides. This cooperation is known as "binocular vision."

The two-dimensional images on the retinas of your eyes are distinctly different. By combining them, your brain creates the effect of depth in a single three-dimensional view.

Two eyes working together—a process known as binocular vision—can send the brain pairs of 2-D images in a continuous stream, from which the brain fashions 3-D pictures of the world. A single photograph can't offer an observer more than one 2-D image. In other words, a single photo doesn't contain enough visual information to reveal the parallax effect. But there's a photographic way to trick the brain into producing a 3-D view. It's called stereoscopic photography.

Stereo for the Eyes

Two lenses side by side are like two eyes side by side. Photographs made with a pair of lenses about 6.5 cm apart record separate 2-D images. If the left eye receives only the left image and the right eye only the right one, the brain can combine them for 3-D viewing, just as if the observer were standing before the actual scene.

A stereoscope is a device for focusing the two separate images of a stereo-photograph like the one in Figure 2–4. The 1851 Crystal Palace exhibition in London displayed a stereoscope that proved to be very popular with the public. Once Queen Victoria took an interest, stereo-photography became a full-blown fad. By 1858 the craze hit the United States, and one newspaper carried a European visitor's estimate of a stereoscope in every American home within twenty-five years. This never came to pass, but stereo-photographs are still with us. For many years toy stores have sold small plastic stereoscopes for viewing pairs of color slides mounted on stiff cardboard disks.

"Three-D movies" became popular during the 1950s, and still

FIG. 2—4 Stereograms—also known as stereographs, stereopticon cards, or simply stereo cards—were very popular a hundred years ago. The difference between the right eye's image and the left eye's is best seen by comparing the edges of the two photos, or by noting the parallax shift of the rock that appears between the horse's ears.

appear from time to time. These achieve a stereo effect by dual filming. In one method, the image the left-hand camera recorded is projected in one color, say blue, while the right-hand camera's image is shown in red. Cardboard spectacles with one blue and one red plastic eyepiece filter out the opposite color and allow each eye only its proper image. Certain effects, such as an on-coming train or a sword thrust toward the audience, can be thrilling.

But there's a limit to the magic of stereo-photography. For no matter how real the appearance of 3-D, a stereoscope produces only a single view from a single pair of 2-D images. Changing your seat in the theater makes no difference in the picture on the screen. And no amount of stretching will let you peek behind a prop in a stereo-photograph. What you need for realistic 3-D viewing are images from every side of a scene, the more the better. What you need is a hologram.

Infinite Stereo

Although you won't be able to find a holographic movie at a theater near you for some time, holography already surpasses stereo-photography in its ability to produce a still-life 3-D effect. That's because a hologram is like a window.

Looking through a window, you can observe anything within your line of sight. Views through a window are dependent on the observer's position. An infinite number of 2-D image pairs is possible, as many pairs as there are different places to look through the glass. No two images are exactly alike. From any single position, your eyes always have two different lines of sight. The infinite number of 2-D image pairs allows your brain to produce an infinite number of 3-D views. As long as you could draw a straight line from a spot on the object through the window to your eye, that spot is visible.

Viewing a holographic image of a face is very much like viewing a real face through a window. As long as it's possible to draw a straight line from a spot on the face to the holographic film, that spot will appear in the hologram. A hologram will record a 2-D image of anything visible from that point on the film (Fig. 2–5 a, b).

As in real life, no matter how small an observer's change in position, a holographic view changes, too. Each eye detects a different 2-D image, and there are an infinite number to choose from. It's almost as if the hologram were a special stereoscope—

(A) (B)

FIG. 2–5a, 2–5b From the first camera position (5a), the left ear of the woman in this hologram is visible.

As you and the camera move toward the left side of the hologram, the 2-D images your eyes detect change constantly, giving your brain the information it needs for an ever-changing 3-D view. From the extreme left (5b), neither eye receives a 2-D image that includes the woman's left ear because her head now blocks it from sight.

one that automatically presents the viewer with an unlimited supply of 2-D image pairs.

Believing Is Seeing

When it comes to believing a holographic image, we have an advantage over the people in the crowds that gathered in New York City to catch a glimpse of some of the first photographs ever made. The closest things to photographs then were drawings, engravings, and paintings. Of course, viewers were amazed to see photographic detail for the first time. It was detail that artists up to that time had been able only to suggest, even with great skill and effort.

Yet strange as the new wonder must've seemed at first, photos quickly became familiar sights. Twenty-one years after photography came to America, supporters of candidate Abraham Lincoln spread his photograph throughout the country during the presidential campaign.

In those days, you could've made an appointment to pose in any of several dozen big-city studios. You even could've had your picture taken by someone working for Lincoln's most famous photographer, Mathew Brady. In only a quarter century in many parts of the country, photography went from magic to matter-of-fact.

It's hard for us to imagine that amazement now. After all, today's wonders—flying machines as big as buildings, viewing machines as fast as light—are far more complicated than those of Lincoln's day. Yet the hologram as an accurate record of a scene is better than a photograph by as much as a photo is better than a drawing.

You'll get used to holography. The more you see of it, the more quickly you'll believe your eyes when you view a hologram. In fact, once holograms become the mass-market product photographs had become in Lincoln's lifetime, you'll probably take them for granted, too.

There's one way to prevent that from happening. That's to dig a little and find out what makes holography work. The closer you look at a hologram, the more magical it can seem. You can start by wondering what our flat penny would look like today if the man who photographed Abraham Lincoln had been a holographer instead (Fig. 2–6).

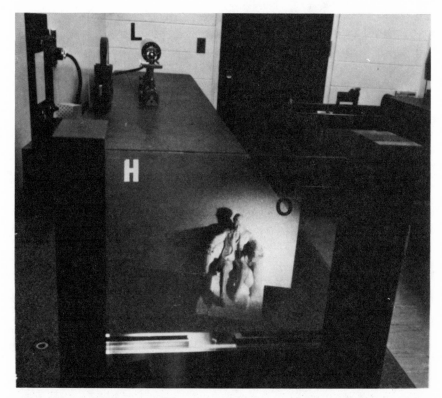

FIG. 2–6 A state-of-the-art portrait of Abraham Lincoln would be a hologram if he were alive today. (L, laser; H, hologram; O, 3-D image.)

RECIPE FOR A HOLOGRAM

Imagine yourself in a room that's empty except for a table and chair. Have a seat—you're going to make the table disappear.

The table is round, made of wood, with enough room for eight people; it must weigh 500 pounds. And you're going to make it vanish, just by flipping that switch in your hand. Go ahead: Try it.

That's it; table's gone. Good work.

I know the lights are out. That's the trick: You can't see a thing without light.

Well, the table disappeared, didn't it?

OK, OK, turn the lights on again. So you didn't like the disappearing table. How about a car? Or an elephant?

Splitting a Spitting Image

You'd probably demand your money back if you had paid for a performance like this, and you'd deserve it. Everyone knows you can't see in the dark. But this little demonstration does prove the relationship of light to image-making. Without light there can be no image. Let's show the recipe for this dependence:

Light + Object = 3-D Image

The recipe shows how important light is for the making of an image. It also suggests that an object must be present as well. After all, that's how a typical disappearing act works—when an object disappears it takes its image with it.

But is it true that a lifelike image <u>always</u> requires the presence of an object? No. For example, stars are so distant their light takes a very long time to reach us, thousands and thousands of years in many cases. It's very likely, then, that some of the starlight you see comes from stars that have changed. Whether they've since exploded or collapsed, the starlight images they made thousands of years ago live on without them.

A hologram is another example of an image existing without its original object. A hologram can split an image from its object and preserve it, as a second recipe shows:

Light + Hologram = 3-D Image

A hologram of an object produces the same image the object does. In many cases, the holographic image is so realistic it fools both eye and brain (Fig. 3–1). That's because the image a

FIG. 3–1 Ordinarily the only way we have of knowing whether an object exists at a distance is by its image. Here the hand is real. But the glass?

hologram makes carries almost as much 3-D information as there is in the actual object.

Preserving Image Information

Our ability to store information enabled the human race to accumulate a great deal of knowledge. Before there was writing, humans relied on the memories of individuals, who passed information from the old to the young by repeating tales.

Unfortunately, spoken messages tend to change with each retelling. And if storytellers died before they'd taught all they knew, some information was lost forever. That's one reason our knowledge of prehistoric humans is so meager–they left little more than bones behind.

Written language enabled the human race to record its thoughts and its spoken words more accurately. Written records supply today's scientists, for example, with discoveries the scientists of yesterday made. In this way, scientific knowledge grows and technology improves. Now each year brings so many discoveries and inventions that it's nearly impossible to keep track of them all. Holography is just one of many wonders developed from written information passed along through time.

Preserving information in written form has its disadvantages, too, however. Sometimes writers don't describe their observations and discoveries as well as they might. In addition, making a written record of some phenomena would be tiresome, if not impossible. Can you imagine trying to describe all the creatures in a drop of water using words alone? That's why it's valuable to record images directly—sometimes a picture is worth more than a thousand words. If the picture is very accurate, it will capture details a writer could never express.

At one time, the best pictures were drawn by hand. Early scientists who studied the creatures they saw through their crude microscopes produced many handsome and detailed drawings. However, recording images this way was a long, laborious task. Although a finished drawing might include an enormous amount of information, it represented many hours of observation and artistic skill.

Later scientists saw more detail with improved microscopes. The invention of photography then allowed them to record as much or more image information in a few seconds or less.

Holography—as a method of recording visual information—is as much an improvement over photography as photography was over drawing. To demonstrate this, let's set up recipes that describe how a photograph and a hologram work. We can find a good model recipe in the type of written language called a code or cipher*.

How a Code Works

A typical language code disguises a message by changing it to a series of symbols according to rules known only to certain people. Call the coded message a cipher. Then the following recipe shows how to encode and decode a message:

(Encoding) Message + Rules = Cipher

(Decoding) Cipher + Rules = Message

Notice that the rules do double duty. In the first version of the recipe, they provide the guidelines for transforming the message into the cipher. In the second, the same rules provide the means to change the cipher back into the message. The following example shows a code whose rules call for substituting consecutive counting numbers for the letters A through Z:

(Encoding)	Message	+	Rules (partial)	=	Cipher
	Hello		e = 5 h = 8 1 = 12 0 = 15		8 + 5 + 12 + 12 + 15

(Decoding)	Cipher	+	Rules (partial)	=	Message
	8 + 5 + 12 + 12 + 15		e = 5 h = 8 1 = 12 0 = 15		Hello

Other ciphers work much the same way. Consider a catcher's signs to a pitcher. Suppose the message is "Throw a fastball," and the code contains a rule that says, "fastball = 2." The catcher encodes the message by flashing two fingers. The pitcher, in turn, decodes the cipher by applying the same rule.

---

*Although codes and ciphers are different, many people use the terms as synonyms; this book will, too.

Recipe for a Photograph

Some devices act like ciphers without having rules in the usual sense. Sometimes a device sets coding guidelines just by the way it's built. Take an ordinary black-and-white photograph, for instance. Whether the photographer was working with glass plates more than a century ago or with the latest equipment today, the recipe for a photograph is essentially the same:

(Encoding) Object's 3-D Image + Light = Photo Negative

(Decoding) Photo Negative + Light = Object's 2-D Image

The photographic message consists of image information from a fully three-dimensional object. But the camera sees and records only one 2-D image of the infinite number available. The cipher is made when this limited image information is transferred to a chemical record in the form of a photographic negative. The purpose is not to disguise the information, of course, but to preserve it. Objects in real life change and so do the images they produce. Image information differs from one moment to the next, and finally is lost.

To preserve one stage of ever-changing image information, photography converts it to a more stable, long-lasting form— into chemical changes in light-sensitive film. The photographic key to encoding image information is the ordinary light that acts on the film in certain predictable ways. The physical rules for the behavior of ordinary light cause changes in the film itself, changes that can be decoded again by ordinary light following predictable rules.

The Photographic Code

Figure 3–2 shows a photographic cipher: It's a negative print. Think of the dark and light portions of the original autographed baseball as the message. As you can see, the photographic code has recorded this message in reverse. What was bright in the original image is changed to dark and what was dark is changed to bright. That's why the black signatures on the actual baseball appear white in the negative while the white leather appears black. This photographic cipher records a single flat view of the original image in a code so simple you can still recognize the baseball.

Ordinary light unlocks the photographic cipher when it shines through the negative onto light-sensitive paper. Bright

FIG. 3–2 The simple photographic code of a white-and-black negative preserves a single 2-D view of a baseball by reversing dark and bright areas of its original image.

areas of the negative (the autographs) are clear and let light through to make dark lines on the paper. Dark areas of the negative (the leather) block some or all of the light to leave matching areas of the paper white. This pattern of clear and dark areas is a guide that produces the more familiar black-and-white image of a positive print (Fig. 3–3). As you know, the image in this positive print is only one two-dimensional version of the many available in the image of the actual object.

FIG. 3–3 The rules for decoding the photographic cipher in Figure 3–2 undo the reversal of dark and bright areas to reproduce this positive print. The image it provides is one 2-D version of the many in the original image. From a different position, the camera would have recorded a different 2-D image— but still only one per photo.

Recipe for a Hologram

A hologram can record much more of the information carried in an object's image than a photograph can because its code is more powerful. It makes the recipe for a hologram look like this:

(Encoding) Object's 3-D Image + Light = Hologram

(Decoding) Hologram + Light = Object's 3-D Image

The holographer first uses light to encode all the 3-D image information from an infinite number of 2-D views of the object, according to certain chemical rules about the way light interacts with film. The same rules later allow light to decode the holographic cipher and recreate the original 3-D view out of all its 2-D images.

The Holographic Code

The two different images of a baseball in Figures 3–4a and b come from the same hologram. The light that decoded the hologram to produce these images also produced many other versions, all of which are visible from various viewing positions.

 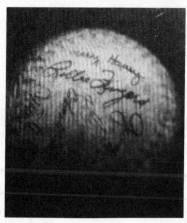

(A)   (B)

FIG. 3–4a A hologram records enough visual information to reproduce multiple 2-D views of an object. The holographic image in this photo reveals the top seam of the baseball. The ball's spherical surface makes Rollie Fingers's signature appear to bend upward at either end.

FIG. 3–4b The same hologram can reproduce many, many images other than the one in Figure 3–4a. From this viewing angle, the holographic image does not show the baseball's top seam, and Mr. Fingers's name appears to bend downward slightly at the ends. This hologram is one of the author's first.

FIG. 3–5 You have to look at a hologram through a microscope to see the holographic code. This pattern of microscopic lines and specks called *fringes* serves as a guide for reproducing an infinite number of 2-D images.

Figure 3–5 shows a magnified view of another holographic cipher. The microscopic pattern of lines in this code is so complex it looks nothing like the original scene. But during viewing, this microscopic pattern produces multiple 2-D images. Each image shows more of one side of the object and less of the other. This is exactly the same parallax effect you get when you view an actual object.

Your brain interprets the many 2-D images in a hologram as one rounded 3-D view. The hologram is a stable recording of most of the changeable information carried in the original image light. If you held the baseball hologram in your hands, you could make the ball seem to turn before your eyes, just as the real ball would.

The Holographic Advantage

A hologram can provide more information about an object because it captures more than one 2-D image at a time. This advantage over a photograph becomes clearer when you consider an image in space.

Photography expanded the ability of scientists to record what their microscopes revealed, but it must have been frustrating at first. Cameras hooked up to microscopes are unable to bring more than a thin horizontal layer of a scene into focus. Living creatures in a drop of pond water seldom hold still for picture-taking. So it can take many exposures to capture a good view of subjects moving constantly under a microscope.

Holography offers a more efficient solution by recording the 3-D view of a whole water drop and its contents all at once. Instead of having to chase a living creature around by constantly refocusing, a researcher can study the "frozen" holographic image at leisure. To examine other specimens, the viewer has only to focus on another part of the now stable image (Fig. 3–6). One

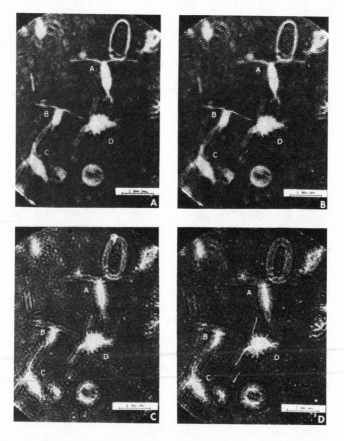

FIG. 3–6 To make these four photos of the same hologram, the camera was attached to a microscope and focused on different layers of the image. Photo A shows creature **A** (a crustacean called a copepod) focused three millimeters (mm) from the plane of the hologram. Copepods **B**, **C**, and **D** are focused 5, 19, and 33 mm from the hologram, respectively. The range of focus shown here means the holographic image is at least 3 centimeters (cm), or 30 mm deep.

hologram could therefore do the work of many photographs, recording visual information about an entire organism or group as it looked in life.

This technique, called holographic microscopy, has been used to record other very fast and very small objects. For example, scientists have made holograms in a few billionths of a second to track the movement of individual tiny particles thrown off by burning fuel. From changes in 3-D position and the time between exposures, they can determine the particles' velocities—information that can help them design better rocket propellants. Holographic microscopy is also helping scientists search for evidence of the most basic building blocks of matter released in rare collisions between subatomic particles. So perhaps the final secret of what atoms are made of will appear first in a hologram.

Drawings, photographs, and holograms represent an increasing capacity for storing visual information. The image in a photograph is the same no matter how you look at it. But it would take an infinite number of photographs to record the same amount of image information in a single hologram.

Redundancy

A hologram has so much image information it can reproduce a good view despite some information losses. Scratch a photograph and part of its image is erased forever. Scratch a hologram and image information on either side of the damaged area enables you to look behind the scratch.

The holographic window gives a viewer a lot of flexibility. If something isn't visible through one portion of the hologram, try another. A hologram has this wider view because it records image light in a different way than a photograph does.

The photographer uses a lens or set of lenses to focus image light from each point on the object to a corresponding point on the photographic film. Because the holographer uses no focusing lens in this way, image light from every visible point on the object strikes all areas of the holographic film within reach in a straight line. This means the hologram's entire surface records image information about every visible part of an object. This "redundant" or repetitive record enables a fragment of a hologram to show a whole image. You saw evidence of redundancy when an intact hologram showing one view of a telephone (Fig. 1–7a) was cut in half to reveal two different—and complete—views of the phone of the same time (Fig. 1–7b).

Beyond Initial Surprise

For casual observers, a hologram may seem unremarkable—just another trick of technology like video and audio tape recorders, stereo phonographs, and computers. But the forces of nature that make holograms work are so intricate, and yet so fundamental, they seem worthy of the name of magic.

Holograms are information storehouses of almost unlimited size. The holographic recipe shows what a hologram is, but it says nothing about the way the power of the holographic code works. For example, how is the laser light necessary for holography different from ordinary light? And how do those little specks and swirls of the holographic code reproduce so many two-dimensional images so faithfully?

Answering the "hows" of holography requires learning more about that form of energy we call light. The explanation of light's movement through space and its relationship with matter and with itself is an astonishing tale. Light is the key, then, for decoding holograms.

PART 2

A LITTLE LIGHT
READING

HISTORY IN A HOLOGRAM

On December 10, 1971, in Stockholm, Sweden, an elderly man received an award he considered the greatest scientific honor of all for work he had once thought a failure. The man was Dennis Gabor. The work was the invention of holography. The award was the Nobel Prize in Physics (Fig.4–1).

"A True Polymath"

The hologram's inventor was born in 1900 with the name Gábor Dénes. Later he became better known outside his native Hungary by its English version, Dennis Gabor.

A polymath is a person of great and varied learning. André Gabor used the word to describe his brother, who "sometimes amused himself by writing little pieces of poetry in one or the other of the five languages of which he had full command, and even played a hard game of tennis."[2]

Bertalan Gabor encouraged his three sons' wide-ranging interests in many ways. The house was full of books and works of

FIG. 4–1 Dennis Gabor accepts the 1971 Nobel Prize in Physics from the King of Sweden.

art, and Dennis was allowed to listen in on the conversations of adults who came to visit. The mere mention of a strange author or title often sent the boy running for the library shelves.

Dennis had a remarkable memory. At the age of eleven or twelve his father challenged him to learn a famous German poem by heart. Within weeks, Dennis was able to recite all 423 lines without a mistake. His gift for recall enabled him to learn Italian at the rate of two hundred words a day. Not everything went as smoothly, however. Once a teacher insisted the ten-year-old Dennis be sent to a special school for unmanageable children. But Mr. Gabor persuaded the instructor his lessons were too easy, and Dennis remained in class with no further trouble.

Shortly after that, father and son visited a science museum in Germany. The exhibits made a strong impression on Dennis. His interest in science became all-important afterward.

Because there were no good advanced math and physics books written in Hungarian, Dennis began studying German textbooks when he was about fourteen. The next year, the Gabor family moved to an apartment where the three boys had room to set up a laboratory. There they experimented and built equipment. André remembers the devices they put together in-

FIG. 4–2 Just about all the scientific knowledge needed to make a hologram was available when Dennis Gabor posed for this photo at about the age of twenty. A quarter century passed, however, before he became the first to understand all the facts.

cluded an overhead projector that could throw the images of drawings or book pages onto a screen, and a high voltage battery.

Dennis's education at home served him well in his university studies later. His solid background in physics and math, combined with his knack for invention, prepared him for his life's work. As a young man in his twenties (Fig. 4–2), Dennis Gabor couldn't have dreamed of the successes to come. But although others might have been able to see how the work of earlier scientists fit together to make a hologram, it was Dennis, grown-up and still curious, who made the connection first.

The Path Roundabout

Although Dennis Gabor was born in Budapest, he studied in Berlin, and lived and worked in England for many years. In fact, he accepted the Nobel Prize as a British citizen. And later, up to his death in 1979, Gabor spent most of his time working in the United States.

This roundabout career path suggests the development of holography in miniature. The hologram didn't spring into existence all at once, or even in the lifetime of a single individual.

The roots of holography reach back centuries to the efforts of hundreds of other scientists. And since Gabor described its basic principles in a 1948 article,[3] holography has passed into the hands of many more students and scientists.

It's difficult to trace all the threads of scientific discovery that led to the first hologram. Some contributions are obvious, some less so, but perhaps just as significant. Trying to compile a list of the most important contributors to our knowledge of optics—the study of light and vision—is a bit like looking at a hologram. What you see depends on your point of view.

Fortunately, we have the opinion of an expert to guide us. Dennis Gabor left us with his view of history in a hologram.

The Men in Gabor's "Holo-Fame"

The first holograms ever made were very different from today's. Because he didn't have the right kind of light source, Gabor was limited to making very tiny holograms. To find a suitable object the right size, he made a list of names. Then he shrunk the list photographically until it was only a millimeter wide. The result was a transparency consisting of tiny black letters on clear film.

The transparency was a photograph, so it held just a single two-dimensional view. This meant each holographic image also was flat. And because such an image was no more than a centimeter (10 mm) across, Gabor needed to magnify it for study. The first holographic images looked like bad photos, indistinct and blurry. But they were unique because they had been formed by a process never used before.

Gabor continued to experiment with his new way of recording images. His original purpose for developing holography was to improve the electron microscope, a special instrument more powerful than the ordinary microscope, but one that fell frustratingly shy of its potential. Gabor lived to see the results of electron holography. And his work has produced even greater success in other areas since the invention of the laser in 1960. Gabor had long been aware of the scientific roots of his development. Perhaps to show the debt he felt to earlier scientists, Gabor used their names as subjects for his early holograms.

The first transparency carried the names Huygens (HI-genz), Young, and Fresnel (fray-NEL). Two later holograms repeated them and added eight more: Newton, Faraday, Maxwell, Kirchhoff (KER-kof), Planck, Einstein, Bohr, and Dirac—all students of light (Fig. 4–3a, b).

Gabor must have thought a great deal of these men to honor them in this way. Without exception, they were extraordinary scientists, although they weren't the only ones whose work was important to optics. Several of them also made important discoveries in other fields.

These pioneers undoubtedly influenced Gabor's own study of light. In later chapters, you'll read about some of their ideas and experiments which helped explain light's behavior. Each of the eleven contributed directly or indirectly to the invention of holography. Their work is a guide to the scientific principles Gabor built upon.

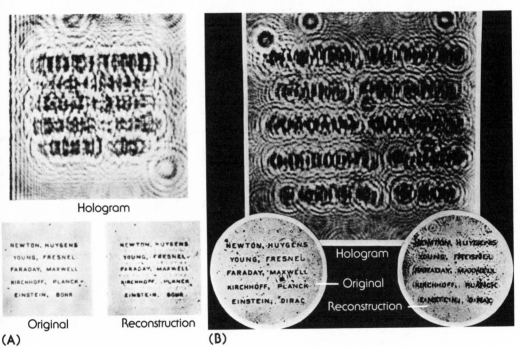

FIG. 4–3a, 4–3b The images of early holograms are crude compared to those of today, which must have been nearly impossible to foresee. André Gabor writes: "Not being a physicist, I completely failed to appreciate the significance of holography when my brother first explained it to me. I could not even understand why he was so elated."[4]

Dennis Gabor's biographer reveals these photos of Gabor's invention were made in 1947, and he suspects the version with Bohr's name came first. This seems likely because the original transparency with Dirac's name is improved. With a sharper transparency, Gabor made a better hologram, which produced a sharper reconstructed image. But no close associates the author contacted were able to explain why Gabor substituted Dirac's name for Bohr's. If there is any significance to the switch, Dennis Gabor's death in 1979 ensures it will remain a mystery.

They're also an excellent example of the way the human race pursues more and more accurate knowledge through the life's work of dedicated individuals.

Isaac Newton

The men in Gabor's "Holo-Fame" represent a radical change in the way science has studied our world during the past three centuries. To compare the work of one of the earliest, Newton, with that of one of the latest, Dirac, is to examine a difference in attitude as well as technique.

Three hundred years ago scientists were called philosophers. For the most part, those who specialized in optics expected light to be revealed as just another aspect of the everyday world. Men like Sir Isaac Newton thought light could be explained in ordinary terms if they only studied it enough. Their method was to observe events and check their conclusions with experiments. Then they applied everyday logic to build a theory for the events they witnessed. A theory is a line of reasoning based on observations and experiments that can be repeated by others.

Isaac Newton (Fig. 4–4) was born in England. As a young man he concentrated on the study of math and mechanics, which is a field concerned with the interaction of forces and matter. One product of this study—Newton's laws of gravity—made a spectacular impression on fellow scientists when he presented the work at the age of forty-two.

Newton established his reputation further with the invention of calculus, an advanced form of mathematical analysis. By the time he died, Newton was easily the most famous and respected scientist in Europe. So it's not surprising that his theories about light were widely accepted and defended long after his death.

Newton believed light consisted of streams of particles, which he called corpuscles. Bodies that shone sent out corpuscles in straight lines. To Newton, light was fundamentally different from sound because although sound waves can travel around obstacles, light is blocked.

Direct observation was the cornerstone of the theories of such well-established authorities as Newton. He knew he could hear around corners, for example, but he couldn't see around them without the aid of a mirror. His belief that the mirror worked

FIG. 4—4 Isaac Newton (1642–1727) demonstrated a knack for invention from an early age, constructing various machines such as windmills and clocks that measured the movement of the sun or of falling water. His later accomplishments brought him renown that lasted well after his death. His reputation as a scientific hero was especially strong in his native Britain. It has since been proved that Newton's brand of physics does not apply under some special conditions. But his equations of gravity, which first explained the motions of the planets more than two hundred years ago, are now used to calculate the flights of spaceships.

by bouncing light particles to the eye was a perfectly reasonable explanation of the facts as known then.

But in time scientists learned more and more about phenomena, observable events, that didn't fit the classical, authoritative models. Mathematics helped explain some of the conflicts between observations and theories. Math became a tool of greater and greater importance, and even led to descriptions of the world beyond the reach of human senses.

P.A.M. Dirac

Some scientists found it hard to accept modern theories that dealt with phenomena beyond direct human experience—for instance, events at or near the speed of light. According to these ideas, the reality of the universe at this velocity must be totally different from the reality of our vastly slower everyday world. But as unreal as some characteristics of light may seem, they are now widely accepted to be as real as the physical objects light illuminates.

Paul Dirac (Fig. 4–5) made a major discovery about atomic structure for which there was no physical evidence in the 1920's. His calculations led him to predict a subatomic particle no one had suspected. The *electron*, with its negative electric charge, had been known for thirty years when Dirac uncovered evidence of its positive counterpart. This particle, which first appeared only in the symbols of a mathematical equation, seemed to be something exactly the opposite of the familiar electron—a sort of anti-electron.

Dirac's math suggested an electron and an anti-electron would annihilate, or wipe out, each other upon contact, giving off bundles of high energy. It also seemed likely from the same reasoning that under certain conditions an energy bundle of the right size could produce an electron and an anti-electron in turn.

FIG. 4–5 Paul Adrien Maurice Dirac (1902–1984) held the same professorship at Cambridge University that Sir Isaac Newton had. Dirac had strong feelings about how the truths about the universe revealed themselves. He once said: "I feel that a theory, if it is correct, will be a beautiful theory, because you want the principle of beauty when you are establishing fundamental laws. Since one is working from a mathematical basis, one is guided very largely by the requirement of mathematical beauty. If the equations of physics are not mathematically beautiful that denotes an imperfection, and it means that the theory is at fault and needs improvement."[5]

Four years later, an experimenter found Dirac's positive electron, dubbed the *positron*. In 1932, Dirac was awarded the Nobel Prize in Physics for his detective work. Many other subatomic particles have been discovered since then. In the process, the atomic model has been greatly refined.

Dirac united the most important theories of modern physics, which counts the laser among its more significant accomplishments. But Dirac viewed his breakthrough as only another step in the search for truth, not as truth itself. For Dirac, physics could describe reality roughly at best. The world was far too complex for perfect explanations. New systems of math would always be needed to improve theories outdated by new knowledge. In this sense, more than time separated Dirac and modern physics from Newton's philosophy.

The Road to Reality

As you've seen, it would be incorrect to assume that knowledge of light has come from individual scientists working in isolation. On the contrary, even the most famous discoveries, including holography, would probably have been made by someone else eventually, although not necessarily in the same way.

It would be misleading to assume that scientists fit neatly into categories. All experimenters theorize to some degree, and all theorists experiment, even if only in their minds. The common language of mathematics enables scientists using different techniques to communicate. Scientific knowledge couldn't have made progress at the rate it has without a great deal of communication. Indeed, holography would be unknown today were it not for the letters, books and articles, lectures, conversations, and debates about light during the past three centuries.

The scientific world Dennis Gabor grew up in recognized two types of reality—the reality of the human scale and that of the atomic realm. The two realities were connected; there was no dividing line between them. But it was useless to try to describe events at the speed of light in terms of everyday experience.

Light embodies this double reality by resembling two drastically different models at different times. While some kinds of energy are wavelike in behavior, and other kinds act more like particles, visible light falls in between these two extremes. Light is changeable in its effects—appearing to be a wave now and a particle then. Perhaps its fickleness is the reason its secrets have taken so long to uncover.

The holographic code is a product of the wave nature of light. But it's also dependent on light's particle nature in the process that produces laser light.

The next few chapters will concentrate first on light's wave effects. Sometimes it'll be helpful to picture some aspects of wave behavior according to physical models. Remember, these are only aids to the imagination. Don't confuse mere models with a reality we do not yet have the tools to see.

LIGHT WAVES

The study of light went back many hundreds of years before Huygens or Newton. For example, in the third century b.c. the Greek mathematician Euclid developed a law to describe the angle at which a mirror should reflect light. Earlier, another Greek, Plato, imagined that the eye saw by means of a stream of particles it emitted. The particles combined with sunlight upon striking an object, which sent them back to the eye to be sensed.

The notion of sight as a kind of reaching out may seem farfetched today, but it was reasonable considering the best scientific knowledge of Plato's day. And as a step in the growth of knowledge it proved valuable. It's likely Plato's belief inspired his student Aristotle to propose the view that light itself is an activity within a substance. Two thousand years later Huygens proposed that light activity was a kind of wave.

Christian Huygens

In the seventeenth century, two great natural pholosophers—Isaac Newton and Christian Huygens—studied light and arrived at conflicting conclusions about its nature. Long after both had died, prominent scientists chose sides and argued, sometimes bitterly, about which was correct.

Huygens (Fig. 5–1), born in Holland, was the earlier of the two philosopher-scientists. Like Newton, young Huygens took great interest in mathematics and mechanics, the study of the effects of forces on matter.

As a student of mechanics, Huygens explained light in physical terms. The most important source of this energy was the sun, whose light came from far away to make life possible on earth. It was difficult for Huygens and others to account for such action between two bodies at a distance without a material connection of some kind. So Huygens became a supporter of an ancient idea—that of ether.

Huygens's ether filled all space. It was thin enough so that the planets could pass through it without being slowed, thin enough to fill even the spaces within gases, liquids, and solids. Yet the ether was also dense enough to transmit motion through

FIG. 5–1 Christian Huygens (1629–1695) deserves credit for successes in areas other than optics. He found a better way to grind lenses, for instance. With them he built a telescope that revealed the strange appearance of Saturn was due to encircling rings. Huygens also greatly improved Galileo's design for a pendulum clock.

its particles, like the passage of an impact along a row of railroad cars nudged by a locomotive.

To Huygens the philosopher, it was enough that the ether made sense. It explained how light got through a glass jar emptied of all air by a pump. There was no need to look elsewhere for an explanation of how light passed from here to there.

For roughly two centuries after Huygens, scientists continued to use the idea of ether to explain behaviors of light. Today we know their logic was a kind of wishful thinking, a way of making mystery more manageable by putting it in familiar terms. Unfortunately, light is not so easily explained.

One of Huygens's most valuable contributions was his description of the way light propagates, or moves forward. His wavelet principle enables us to understand certain aspects of light behavior in ways that are still satisfactory today. And his model helped others make discoveries that apply to holography.

Sound Waves

Huygens used sound as a model for his light waves. To compare the two, suppose you strike a big bass drum. This sets the drumhead vibrating. You can actually see this vibration if you look closely. Imagine its effect on the air (Fig. 5–2).

The individual air particles don't advance with the sound wave that passes through them. They only move back and forth—back when the group of particles is compressed (made more dense) and forth when the group is rarefied (made less dense). The overall effect is that the particles oscillate, or vibrate, in time with the drumhead. You hear the sound when your eardrum joins the dance. The to-and-fro path of an oscillating particle matches the direction along which the rarefaction and compression pulses expand, or propagate. When the directions of expansion and oscillation of waves are the same, as is the case with sound, they are called *longitudinal waves*.

Sound also propagates, or advances, through other materials by means of oscillating particles. Of course, the movement of individual particles of water or steel is less than that of vibrating air, but the principle is the same.

Likewise, according to Huygens's theory, the vibrating of ether particles allowed light's effects to propagate in longitudinal waves.

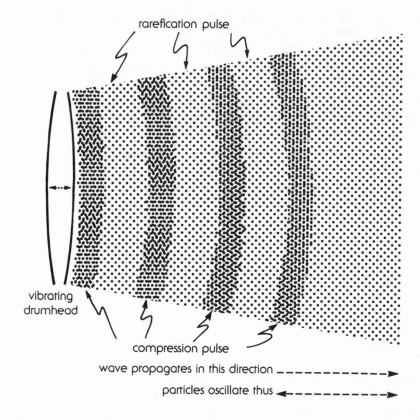

rarefication pulse

vibrating
drumhead

compression pulse

wave propagates in this direction ──────────▶

particles oscillate thus ◀──────────▶

FIG. 5–2 As a vibrating drumhead draws inward, air particles next to it rush in to fill the space the drumhead used to occupy. The air in that volume becomes less dense. This rarefication effect rushes away as the drumhead springs back. The new drumhead position compresses the nearby air, making it more dense. This compression effect advances in turn, right behind the rarefying effect, and the cycle repeats.

A sound wave is the product of alternating pulses of compression and rarefication. Particles of water, steel, or other substances also can transmit these forces. The vibrating particles are said to be oscillating. One complete oscillation of compression and rarefication is one cycle.

Taking Huygen's Pulse

Huygens used a row of hard spheres to illustrate the longitudinal, or lengthwise, way he thought ether oscillations advance in the form of light pulses. You can do the same with a row of marbles. When a loose marble crashes into the end of the row, the first marble it hits recoils from the impact. This marble strikes the second, which rebounds against its neighbor in turn. The impact travels from one marble to the next down the length of the row. At the far end it kicks out the last marble with a force roughly equal to that striking the first marble.

According to Huygens, ether filled all space like marbles in a box. The ether particles were so small, they even filled the spaces between the particles of glass in a window, for example, enabling the windowpane to transmit light. And because each ether particle touched others on all sides, it could transmit a pulse in all directions.

Huygens's model is typical of attempts to describe light's behavior based on familiar experience. But although light waves have physical effects, they're not physical in the way their various models suggest. A light wave is not an object; it's a *change*.

In the models you're about to consider, some waves represent changes in the shape of whatever substance, or medium, they're traveling through. But a wave of light needs no medium to propagate, or advance. A light wave is a change in energy.

Wave Symbols

Modern theories of light make no mention of ether or any other medium as being necessary for the movement of light. Light travels just as easily through the empty space between the stars as it does through the air to your eyes.

As basic as light is to human existence, it's very difficult to imagine. All models of light are attempts to "draw a picture" of it. In two dimensions, these pictures consist of certain lines (Fig. 5–3).

The light *ray*, *wave*, and *wavefront* are helpful, each in its own way. They'll all appear on the following pages, almost interchangeably, depending on which one best illustrates light's behavior at that point. But remember the lines are no more real than the particles of ether Huygens imagined.

Huygens's Principle

Huygens explained the forward motion of a wavefront by picturing each point on the front as a separate source of light or sound. From each point, particles of air (in the case of sound) or particles of ether (light) were set vibrating in the direction of the wave's advance, creating tiny wavelets. Figure 5–4 depicts the wavefronts he imagined to exist along a line connecting the front edges of neighboring wavelets. According to Huygens's principle, each wavefront in a series arises in the same way—

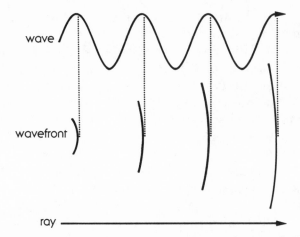

FIG. 5–3 A wave takes its shape from the familiar rise and fall of the surface of a body of water, as if seen from the side.

A wavefront represents an overhead view of the same motion, as if a line connecting the wave's high points were seen from above.

A ray is the simplest way to depict a light wave. The arrow shows the direction the wave or wavefronts are traveling. Think of the commonly used term "beam of light" as a bundle of rays headed in the same direction.

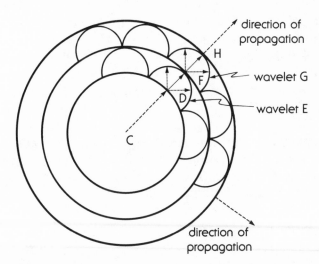

FIG. 5–4 A wavefront of light in Huygens's model propagates, or advances, as though it were the leading edge of a series of overlapping wavelets. In this diagram, point **C** is a source of light. The smaller circle **D** is a wavefront expanding from **C**. All points on wavefront **D** act as sources of an infinite number of wavelets like **E**.

The next wavefront (**F**) forms along a line connecting the forward edges of wavelet **E** and its neighbors. Points along wavefront **F** then act as sources of another series of wavelets like **G**. And the leading edge of this series forms still another wavefront, **H**, as the process repeats itself until the wave energy dies out.

as a result of wavelets produced from points of disturbance behind it.

On this two-dimensional page, Huygens wavefronts advance in the shape of concentric circles, that is, circles having a common center. In three dimensions, of course, the pulses grow in the shape of concentric spheres, expanding like so many balloons one inside the next.

Huygens's principle shows how a drumbeat travels through the air. It also provides a picture of how light pulses expand from any visible object no matter what its shape. All that is necessary is to imagine that each visible point on the surface of the object acts as though it were an isolated light source. The forward edge of neighboring wavelets combine to produce a wavefront that is the shape of the object itself, however complex.

As you'll see in the next chapter, Huygens's pulses are still an effective way to visualize some light behavior such as reflection. But a longitudinal wave model can't explain other effects. Before looking at one example of these other effects, let's examine a more suitable model.

Rope Wave

If you've ever jumped rope or watered a garden, you've probably played with a wave model. By pumping the free end of a rope once, for example, you can make a pulse-like hump move from your hand to the far end. Obviously the rope itself doesn't advance as the wave pulse propagates. The rope merely passes the wave energy along as its different sections rise and fall and rise and fall and so on. Pumping the rope repeatedly and rhythmically creates a continuous series of pulses, a wave train.

The rope wave at its highest point is at its *crest*. Its lowest point is a *trough*. The terms *crest* and *trough* sound as though they're naming entirely different parts. This is true of some waves, as any sailor can tell you. But light waves have no up and down. You can just as easily call a crest an upside-down trough and vice versa—they're merely opposite phases of a cycle.

An ideal simple wave train has all crests of equal height, all troughs of equal depth, and equal spacing from crest to crest all down the line. But as a wave of this type propagates, it reveals a motion different from that of oscillating particles in a sound wave (Fig. 5–5).

The up-and-down path of a point on a rope wave lies along a line that's perpendicular, or at right angles, to the direction of

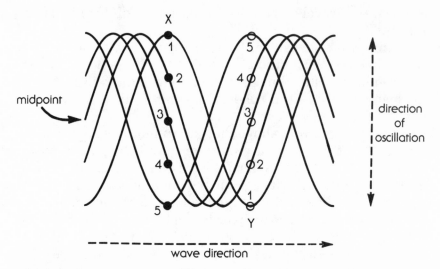

FIG. 5–5 Over time, a wave makes individual points oscillate through all phases of the wave cycle. At instant "1", for example, point **X** reaches a crest at precisely the same time point **Y** reaches the first trough beyond. As **X** falls, **Y** rises. When **X** reaches a trough, at instant "5", **Y** will be at crest. Then as **X** rises, **Y** falls. At all times during a wave cycle, **X** and **Y** are the same distance from the mid-point of the oscillation.

propagation. Waves that oscillate in this way are termed *transverse waves*. Let's examine another familiar transverse wave.

Water Waves

Imagine a still pond before a storm. When the first raindrop strikes the surface of the water it acts as a point source for a disturbance—an expanding circular wavefront. As the water's surface continues to vibrate, concentric circles form behind the first wavefront, which advances as the leading edge of wavelets from the wavefront immediately behind. A bobber on the water's surface makes the ripples or transverse oscillation of the water wave more obvious. The bobber doesn't go anywhere but up and down.

Seen from directly above, the series of water wave crests form the same pattern of concentric wavefronts you saw in Figure 5–4, in the beginning at least. As you know, the crests of water waves often appear as straight lines on a pond. That's partly because the larger a circle becomes, the flatter any small section of it seems. At some distance from their source, circular wavefronts begin to look like a series of parallel lines.

A spherical wavefront undergoes a similar transformation as it propagates in three dimensions. Imagine an expanding balloon. The larger it becomes, the flatter any small section seems. In three dimensions, the growing sphere comes to resemble a plane surface more and more. Discussions of holography often include references to spherical and plane waves as if they were different things entirely. But a plane wavefront is often just a spherical wavefront that grew up.

Huygens based his principle on longitudinal waves, that is, waves that oscillate in the same direction as they advance. The wavelet model also works with transverse waves, however, those waves that oscillate crosswise, or perpendicular, to the direction of travel. Watch the V-shaped wake that trails boats, ducks, or anything else that moves on water. At the point of the V, you'll see the wavelets whose leading edges merge to form the V's legs.

Transverse oscillations have the advantage of explaining other wave phenomena besides propagation.

Polarization

About a century after Huygens died, scientists discovered light waves have both an electric effect and a magnetic one. The spaces over which these effects operate are called fields, which vary in unison, but are perpendicular, or at right angles, to one another (Fig. 5–6a, b, c, d).

Light wave diagrams in this book will follow custom and show only one of the oscillating electromagnetic fields, the electrical. In the following discussion, for example, the oscillating magnetic field is always present, even though it's omitted from the illustration.

Certain materials have the ability to transmit some light while blocking the rest (Fig. 5–7). Huygens observed this effect, called polarization, in a special crystal known as Iceland spar, or calcite. He adapted his wavelet principle to account for the phenomenon. But his longitudinal wave model prevented him from discovering its cause.

The action of Iceland spar or of polarizing sunglass lenses is easily explained if light is considered to be a transverse wave, one that oscillates at right angles to its propagation. Imagine a simple wave approaching you head on. Using a clock face as a reference, you could say the wave is just as likely to oscillate from 12 o'clock to 6 o'clock as from 9 o'clock to 3 o'clock, or

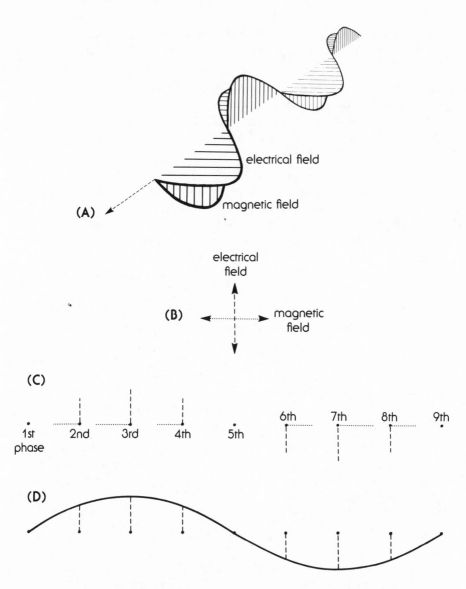

(A)

electrical field

magnetic field

(B)

electrical
field

magnetic
field

(C)

1st
phase

2nd

3rd

4th

5th

6th

7th

8th

9th

(D)

FIG. 5–6a, 5–6b, 5–6c, 5–6d An electromagnetic wave consists of electrical and magnetic fields that oscillate at right angles. In diagrams, the energy fields appear as a pair of interlocked line waves (6a). Seen "head on," the fields would form a cross (6b). At any instant, each of the fields might occupy the crest or trough phase of its cycle, or be in transition between the two extremes (6c—first through ninth phases).

The electrical and magnetic components of a light wave are inseparable, but for the sake of simplicity usually only one is drawn (6d, side view). This single line wave is considered to represent the oscillating electrical field. Notice how the shape of the line wave in 6d traces the changing strength of the energy in the electrical field in 6c, as seen head on.

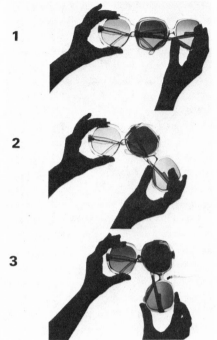

FIG. 5–7 The lenses of these sunglasses are made of a material that transmits only light waves that oscillate in the same plane as the material's main structure. The transmitted light is said to be *plane polarized*, that is, oscillating almost exclusively in one plane. Each lens transmits only vertically plane-polarized light. Crossing them blocks nearly all light. Figure 5–8 explains why.

between any other pair of opposite points on a circle. A polarizing material acts to filter out all transverse waves except those oscillating in a certain plane (Fig. 5–8a,b).

The rate at which a transverse light wave oscillates is related to the energy it carries. So measuring waves is a good way to identify different types of light.

Wavelength and Frequency

In thinking of light as a series of isolated pulses in the ether, Huygens overlooked the regularity of its cycles. This characteristic provides a means of measuring and comparing light waves in terms of space and time.

The distance between two successive crests is a wave's length (Fig. 5–9). Of course, because a trough is nothing but an upside-down (or inside-out) crest, you also can describe the length of a wave as the distance between successive troughs. In fact, you can measure a wave between any two corresponding points of successive wave cycles.

Waves can be measured in time as well as space. The number of times a wave reaches its crest each second is its frequency. A longer wave of light or water forms fewer crests per second

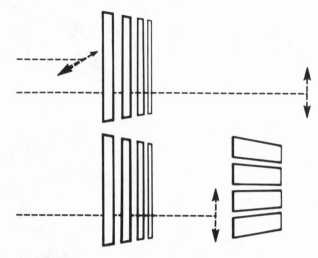

FIG. 5—8a, 5—8b A wave oscillating in a vertical plane will pass through a vertical fence, while a horizontal wave will be stopped (8a). The vertical fence acts to filter out all waves but those that are vertically plane-polarized.

Two fences set at right angles block all waves no matter what their plane of oscillation. A wave that passes through the first fence cannot make it through the second (8b). A polarizing sunglass lens has the same effect as the first fence. Crossed lenses have the same effect as this pair of fences.

FIG. 5—9 The crests of these water waves reflect sunlight onto the wall, showing how far apart the plane wavefronts are. The length of these waves is about 30 centimeters, or 30 hundredths of a meter. The wavelengths of visible light are measured in billionths of a meter.

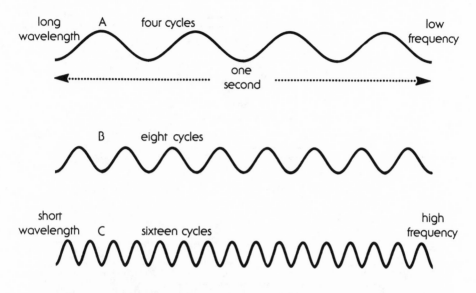

FIG. 5–10 Wavelength and frequency are inversely related—an increase in one means a decrease in the other, as long as wave speed remains the same.

Waves **A**, **B**, and **C** propagate, or travel, at the same speed. That means wave **A**—which has *twice the length* of **B**—oscillates at *half the frequency* of **B**. And wave **C**—which has *half the length* of **B**—has *twice* **B**'s *frequency*.

than a shorter wave of the same type. The relationship between wavelength and frequency is such that as one increases, the other decreases (Fig. 5–10).

Because frequency and wavelength are related, a wave of certain frequency will always have a specific length as long as its speed remains the same. Either measurement, then, describes only one particular light wave at that speed. According to scientific custom, visible light is usually described by its wavelength in a vacuum, which is space emptied of everything.

There are several means of determining wavelength, even though light waves themselves can't be seen. The most basic detector is your eye because it senses a difference among wavelengths of visible light as a difference in color. And color, as you'll see, plays a central role in holography.

COLORS SEEN AND UNSEEN

In an 1893 short story by Ambrose Bierce, "The Damned Thing," the tale is told of a frontiersman killed by a mysterious beast. The man's diary left a record of his growing terror at being stalked by a creature he never saw.

At the inquest into the death, a witness reported he saw nothing but a movement in the grass as his friend struggled with what seemed to be empty air. The coroner's jury scoffed at the testimony and ruled the man died of a mountain lion's attack.

But the diary's last entry explained all:

There are sounds that we cannot hear. At either end of the scale are notes that stir no chord of that imperfect instrument, the human ear. . . .

As with sounds, so with colors. At each end of the solar spectrum the chemist can detect the presence of what are known as 'actinic' rays. They represent colors—integral colors in the composition of light—which we are unable to discern. The human eye is an imperfect instrument; its range is but a few octaves of the real 'chromatic scale.' I am not mad; there are colors that we cannot see.

And God help me! The Damned Thing is of such a color![6]

Fortunately for Bierce's reputation, he was a much better storyteller than scientist. His "invisible" creature really would have appeared to observers as pure black, which is the absence of visible light.

But "The Damned Thing" dramatizes the idea of radiation as a range of colors. The light we see is merely a small portion— the range extends into invisibility.

Note about Wavelength and Color

Objects are commonly said to appear a certain color because of the wavelengths of light they send to the eye. This is not strictly true because light's wavelength is affected by the medium through which it travels, while its frequency is not. Although the wavelength of a particular kind of red light in water will differ from its wavelength in a vacuum, its frequency remains constant for reasons that must wait until the next chapter. Just remember that light's frequency is the truer measure of its color.

That said, also remember that wavelength is the customary way to describe color. So whenever you see a color mentioned in terms of wavelength, the measurement is understood to be that light's wavelength in a vacuum.

Now let's investigate the relationship between wavelength and color further to see how common everyday colors compare to Bierce's invisible ones.

Dimensions of Visible Light

With rope in hand, you can produce a fairly steady wave by pumping the free end up and down. Such a rope wave typically might have a wavelength of a meter or two and a frequency of perhaps a cycle a second. By tossing a stone into a pond, you might produce a wave a tenth of a meter long with a frequency of several cycles per second.

As handy as these models can be in some respects, they are completely inadequate for suggesting the dimensions of light waves. Suppose you rigged a bell so that successive crests of a rope wave rang it. To more accurately portray the size of a single wave of light, you'd have to pump the free end of the rope fast enough to make the bell ring about four hundred million million times a second!

At a frequency of 400,000,000,000,000 cycles a second, light waves have a length of only about seven ten-millionths (.0000007) of a meter. Light at this wavelength forms 70,000,000 crests every meter.

Numbers such as 400,000,000,000,000 and .0000007 are awkward to write and work with. Because such large and small numbers are characteristic of the dimensions of visible light, scientists working in this area find it handy to write them in abbreviated form—4×10^{14} and 7×10^{-7}—called scientific notation. Turn to the back of the book for a brief explanation.

The Visible Spectrum

Visible light varies in wavelength from roughly 4×10^{-7} meters to 7×10^{-7} m. In nanometers (nm), which are billionths of a meter, this range is somewhat wider than 400 nm to 700 nm. You can't see light waves themselves, of course, but they have an effect on your eyes that differs with wavelength. You perceive this difference in sensation as a difference in color.

You recognize light at the shorter end of the wavelength range as violet. As wavelength increases from there, the light is called blue, then green, yellow, and orange. Visible light with the longest wavelength appears to be red. This array of colors is the visible spectrum (Fig. 6–1).

Figure 6–1 shows the approximate wavelength range for each color in the visible spectrum. There is no distinct dividing line between colors; in reality they blend one into the next.

White and Black

When light waves strike an object, the object may absorb some waves, transmit some, or reflect some, depending on its surface and the material it's made of. The difference in the way objects absorb, transmit, and reflect light determines the colors they appear to be.

For example, the commonsense advice to wear white clothing outdoors on a hot, sunny day is based on the difference in the ability of certain materials to reflect light. Some materials reflect poorly, absorbing most of the incoming light waves, which are then converted to heat. Black cloth appears black because it

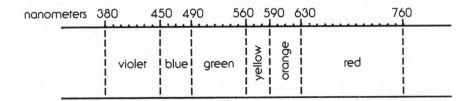

FIG. 6-1 The wavelength ranges of colors in the visible spectrum, as measured in a vacuum in billionths of a meter. Divisions between colors are exaggerated—the perception of color differences is gradual.

reflects very little light of any wavelength you can see. Black clothing can be uncomfortable in the summer because absorbed light heats it.

Other materials reflect light with wavelengths throughout the visible spectrum. Under white light—which contains most if not all visible wavelengths—these surfaces appear white. They absorb few of the light waves, making white clothing more comfortable under full summer sun.

But if all visible wavelengths aren't represented in the light striking a surface, then the reflected image doesn't carry them either. That's why "white" objects appear red under red light, blue under blue light, and so on. White objects reflect any and all visible wavelengths available. If there's nothing but red wavelengths coming in, that's all that can be reflected.

The Appearance of Color

In our colorful world, as you can see, many objects are very selective, reflecting only certain wavelengths of light while absorbing the rest. Objects that reflect light whose wavelength is 630 nm or longer, for example, appear red even in white light. And if the light illuminating it contains few waves in this range, a "red" object, which by its nature must absorb all other visible wavelengths, has little to reflect—it appears black.

In the same way, "blue" objects appear blue because they selectively reflect light only in the blue range of the spectrum. In "blueless" light, such objects also appear black.

It's possible to perceive colors whose wavelengths aren't included in the light reaching your eyes. That's because combinations of certain wavelengths in certain strengths can affect your retinas in the same way as a single wavelength between them on the spectrum. You see green, for instance, in the presence of the right kinds of blue and red (Fig. 6-2).

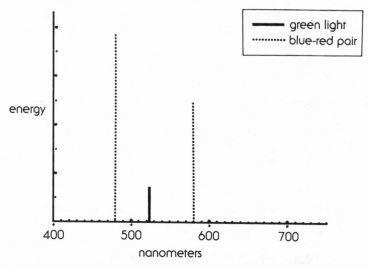

FIG. 6–2 Your brain can see green even though the light striking your eyes contains no wavelength from the green portion of the spectrum. As the graph shows, wavelengths from the blue and red portions of the spectrum can stimulate your retinas in such as way as to produce the sensation of green. The lengths of the dotted lines indicate how bright the lights of the wavelength pair have to be to have the combined color effect of the weaker green light. Other wavelength pairs of red and blue light (not shown) also can match this same green as far as the human eye is concerned.

Some holograms require light of a single color for decoding. So you need a laser or similar source to get the best image. But others are viewable in white light, such as that from the sun or a spotlight. A hologram of this type uses only a narrow range of wavelengths from the incoming white light. Other holograms can selectively reflect several different wavelengths, producing images in a rainbow of colors.

Thomas Young—one of Dennis Gabor's "Holo-Famers"—proposed that our eyes need to detect the right combinations of only three wavelengths to perceive white and all the colors of the spectrum. These three are called primary colors. The degree to which your eyes detect the wavelengths of the primary colors in an image determines the overall color sensation your brain perceives.

Primary Colors

Consider the color sensation known as white. You perceive whiteness when your eyes detect all visible wavelengths. But an object also looks white to you when its image contains the proper mixture of primary wavelengths that affect your eyes in the same way as a mixture of all wavelengths.

The primary wavelengths that add their effects together to produce white are red, blue, and green. Shining lights of these three colors on a screen shows how additive primaries produce other color sensations. White appears where all three overlap. Where red and green lights overlap, yellow appears. Red and blue lights produce a color called magenta. And blue and green lights produce cyan, a greenish blue.

Now consider black, the absence of all visible wavelengths. Certain substances produce the sensation of blackness by absorbing, or "soaking up," all visible wavelengths. But other substances that don't absorb all wavelengths can be combined to absorb them all. The colors of these substances are yellow, magenta, and cyan, which are known as subtractive primaries.

Mixing yellow, magenta, and cyan inks or paints produces black because wavelengths not absorbed by one of the three will be absorbed by the other two. As a result, no visible wavelengths are reflected to your eyes. Yellow, magenta, and cyan filters also produce black by subtraction when they overlap because wavelengths that pass through one filter will be absorbed by the other two. Consequently, no visible wavelengths are transmitted to your eyes. The subtractive primaries produce the additive primaries through other combinations. Yellow and magenta filters produce red. Magenta and cyan produce blue. And cyan and yellow produce green.

Using filters to subtract certain wavelengths from white light can have beautiful effects, as you know if you've ever seen the panels of a stained glass window, which act as filters. But as beautiful as these subtractive effects can be, filtered light isn't pure enough for some scientific research. And it isn't pure enough for making quality holograms.

Monochromatic Light

Making a hologram requires a light source that produces light of as close to a single wavelength as possible. This is known as *monochromatic* light, which means "light of one color."

Perfectly monochromatic light doesn't exist because all sources emit light whose waves vary in length to some degree. Recall that the sun sends out light of all visible wavelengths. Sunlight produces a spectrum that appears as a continuous blend of colors from violet to red.

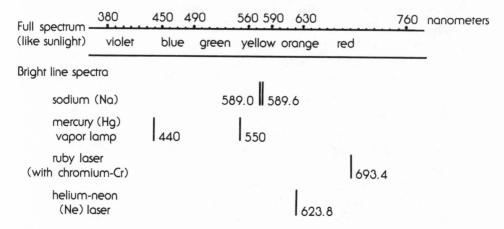

FIG. 6–3 A continuous band spectrum represents all the components of white light. Under the right conditions, different materials—elements, compounds, or mixtures—give off light whose wavelengths fall within characteristic bandwidths. Here, lines represent some prominent characteristic colors, slices of the full visible spectrum.

Other objects produce much different spectra when heated, however. The wavelengths they emit may be clustered in distinct and narrow ranges, or bandwidths. The spectrum of light emitted by hot sodium, for example, shows several slices of color separated by black. The portions of a continuous spectrum missing from sodium's line spectrum represent wavelengths this hot substance doesn't produce.

The bandwidths sodium does emit are, most noticeably, narrow bands or lines of orange and yellow. The brightest of sodium's several spectral lines are two bands of yellow between 589 nm and 590 nm (Fig. 6–3). These bandwidths are distinctive enough that their presence reveals the existence of sodium in whatever material is being tested.

Dennis Gabor put the spectral lines of mercury to work to demonstrate his principles of holography.

Laser Light

Real progress in holography after Gabor discovered it awaited the invention of the laser about a decade later. Gabor was hindered in the beginning by lack of a source of sufficiently monochromatic light. Instead he used the best lamp of his time, which worked by passing an electric current through mercury vapor at high pressure. The resulting light formed two main spectral bandwidths, one violet and one green (Fig. 6–3).

Gabor limited the wavelengths by filtering all but one band. He then organized the remaining waves by passing them through a pinhole (Fig. 6–4). But the filtered bandwidth was too wide. In addition, filtering the light absorbed most of it, and the usable beam was very weak. As a result, Gabor's holographic subjects had to be very tiny, two-dimensional objects, and his holograms were only a few millimeters square.

A laser can produce light in a much narrower bandwidth— and with much greater power—than Gabor's lamp (Fig. 6–5). The first laser used a ruby to emit light about 693.4 nm in length. The popular and relatively inexpensive helium-neon laser emits light of a brilliant cranberry color; its visible band is 623.8 nm (Fig. 6–3). The laser's very narrow range of wavelengths, its bandwidth, allows holographers to record objects as large and as 3-D as human beings.

The discussion of how bandwidth affects a hologram must wait—other aspects of light need looking at first. So let's turn from a narrow range of wavelengths to an infinite range. Just as blue blends into violet and orange into red, violet blends into even shorter wavelengths and red into even longer ones. These are the invisible colors.

FIG. 6–4 When light of many wavelengths strikes a screen with a pinhole in it, most of the light is stopped. Waves that pass through the pinhole emerge in a more orderly fashion. That's because the pinhole acts as a point source for each emerging wavefront. The size of the wavelets forming each wavefront varies according to the wavelengths in the original light. But after passing through the pinhole, the different wavefronts are concentric.

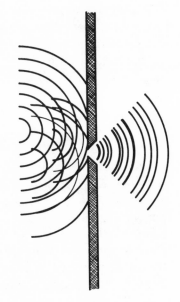

Gabor's Holo-Fame contains two men who had a great deal to do with describing the nature of the energy that made up this spectrum.

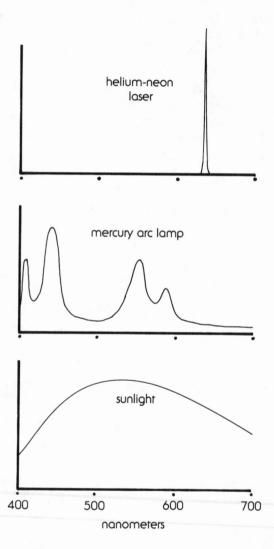

FIG. 6–5 Three graphs compare the bandwidths of three light sources. All wavelengths are present in the light of the noonday sun, although not with equal intensity, or what's commonly thought of as brightness.

The spectrum of a mercury vapor lamp shows several pronounced peaks—wavelengths characteristic of this source. Dennis Gabor used a filter to isolate the wavelengths in the peak around 436 nm to make his early holograms.

Compared to these two sources, laser light is highly monochromatic.

Michael Faraday

The word "scientist" was new in Michael Faraday's time. He preferred to call himself a philosopher, in the manner of Newton. Some believe Faraday was the greatest experimenter the world has ever known. Certainly he was one of the hardest working. Detailed diaries tell the story of his laborious search for a connection between electricity and magnetism—and between them and light.

Faraday (Fig. 6–6) was born in England and was largely self-taught. He made the most of opportunities to gain the respected position of director of the Royal Institution, a laboratory funded by research contracts with industries and the British government.

Faraday had little knowledge of math and expressed his experimental results in physical terms instead. For example, he developed the idea of "magnetic lines of force," over which a magnet acts to attract or repel. These lines appear when a paper is placed over a magnet and sprinkled with iron filings. Faraday thought light waves might originate in vibrating electrical and magnetic lines of force.

Electromagnetism

Michael Faraday conducted experiments that led to discoveries about the nature of light and related phenomena. In the early 1820's, reports of a relationship between electricity and magne-

FIG. 6–6 Michael Faraday (1791–1867) was a blacksmith's son who rose to the distinguished position of director of England's Royal Institution. This remarkable turn of fortune can be traced to the kindness of a bookseller who encouraged his young apprentice's scientific curiosity.

Faraday was a self-disciplined and methodical experimenter. Despite his lack of formal education, he invented the electric motor and electric generator. Faraday was also a popular lecturer with a special fondness for children. His account of "The Chemical History of a Candle" is evidence he remembered as an adult what it had been like to be a curious youngster.

tism aroused Faraday's curiosity while he was assistant to the director of the Royal Institution at the time, Sir Humphrey Davy. The two of them repeated key experiments in the reports. In one, a magnetized needle moved when brought near a wire carrying a continuous electric current from a battery. In another, two wires carrying electricity showed a magnetic attraction or repulsion between them, depending on the direction of current flow. These results inspired Faraday to conduct a long series of experiments to explore this relationship further. Although he suffered many, many failures, his overall work is a perfect example of how the reasoning mind builds its own stepping stones. In the course of about twenty-five years, Faraday made discoveries that included the following:

An electromagnet induced, or stimulated, a momentary current in one direction through a nearby coil of wire when the electromagnet was connected to a battery, that is, when it was turned on. A momentary current in the opposite direction appeared in the coil of wire when the electromagnet was turned off.

A related, but simpler experiment revealed that merely thrusting a bar magnet into the center of a coil of wire produced a momentary current in one direction through the wire. And pulling the magnet out again produced a momentary current in the opposite direction.

An electric current flowing through a wire induced a similar current to flow in the opposite direction through a circle of wire as it was brought close or withdrawn.

One conclusion seemed to be that although magnetism could exist alone, as in an ordinary bar magnet, this was not true of electricity. Faraday imagined that an electric current was a kind of energy wave whose electrical and magnetic effects were perpendicular to each other and across the direction of current flow. He was able to put these right angle effects to good use when he finally succeeded in affecting a beam of light with a magnet.

The Magnetization of Light

Faraday hoped to show a relationship between light and other forms of energy by proving that magnetic force could influence a light beam. He worked with polarized light, which was a well-established phenomenon in the nineteenth century. Quite a few substances were known to be able to screen light like the crossed sunglass lenses in Figure 5–7. With characteristic thoroughness, Faraday tested as many polarizers as he could get his hands on.

Faraday tested both liquid and crystal polarizers with the same basic technique (Fig. 6–7). His diary during four months

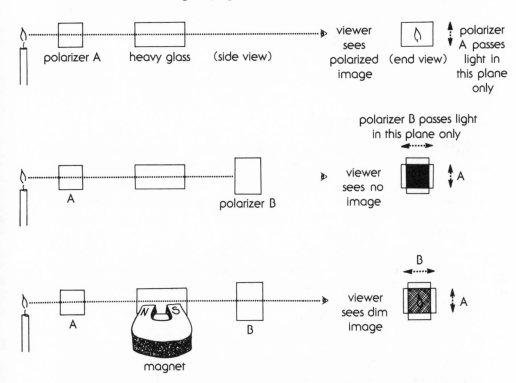

FIG. 6–7 Faraday's apparatus for magnetizing light. The first polarizer (**A**) passes only light oscillating in a vertical plane. Looking through it, you see an image of the candle flame. But place a similar polarizer (**B**) in line so that it passes light only in a horizontal plane. Because **A** screens out all horizontally oscillating light, there is none for **B** to pass, and the viewer sees no image. (This is the same as what happens when you cross polarizing sunglass lenses.)

Now add a magnetic field to the line of sight between **A** and **B**. In the position shown, the magnetic lines of force twist the vertically polarized light waves as they pass by. Faraday found that a piece of heavy glass, which contained a large amount of lead, was good for concentrating the magnetic field. (The glass is needed in all cases so that the magnetic field is the only part of the experiment that changes and, therefore, is tested.) By rotating the passing light, the magnetic field turns it enough from the vertical plane so that some gets through the horizontal polarizer **B**, and the viewer sees an image once again.

of 1845 chronicles his painstaking efforts to find the right combination of light, magnet, and polarizer that would reveal the connection he suspected. At last, Faraday found he could affect polarized light with magnetic effects alone or with a magnet made by passing an electric current through a coiled wire. This was the first definite evidence of a link between light and electromagnetism.

As dramatic as the results of Faraday's experiments were, they were also difficult for other scientists to build on. Someone would first have to transform Faraday's ideas into mathematical terms to make it possible to predict other results, test them, and improve his theories.

James Clerk Maxwell

When James Maxwell (Fig. 6–8) was born in Scotland, Faraday was forty years old and well into his study of light. Maxwell later followed, writing a paper entitled "On Faraday's Lines of Force" soon after college. Maxwell thought it unfortunate that Faraday's important ideas were not widely understood. He wrote:

> I was aware that there was supposed to be a difference between Faraday's way of conceiving phenomena and that of the mathematicians, so that neither he nor they were satisfied with each other's language.[7]

FIG. 6–8 James Clerk Maxwell (1831–1879) dedicated his life to explaining Faraday's work in mathematical terms. One observer described the uproar these calculations caused in the scientific world by comparing Maxwell's work to the grin of the Cheshire cat. It wasn't until several years after Maxwell's death that someone demonstrated the existence of the invisible electromagnetic waves Maxwell's equations suggested. And so the mathematical grin had the last laugh.

COLORS SEEN AND UNSEEN =81=

But Maxwell found common ground and did much to translate Faraday's results into "the conventional form of mathematical symbols." Once rewritten, the results could be "compared with those of the professed mathematicians."[8]

Faraday had shown that electrical and magnetic fields were related—under the right conditions, one could produce the other. And when Faraday speculated on the way electromagnetic effects traveled through space, he considered how magnetic forces seemed to exert themselves along certain lines, as shown in his magnet and iron filings demonstration.

Maxwell converted this and other observations into mathematical equations. He then used his mathematical translations to calculate new descriptions of the way light works. For instance, he thought of Faraday's lines of force around a wire carrying an electric current as a field of energy. Then Maxwell figured out how this energy field could radiate, or travel through space in all directions. The result was a mathematical proof of Faraday's feat—magnetism and electricity and light were aspects of the same kind of energy.

The Electromagnetic Spectrum

Maxwell showed how a disturbance in one of Faraday's lines of electromagnetic force could produce an energy wave that radiated away from the point of disturbance. Maxwell's theory said that light consisted of electromagnetic waves, later found to be part of a family of longer and shorter waves of invisible radiation. Today's map of the electromagnetic spectrum is, in a sense, Maxwell's epitaph (Fig. 6–9). His work illuminated this unseen world. The full electromagnetic spectrum increases by a factor of 10^{16} from one end to the other. In other words, the longest waves indicated here are 10,000,000,000,000,000 times longer than the shortest ones. And it probably extends to further extremes in either direction. Considering how narrow the range of radiation we can see, who can say what "invisible creatures" we're missing.

In theory, if the right kind of laser-like device existed, a narrow slice of any part of the electromagnetic spectrum could make a hologram. Such a slice of the microwave region used in radar—one of Bierce's unseen colors—made radar holography useful long before visible light holography was. Ultraviolet holograms also exist. But other slices of the spectrum have proved harder to use.

The attraction of holography in the visible range is obvious. Visible light holograms are immediately appealing because they mimic everyday experience so well. And they do it using the behaviors of ordinary light as well as the extraordinary aspects of laser light.

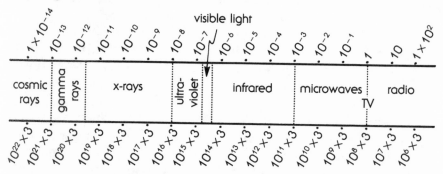

FIG. 6–9 Just as individual colors occupy places in the spectrum of visible light by virtue of their wavelengths, so does visible light occupy a position in the much larger spectrum of all electromagnetic waves.

Types of electromagnetic waves become longer and longer, and oscillate at lower and lower frequencies, as you move from left to right along this diagram. And moving from right to left means encountering waves that behave more and more like particles. Visible light seems to act as waves or as particles under different circumstances.

Although we can't see most types of electromagnetic radiation, we can detect them in other ways. For example, ultraviolet waves tan, even burn the skin, and shorter waves destroy tissue even more quickly. We sense infrared as heat, and machines such as radio and television put longer wavelengths to use. Of course, there aren't distinct divisions in the electromagnetic spectrum, any more than between colors in the visible spectrum.

REFLECTION AND REFRACTION

Without looking, see if you can describe the ceiling of the room you're now in.

Come on—no peeking.

Most people find themselves unable to respond to this sort of request with any certainty. Most are surprised to check their memories against the roof over their heads. And it's not so much because they're inobservent as selectively observant. Humans tend to concentrate on what's most important in their surroundings and ignore the rest until it's needed.

Of course, if ceilings were important to you, because you're a painter, say, or a human fly, you'd notice them in greater detail. It's not too hard to think of other objects or phenomena commonly taken for granted—the ways light waves change direction, for instance. You've experienced the effects of reflection and refraction from an early age, and you don't usually pay attention to them any more.

But suppose your life depended on these behaviors of light. Pretend for a moment that you're a member of a primitive clan that lives mainly on the fish you spear. Under those circumstances you'd pay a lot of attention to reflection and refraction, or you'd go hungry. That's because unless you positioned yourself properly, the glare of sunlight reflected from the lake's surface would hide the fish underneath. And unless you considered what the water's surface did to light coming from fish underneath, you'd aim your spear too high and miss.

Reflection and refraction are some basic light behaviors involved in making a hologram and in forming a holographic image. They make a good starting point for a discussion of optics because they're so familiar. But don't take reflection and refraction for granted—there's much more to them than meets the eye.

The Meaning of Light

The wave models you've seen so far have been fairly simple: the line of a rope, the rippling surface of a pond, and Huygens's pulses in the ether.

But as you probably suspect by now, actual light waves are anything but simple. A model of light is no more like light itself than a toy car is like a working Chevrolet.

Light waves in nature are complicated in part because they never exist in isolation. Light waves constantly pass through each other and interact with matter. They bend, rebound, orient themselves in new ways, and change length with changes in their speed. We live in light, awash in an ocean of visible energy.

The light waves you recognize as images come to your eyes only after being transformed by the world around you. The chair across the room, for example, altered the light that struck it in a way that says "chair" to your brain. The changed light waves may also say "green," or "small," or "wooden," or any of dozens of other visible characteristics chairs can have.

To carry such rich messages, image wavefronts must have a meaningful shape—their many waves must react to each other and to matter in orderly ways. Careful observers of centuries past described some of the rules light waves follow.

The Law of Reflection

The predictability of reflected light was known in ancient times. The easiest way to depict this principle is with a light ray, which is merely an arrow pointing in the direction of wave advancement, or propagation. The *law of reflection* states that a reflected light ray will "rebound" from a surface at an angle equal to the angle at which it struck. This angle is measured between the ray and an imaginary line drawn perpendicular to the surface at the point of the ray's impact. The imaginary perpendicular line is known as a *normal* (Fig. 7–1). The law also states that the reflected ray will continue in the same plane as the *incident*, or incoming, ray.

A dull surface is rough enough to send reflected light rays off in all directions. Rough surfaces create diffuse reflections. A shiny surface, like a mirror's, is smooth enough to reflect incident light faithfully, preserving any image information it may carry. Reflections from mirror-like surfaces are called *specular* reflections (Fig. 7–2).

Flat, or plane, mirrors produce our most familiar images. Yet a mirror image does not match an object exactly. The image in

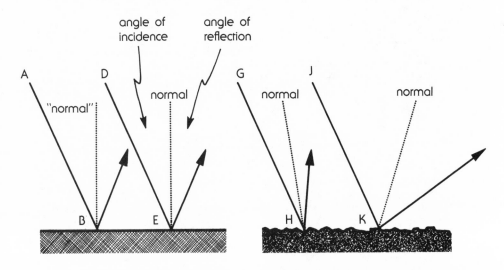

FIG. 7–1 The law of reflection: The angle of incidence for any light ray equals its angle of reflection. The angle is measured in relation to the *normal*, an imaginary line drawn perpendicular to the surface at the point where a light ray strikes. The surface on the left is so smooth its normals are parallel to one another like candles in a birthday cake. Parallel rays **AB** and **DE** remain parallel after reflection. Any image information they carry remains intact, and the reflection is said to be *specular*.

The right-hand surface, in contrast, is so rough its normals are tipped in many directions. Parallel rays **GH** and **JK** follow the law of reflection and therefore lose their parallel relationship. Any image information they carry is jumbled and lost as well; this reflection is *diffuse*.

FIG. 7–2 Specular reflections preserve image information. The mirror redirects light from the candle and the girl's face faithfully, and their images reach us intact.

But consider another reflector in this scene, the girl's skin. Her skin sends to the mirror a diffuse reflection of the candle—which you see as a glow on her face.

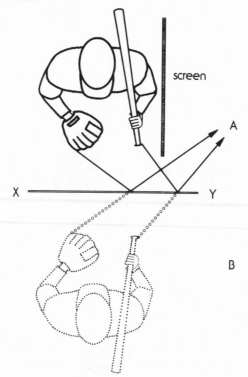

a specular reflection is reversed left to right (Fig. 7–3). That's why you'll never see the real you in a mirror.

Huygen's wavelet model works well to describe what happens when image light encounters the surface of a mirror (Fig. 7–4).

A beam of light passes through the same medium, or substance, before and after reflection. As a result, its speed of propagation stays the same. But light traveling from one medium to another changes speeds, and that makes things more complicated.

The Speeds of Light

Before the eighteenth century, arguments about how fast light travels pitted those who thought its speed was infinite—that it took no time at all to get from here to there—against those who thought its speed was limited in some way.

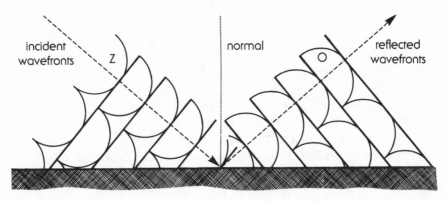

FIG. 7–4 According to Huygens's model of reflection, an incident wavefront produces a series of wavelets as it strikes a surface at one point after another. The reflected wavelets, such as **O**, advance at the same rate as the incident wavelets, such as **Z**. This means the reflected wavefront leaves the surface at the same angle (to the normal) as the incident wavefront struck the surface.

◀ **FIG. 7–3** A specular reflection carries an image that remains faithful to its source in all but one respect: Light rays from various points are reversed by the act of reflection. If **XY** were a window, an observer at **B** would see a ballplayer wearing a glove on his right hand. If **XY** were a mirror, however, and a screen prevented a direct view of the ballplayer, an observer at **A** would see the glove on the player's left hand.

In addition, the second observer would see the mirror image as if it came from a source behind the mirror—apparently as far behind the mirror as the actual source is in front of it.

Early experiments proved little except that light's speed was beyond the ability of human reflexes to measure. The first reasonable measurement came in 1675, when a Danish scientist named Roemer used his knowledge of astronomy to observe a difference in light's travel time to Earth. Roemer knew when one of Jupiter's moons was due to pass behind the planet and disappear. But he noticed that time of actual eclipse varied from the expected time depending on the date of the observation. When Earth and Jupiter were nearer, the times of the eclipses were a little earlier than expected. And when Earth and Jupiter were farther apart, the times of the eclipses were later than expected.

Roemer concluded that the difference in distance between the planets was responsible for the difference in the actual times of eclipse. Light took more time to travel a greater distance, therefore, its speed wasn't infinite. Roemer calculated a speed that turned out to be about 25 percent less than the actual 2.99793×10^8 meters per second, which is usually rounded off to 3×10^8 m/s.

This great speed is very difficult to imagine. By way of comparison it might help to imagine a trip by car at the legal highway speed. At the end of one hour you would've traveled fifty-five miles. But in an hour a beam of light could have made the same trip more than twelve million times!

The speed of light is greatest in a vacuum such as exists between the planets. In other media, light travels more slowly. It covers about 88,000 meters less per second in air at sea level and 0° Celsius. In water, its speed differs from top speed by nearly 75 million meters a second. And in a diamond, light's speed is less than half what it is in empty space.

This variation in the speed of light according to the medium through which it travels accounts for a bending of light that the ancients found far more difficult to explain than reflection.

The Law of Refraction

With the help of a friend, you can observe that light bends when it passes from one medium to another. Sit comfortably at a table and support your head in your hands. Have the friend put a coin in a cup and place the cup on the table so the coin is just barely out of sight behind the cup's rim. Then have your friend gently pour water into the cup. Without moving anything, the coin will reappear as the water covering it bends the reflected light toward you over the edge of the cup. This shows why you'd miss a fish with your spear unless you aimed below the refracted image you saw.

This bending or *refraction* of light is as predictable as reflection, although the rule is harder to express. Once again, let a ray represent the direction of propagation of a light beam. The *law of refraction* describes the way the path of this ray is altered as it leaves one transparent substance and enters another (Fig. 7–5a).

Light passing from air into glass loses speed at the boundary, causing it to take a new course closer to the normal, that imaginary perpendicular line at the point of impact. Light traveling in the opposite direction gains speed, and is also refracted— this time away from the perpendicular (Fig. 7–5b).

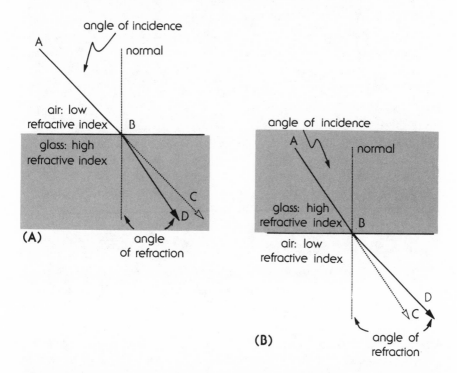

FIG. 7–5a The law of refraction: A change in light speed causes a change in its direction. Light travels faster in air than in glass. When ray **AB** enters the glass, it slows and is bent toward the normal, which is perpendicular to the surface at that point. As a result, the light arrives at point **D** instead of continuing on to **C**.

FIG. 7–5b When ray **AB** passes from glass into air, its speed increases. This causes a change in its course away from the normal. Instead of continuing on to point **C**, it arrives at **D**.

A piece of glass with parallel sides refracts light in such a way that it emerges along a path that's displaced to one side, but parallel to the original course. In this case, the second refraction "undoes" the effect of the first. In resuming its "airspeed" after leaving the parallel-sided glass the light also resumes its heading (Fig. 7–6). The *principle of reversibility*, as illustrated in Figure 7–6, will reappear later, in the discussion of the way holograms form images.

Dividing the speed of light in a vacuum by its speed in another medium produces a ratio known as the *index of refraction*. The index of refraction for air is very nearly one, indicat-

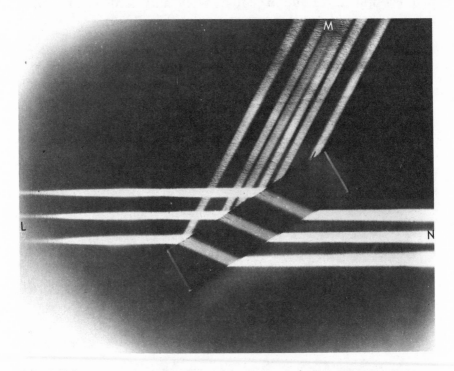

FIG. 7–6 Light's path is reversible. A beam gets from one point to a second by the same path it would take from the second point to the first. Three light beams approach this glass bar from the direction of point **L**. The first glass surface reflects part of each beam toward point **M**. But if the beams were to approach from the direction of point **M**, they would be reflected toward **L** along the very same path.

In the special case of passage through a medium with parallel sides, such as this glass bar, the second surface refracts the light beams back onto their original heading, whether they're moving from point **L** toward **N** or vice versa. As far as the paths of reflection or refraction are concerned, it makes no difference whether the beams enter the glass from the left or from the right.

ing that sunlight entering our atmosphere is bent a relatively small amount. Still, at day's end the angle of incidence for sunlight entering our atmosphere is so extreme the rays are refracted enough to allow us to see the sun for a few minutes after it has actually set!

Other transparent substances have higher indexes of refraction. The index for water is about 1.333, for example. And the index for a diamond is 2.417. Huygens's wavelets account for refraction as neatly as they describe reflection, whether light is traveling from a medium with a low index of refraction into one with a high index (Fig. 7–7a) or vice versa (Fig. 7–7b).

The diagrams in Figures 7–7a and b illustrate how light's wavelength but not its frequency changes when it's refracted. Light waves slow down when they enter a medium of higher refractive index. They continue to oscillate at the same rate, but don't travel as far with each cycle—that is, the forward distance covered during each cycle is less. Despite the practice that connects color with wavelength, refraction shows color to be determined by light's frequency, which remains constant no matter what the medium through which light travels.

The law of refraction has been put to use with lenses for hundreds of years.

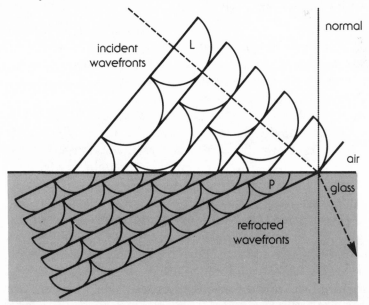

FIG. 7–7a When light passes from a medium of low refractive index to one of high refractive index, it slows down. According to Huygens, the refracted wavelets such as **P** expand more slowly than the incident wavelets such as **L**. This means the refracted wavefront advances at an angle closer to the perpendicular than the incident wavefront.

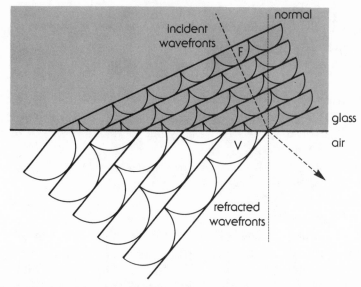

FIG. 7–7b When light passes from a medium of high refractive index to one of low, it speeds up. The refracted Huygens wavelets such as **V** expand more rapidly than the incident wavelets such as **F**. This causes the refracted wavefront to advance at an angle farther from the perpendicular than the incident wavefront.

Focusing Light by Refraction

A lens is basically a piece of transparent material, carefully shaped to bend electromagnetic rays precisely. You're most familiar with lenses of glass or plastic in eyeglasses, cameras, and so on. These—like the lens of your eye—bend visible light and focus it into images. But it's possible to make lenses of other materials to refract radiation of other wavelengths.

A scientist named Hertz, for example, used a lens made of pitch to refract the invisible radio waves James Maxwell's equations predicted. Although pitch is opaque to visible light, it's transparent to much longer waves in the electromagnetic spectrum. Showing that radio waves were refrangible, that is, able to be refracted, was further proof of their similarity to visible light.

Lenses bend radiation because their surfaces are curved in a certain way to cause incident light to pass through the refractive material at various angles. Lenses with outward-curving surfaces are called *convex*. They cause light to converge, or bend inward to a point (Fig. 7–8a,b,c).

Lenses with inward-curving surfaces are called *concave*. They cause light to diverge, or spread outward (Fig. 7–8b, c).

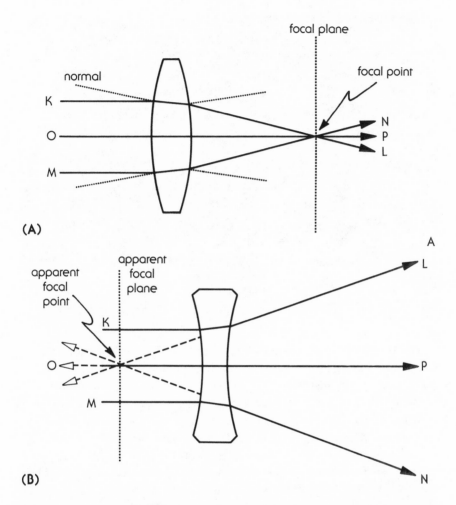

FIG. 7–8a An imaginary line drawn perpendicular to a surface at the point where a light ray strikes is called a normal. Normals to a flat surface are parallel. Normals to curved surfaces, such as the sides of this double convex lens, are not parallel. This causes parallel rays of light to converge to a point, the focal point. Note that ray **OP** is not bent because it enters and leaves the lens along normals. That is, the incoming ray **OP** strikes both the front and back surfaces of the glass at a perpendicular angle. Any other ray entering or leaving the lens along any other normals won't be refracted either.

Parallel rays approaching the lens at different angles than the one shown here will be focused somewhere else on this focal plane. Nonparallel rays will be focused on other planes.

FIG. 7–8b A concave lens causes parallel rays to diverge. Of course, this means they aren't brought to a real focal point. But to an observer at **A**, the rays appear to originate from a virtual image point on the other side of the lens. This focal point doesn't exist, but a virtual image that appears on a virtual focal plane can seem real nonetheless.

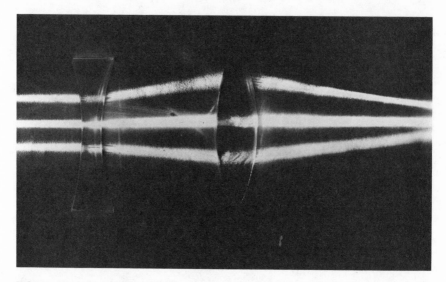

FIG. 7–8c Light striking a lens along a normal is not refracted. Light striking a lens at an angle other than a perpendicular angle is refracted.

Those who design and make lenses can control refractive effects by changing the curvature of lens surfaces, sometimes pairing one convex and one concave surface, or even one flat surface. They also select materials with various indexes of refraction for different focusing effects.

But lens designers can't overlook the wavelengths of light to be refracted because the amount of refraction depends on the wavelength of light was well as the nature of the material through which it travels. Red light is refracted to a lesser degree than blue and violet, as Isaac Newton observed.

Newton's Color Research

Once Newton painted a piece of cardboard half red and half blue. He then wrapped the cardboard with a thin black thread. Using the light from a candle, Newton arranged a converging lens to collect the colored light reflected from the single flat surface and focus it on a white paper (Fig. 7–9). Newton was able to tell if either part of the cardboard image was in focus when the black lines of the thread appeared sharpest. He found he couldn't see a focused image of both halves of the painted surface at the same distance from the lens. Where the blue image appeared most distinct, the red half was blurred, and vice versa.

Newton's demonstration helped explain chromatic aberration—a problem that had annoyed astronomers since the invention of the telescope. It was impossible to focus images of stars without surrounding rings of color. As Newton had concluded, differences in the refrangibility of different colors were beyond the power of the simple lenses of the time to correct. Years later, special combinations of lenses were designed to focus all wavelengths equally.

Newton found a simpler solution to chromatic aberration. He invented a telescope that used mirrors, which have the same effect no matter what the wavelength of incident light. In the right shape, mirrors bring all wavelengths to the same focal point.

Others before Newton had noticed that a wedge of glass called a prism could produce the color spectrum from white light. But the commonly held explanation was that the prism somehow transformed white light into the colors of the rainbow. Newton understood that rather than imposing colors on white light, a prism dispersed, or separated the colors contained in the whiteness.

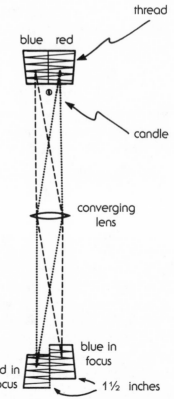

FIG. 7–9 Newton observed: " . . . the distance of the white paper from the lens, when the image of the red half of the colored paper appeared most distinct, was greater by an inch-and-a-half than the distance of the same white paper from the lens, when the image of the blue half appeared most distinct. In like incidence, therefore, of the blue and red upon the lens, the blue was refracted more by the lens than the red, so as to converge sooner by an inch-and-a-half, and therefore is more refrangible."[9]

This phenomenon is the cause of chromatic aberration—the appearance of rainbow-colored outlines around images—which lensmakers must always overcome.

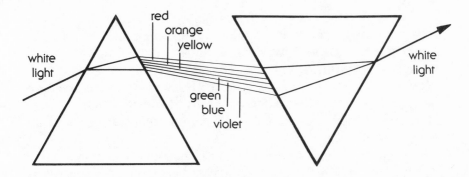

FIG. 7–10 A piece of paper placed between two prisms arranged like this will intercept the first prism's spectrum. Removing the paper allows the dispersed colors to continue through the second prism and recombine into white light. In each prism violet light waves are refracted more than red ones.

Furthermore, Newton realized that the prism's effect was reversible. By using two prisms, he recombined the dispersed colors into white light again (Fig. 7–10).

Some holograms are able to disperse light and produce images in bands of spectral colors. As the viewer's position changes so do the colors shift. It's fitting that they're popularly known as rainbow holograms.

Ordinary Image-Making

Refractive and reflective images are part of everyday experience. Although lenses and mirrors affect light according to different rules, they produce similar images. These fall into two categories—*real* and *virtual*.

A concave mirror—like a convex lens—can form both real and virtual images (Fig. 7–11a,b,c). A convex mirror—like a concave lens—can by itself produce only virtual images (Fig. 7–11d), which only seem real.

Real images consist of actual light waves in space. A piece of paper or a movie screen or your retina can intercept a real image where it appears in space (Fig. 7–12a,b).

If you've ever used a magnifying glass to refract sunlight, which becomes hot enough at the focal point to set paper afire, you've had first-hand experience with a *real image*. The same is true if you've gone to the theater to watch a real image of your movie heroes projected onto a screen.

Virtual images, on the other hand, can't be intercepted by a screen where they seem to be. In a virtual image, like the one

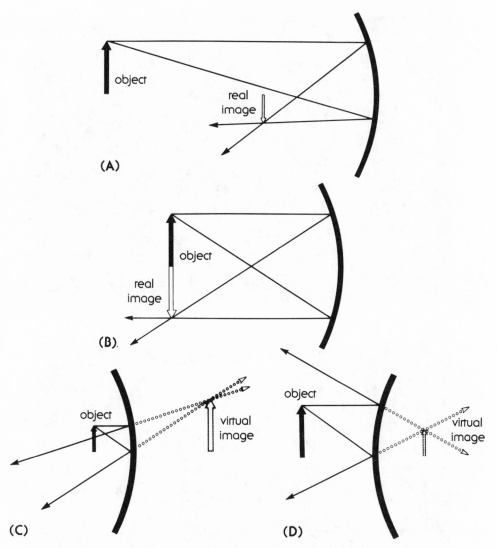

FIG. 7–11a, 7–11b, 7–11c, 7–11d The image a curved mirror forms depends on the position of the object. A concave mirror produces an inverted real image of a distant object (11a). As the object approaches the concave mirror, it reaches a point at which its inverted real image is exactly the same size and distance from the reflecting surface (11b). If the object moves very close, the mirror can no longer produce a real image because reflected light does not converge. Instead, diverging reflected rays show the position of the upright, larger virtual image behind the mirror (11c).

A convex mirror can only produce a virtual image (11d).

Figure 11b shows how the mirror in Figures 12a and b creates a real image. Figure 11d shows how the tree ornament in Figure 13 reflects a virtual image of an entire room. Figures 11c and 11d will appear in slightly different form later, when it's time to discuss how holograms use reflection to make images.

FIG. 7–12a, 7–12b A concave mirror can focus light to make a real image. In this case, a toy car is mounted upside down in a plane running through the mirror's focal point (12a). It appears right-side up in the same plane when viewed head-on, however (12b). The mirror projects light from every point on the toy into space. The real image is not an illusion—it consists of light waves focused in thin air. Focusing the camera on the real image but not the distant mirror proves the image is not on the mirror's surface.

FIG. 7–13 The convex surface of a tree ornament reflects diverging light rays that appear to come from behind the mirror. The virtual image is reduced from life size because all the diverging reflected light seems to emerge from points within the sphere.

in your medicine cabinet mirror, light from the image doesn't exist in the space behind the mirror. It's only an illusion that the *virtual* image you see and can photograph resides there (Fig. 7–13).

Holo-Images, Real and Virtual

Later, you'll see how holograms act like lenses and mirrors, such as those pictured in this chapter, to form real and virtual images. Gabor's original holograms produced both, in a straight line, one on either side of the holographic film. An observer could bring either tiny image into focus with a viewing lens. But because they overlapped, the out-of-focus image obscured the other. The laser made it possible to separate the real and virtual holographic images at an angle to permit viewers to observe one at a time.

Reflection and refraction are the basis for much image-making, such as you saw in Figures 7–12 and 7–13. Holograms, too, rely on reflected and refracted light. But light waves display other, less obvious, effects equally important to holography.

DIFFRACTION AND INTERFERENCE

Etienne de Silhouette was a somewhat less than successful minister of finance in the French government of 1759. During his brief term of office, from March to November, he made a name for himself among the citizenry for his stinginess.

To the public, de Silhouette was so tightfisted, his hobby—cutting portraits out of black paper—became a symbol of cutrate substitutions. The phrase "a la Silhouette" meant "on the cheap." Luckily for his memory, the art form has taken his name as well.

Stone Age cave dwellers painted silhouettes on their walls. Greeks used the technique. But it may have been most popular with Europeans in the half a century before photography was invented. Artists typically cut silhouettes from paper or traced the subject's shadow and painted in the outline.

The silhouette's outline carries its only detail. It resembles an ordinary shadow that way. But a silhouette, with its well-defined edges, is like no shadow you'll ever see. Because as sharp as a shadow's edge appears to be, close examination proves it's indistinct. A shadow's really no match for the artist's scissors or pen.

The Shadow's Edge

Everyday shadows are sharpest when the light source is bright and small, or the background close to the object. Should the source become larger or the background move away, the shadow will become fuzzier. Compare your shadow in the full sun as you lie on the ground to your shadow standing up, or your shadow on a cloudy day. Standing up allows reflected light from other sources to soften the shadow's edge. And the diffuse light of an overcast sky almost wipes out the shadow completely.

A better way to test for shadow sharpness is to filter the sunlight by sending it through a tiny hole or slit. This ensures that the illuminating light comes from a single point source. If light consists of corpuscles as Isaac Newton believed, it would travel in straight lines. Objects that block the light would block a portion of the incident wavefronts and cast a shadow like a "hole of darkness."

But some of the light in this arrangement doesn't travel a straight line from source to screen. Light that passes the edge of an object turns slightly inward behind the object. This is an area Newton's corpuscles would miss. This tiny amount of bent light means the shadow's edge is not perfectly sharp. The effect is *diffraction*, and it shows up in water waves.

Diffracted Water Waves

Engineers often can improve the safety of a harbor by building a massive wall to absorb some of the force of ocean waves. The *breakwater* helps block the waves, producing a sort of shadow of relatively calm water behind its protective arm. That the water wave shadow isn't perfectly calm is partly due to winds, currents, tides—but it's also partly due to diffraction.

To isolate the effect, picture a straight channel filled with calm water. A stone wall inside the channel juts halfway across.

Now introduce a steady surf whose wavefronts enter the channel in parallel lines. When the first wave crest meets the narrowed passage, the wall allows part through and blocks the rest. But the part of the wavefront that moves on doesn't continue as a chopped-off wavefront. Instead it gradually stretches, widening into the calm surface behind the wall (Fig. 8–1).

Diffraction also explains why water waves passing through a hole don't continue in a wavefront the size of the hole. Instead they expand in a circular shape (Fig. 8–2).

Light waves from a point source mimic the behavior of water waves as they encounter the edges of a barrier. It should come as no surprise that Huygens's wavelets show why, as in the special case of a pinhole (Fig. 8–3).

A barrier to light affects those waves passing close by its edges. Shapes more complicated than pinholes act on passing light waves in the same way. If a person's head is the barrier to light from a point source, each point on the outline of the head creates a disturbance that produces a Huygens wavelet. These expand along with the wavelets passing by. And like the wave behind the breakwater, the passing wavefront expands into the shadow area behind the head.

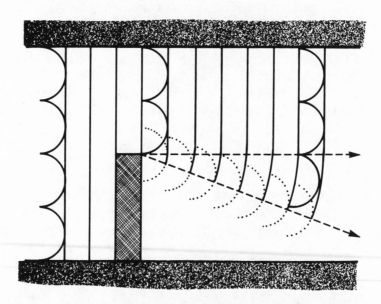

FIG. 8–1 A plane wavefront is the product of circular wavelets whose points of origin lie on the straight line of the wavefront behind. A wall removes part of the plane wavefront, and in so doing, the wall's tip acts as a point source for a new wavelet, whose expansion also is circular. But because it's on the end with no neighboring wavelets to one side, the line of leading edges now forms a wavefront in the shape of a gently curving hook.

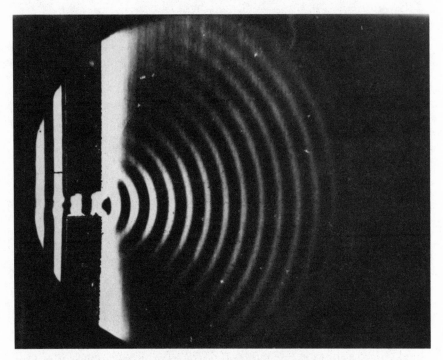

FIG. 8–2 When a plane wave of water strikes a barrier, most is blocked. The portion that passes through a hole emerges in the form of circular wavefronts because of diffraction.

FIG. 8–3 A pinhole transforms an incident plane wave of light into a diffracted spherical wave, as Huygens's wavelets show.

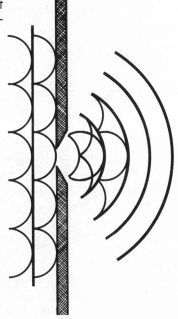

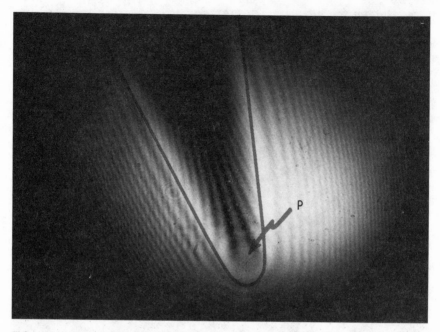

FIG. 8—4 Fringes appear around the edges of shadows when objects are illuminated with monochromatic light. Here, the outline of a pin's tip is laid over its shadow. The roundish spot (**P**) at the end of the pin's shadow is known as Poisson's bright spot, which is described later in the chapter.

You can observe shadow fringes by looking at a mercury or sodium streetlamp at night through the thin gap between two fingers. The narrow slit diffracts the lamp's light, and wave interference creates fringes on your eyes' retinas.

Diffraction of Light

Grimaldi, an Italian scientist of the seventeenth century, discovered diffraction. He found that when objects are illuminated by sunlight that has been passed through a small hole, their shadows are not merely blurred—as we see them everyday—they're surrounded by thin lines (Fig. 8–4).

Newton studied diffraction, but couldn't fit it in with his particle theory of light. He called the shadow lines *fringes* and noted they could often be resolved into colors of the spectrum. He posed a question for further research: "Are not the rays of light, in passing by the edges and sides of bodies, bent several times backwards and forwards, with a motion like that of an eel?"[10]

The fringe colors suggested a connection with a prism's dispersion of colors in white light. But, color aside, the shadow fringes were a puzzle. As it turned out, the fringes were the result of another of light's effects, which diffraction made possible. The phenomenon is *interference*, and it too is evident wherever there are waves of water.

Interfering Waves

A lake or pond is usually covered with waves of many lengths from many sources. Finding a pattern on the surface can be hard because of the abundance of waves. It helps to limit the sources and make the wavelengths more uniform (Fig. 8–5).

Before two waves meet, each set of wave crests has a particular height, or *amplitude*. But wherever waves are *superimposed*, that is, occupying the same place, their amplitudes combine. Their combined crests are higher and combined troughs are lower than either alone.

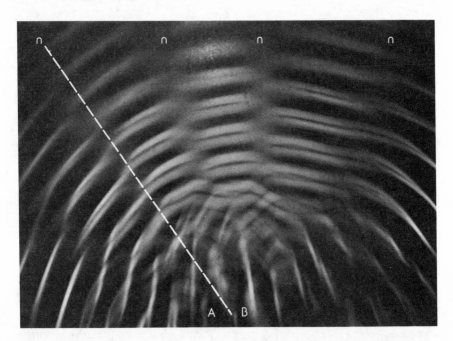

FIG. 8–5 Two circular water waves (centered at points **A** and **B**) having the same frequency interfere to form higher crests and lower troughs. Along certain lines—the nodes—the water seems almost flat, as if all wave action had disappeared there. The nodes resemble spokes of a wheel (the dotted line shows one), extending from the points labelled **n** toward **A** and **B**.

Two superimposed wavefronts act on the same particles of water at the same time. The result of this interference is that their individual amplitudes, or heights, are added together. The interference is called *constructive* when the amplitude of the combined wave is greater than the amplitudes of either individual wave before they were superimposed.

The interference is *destructive* when the amplitude of the combined wave is less than that of either individual wave alone. In other words, constructive interference makes two superimposed wave crests into a taller single one. Destructive interference makes the combination shorter (Fig. 8–6a,b).

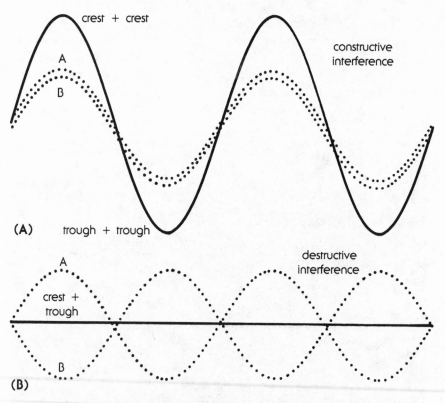

FIG. 8–6a, 8–6b Waves **A** and **B** are said to be *in phase* when the crests and troughs of one line up with the crests and troughs of the other. Waves superimposed in phase form a single wave with an increased amplitude equal to that of **A** plus that of **B**. This is *constructive interference* (6a).

Waves are *out of phase* when crests and troughs don't line up. When **A** and **B** are as far out of phase as they can be, crests are opposite troughs. The superimposed wave **A** + **B** has zero amplitude, because adding the height of a crest to the depth of a trough cancels out both. This is *destructive interference* (6b).

Wave interference can make patterns in which wave forms seem to stand still.

Standing Waves

The portions of a wave pattern like that in Figure 8–5 that are most noticeable are the crests, troughs, and the spots halfway between, the nodes. Wave energy at a node is passing from crest to trough and vice versa. The energy of each wave is clearly radiating outward from its source because the outermost wavefront is advancing. But the pattern of interfering wavefronts behind the outermost one doesn't seem to expand at all. On the contrary, the interference pattern seems to be fixed, as if the waves were "running in place." The phenomenon is said to be a *standing wave pattern.*

Standing wave patterns of light, such as the fringes around the shadow of the pin in Figure 8–4, require waves of roughly the same length. Long ago, the best way to isolate uniform wavelengths was to filter sunlight. That's how Grimaldi and Newton were able to observe faint interference fringes.

Newton never explained the fringes satisfactorily. But his reputation was so great few scientists dared question his corpuscular theory of light. Finally, about seventy-five years after Newton's death, careful experimenters made discoveries that contradicted the great philosopher. A physician began the assault on Newton's optics.

Thomas Young

Thomas Young (Fig. 8–7), born in England, was a child marvel who could read at the age of two. Young applied his genius to a wide range of subjects throughout his life. He was only in his twenties, for instance, when he was the first to translate ancient Egyptian hieroglyphics for the modern world.

Accomplishments such as this brought Young the respect of fellow scientists. Yet when Young announced the results of a rather simple experiment in 1801, most disbelieved and some ridiculed him. This experiment conflicted directly with Newton's particle theory of light. Young's reputation couldn't stand up to Newton's, perhaps because Young was a medical doctor with little mathematical background.

But the results couldn't be ignored.

FIG. 8–7 Thomas Young (1773–1829) is responsible for several discoveries that added a great deal to our understanding of vision. While dissecting the eye of an ox in medical school, he observed that the lens, rather than the entire eyeball, changed shape to focus objects at different distances.

Young also discovered that an uneven cornea was the cause of a kind of fuzzy vision known as astigmatism. And he helped develop a theory of color vision in which the eye detects all hues as various mixtures of red, green, and blue light. This theory has been put to work in color photography and color television, for example.

Young's Interference

The apparatus Thomas Young used in the experiment that finally undid Newton's particle theory of light is remarkable for its simplicity. His light source was the sun, which he allowed to shine into an otherwise dark room through a narrow slit in a screen. The narrow beam that entered the room illuminated a second screen with two more narrow slits side by side. The two identical beams of light that passed through the pair of slits fell on yet another screen, this one without holes.

Now if the beams consisted of light particles, you would expect them to form two bright rectangular spots that overlapped on the final screen. But instead, Young saw alternating bright and dark parallel lines (Fig. 8–8).

Young discovered that the line pattern his setup made depended on there being two slits in the second screen (Fig. 8–9). When he covered one of them up, the light from the remaining slit appeared as a single bright spot.

The interference of diffracted light waves caused the fringe pattern Young saw. The first slit acted as a pinhole does to organize sunlight into concentric wavefronts. In other words, the

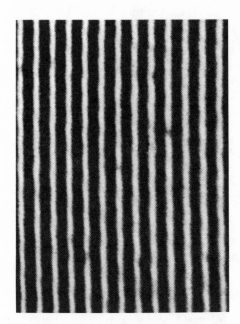

FIG. 8–8 Young observed this kind of standing wave pattern when light from two slits overlapped on a screen.

light striking the first slit came from the sun and reflections from the sky and other surroundings. But after entering the room it came from only one source, the slit.

Each wavefront from the first slit expanded until it struck the second screen, which contained two identical slits. These slits were positioned so that the expanding wavefronts from the first slit passed through both openings at the same time. As a result, each wavefront passing through the slit pair became a pair of identical wavefronts, which expanded until they overlapped.

Phase Differences

A standing wave pattern of interference fringes occurs when separate, roughly monochromatic wavefronts overlap *in phase* (bright) and *out of phase* (dark). The central bright line in Figure 8–8 forms on the screen at a point equally distant from the two slits. To reach that point, one wavefront travels just as far as the other, and because they both leave from point sources (the slits) at the same time, they arrive at the screen in phase. The difference between their phase at the time of arrival is zero, and the central bright fringe is called the *zero-order fringe.*

The first dark fringe on either side of the zero-order fringe is the result of wavefronts that are a half-step out of phase. Instead of meeting as two crests (or troughs), they overlap when one is in crest and the other in trough.

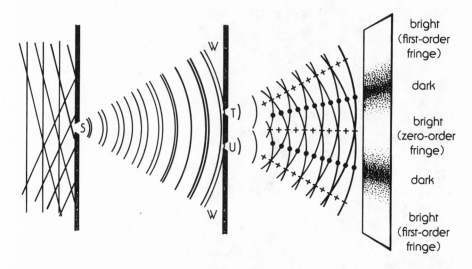

FIG. 8–9 The first slit (**S**) Young used helped organize sunlight into concentric wavefronts, which appear circular in two dimensions. Light from the same wavefront (**W**) passed through slits **T** and **U** at the same time. It then emerged as a pair of matched wavefronts, that is, wavefronts in phase. These overlapped and added their individual amplitudes together. In the diagram, *pluses* mark points of constructive interference, where crest met crest, or trough met trough.

Destructive interference occurred wherever wave crests met wave troughs. *Dots* mark points of canceled wave amplitude. When the overlapping wavefronts struck the final screen, points of constructive and destructive interference appeared as bright and dark fringes, respectively.

In this cross-section view, the slits referred to appear as holes. Think of similar diagrams stacked on top of this one. Then you can visualize how the stacked holes would be slits and the stacked points of interference would appear as fringe lines perpendicular to the plane of this page.

Bright fringes appear on either side of the first dark ones. These have a phase difference of one full cycle between the two incident wavefronts. To the bottom of Figure 8–9, a crest of Wave T interferes with a crest of Wave U that's one cycle behind it because it had one wavelength farther to travel to the screen. Similarly, the other "first-order" fringe above the zero-order line occurs when Wave T's crest is the one that lags a full wavelength behind.

In summary, bright fringes appear on the screen wherever the phase difference between interfering wavefronts is zero or differs by full cycles. Dark fringes appear wherever the wavefronts differ by a half cycle or multiples of a half cycle (Fig. 8–10).

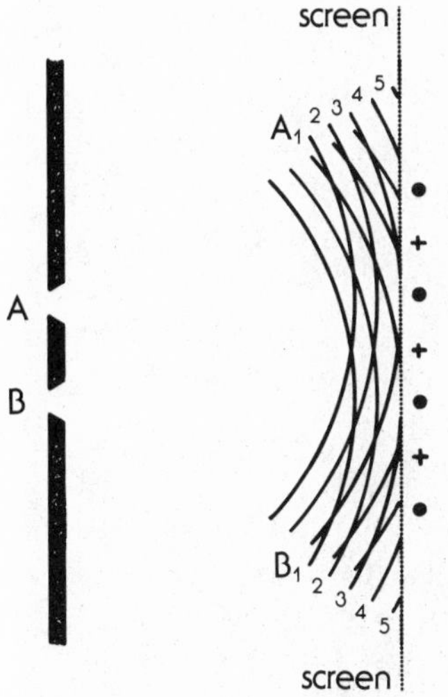

| Phase | | Phase | |
A	B	Difference	Appearance
• 3½	5	3/2	dark
+ 3	4	2/2	bright (first-order fringe)
• 3	3½	1/2	dark
+ 3	3	0	bright (zero-order fringe)
• 3½	3	1/2	dark
+ 4	3	2/2	bright (first-order fringe)
• 5	3½	3/2	dark

FIG. 8-10 Slits **A** and **B** are between 0.1 mm and 0.2 mm wide and less than 1 mm apart. The concentric wavefronts they emit are intercepted by a screen a few meters away. The crests of each set of wavefronts are identified by whole numbers; troughs are numbered by halves. Two troughs interfere in the center of the pattern to form the zero-order fringe. These troughs left **A** and **B** at exactly the same time and traveled the same distance to that point on the screen—there is no phase difference between them.

Dark fringes appear on either side of the zero-order fringe because one or the other wavefront must travel one-half wavelength farther from its slit to that point. With a phase difference of one-half, the two wavefronts interfere destructively and produce darkness.

In the same way, first-order fringes form because one or the other wavefront must travel a full wavelength farther to the screen. With a phase difference of one (2/2), the wavefronts here interfere constructively to make a bright fringe.

Higher order bright fringes form farther out from the center of the pattern, wherever the difference in the distances the two wavefronts travel varies by even multiples of one-half wavelength (1, 2, 3, etc.). Dark fringes form wherever the phase difference equals odd multiples of one-half wavelengths (1/2, 3/2, 5/2 etc.).

Young announced the results of his interference experiment at a time when the idea of diffraction was still new. Some critics were reluctant to accept the physician's explanation of the fringes because it was based on slit diffraction. Besides, Young's theory contradicted Newton's corpuscular theory, and such conflict with the master was still unthinkable to many. But slowly evidence began to pile up in Young's favor.

Augustin Jean Fresnel

Perhaps the strongest support for Young came from the French-man Augustin Fresnel (*fray-NEL*—Fig. 8–11). Fresnel measured the edges of shadows carefully under special conditions. The shadows were not as sharp as Newton had claimed they should be. He also repeated Young's results, using other means to separate light from one source into two interfering wavefronts. Fresnel produced phase differences by reflection and refraction instead of diffraction. This sidestepped the objection of Young's critics, who weren't convinced slit edges bent passing light, much less that the diffracted wavefronts that resulted formed interference fringes. Fresnel mathematically described the way light interfered with itself, something Young wasn't able to to. These equations backed up Young's belief that light traveled in waves, not particles.

Interference patterns don't always form fringes in parallel lines. Fringes also appear when two layers of transparent mate-

cross section of comparable conventional lens

cross section of Fresnel lens

FIG. 8–11 Augustin Jean Fresnel (1788–1827) is known to this day for a special lens he perfected (inset). The Fresnel lens makes it possible to concentrate light in a narrow beam without the glass bulk of an ordinary lens. Its first use was in lighthouses, where a conventional lens big enough to focus the signal light would have been too thick and heavy to support its own weight. Today Fresnel lenses are used in such devices as traffic signals, stage lighting, and film projectors.

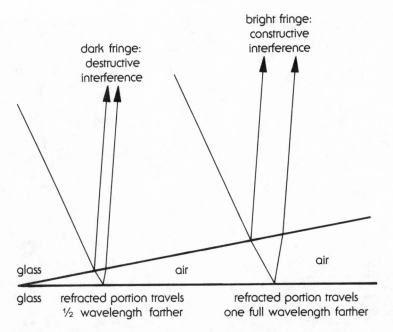

FIG. 8–12 Light partially reflected from glass surfaces separated by air of varying thickness travels different distances to the eye. Because the light is divided into two identical wavefronts with phase differences between them they form interference fringes that we can see.

rial overlap. Then partial reflection from each layer sends light from the same source back to the eye over different distances, which throw the separated wavefronts in and out of phase (Fig. 8–12).

Newton, in fact, had noticed and described circular fringes he saw when he placed one piece of glass atop another (Fig. 8–13). Ironically Newton's rings are now understood as prime evidence of light waves, not of light corpuscles.

Diffraction and interference both figure in the making and viewing of holograms. In that respect, a hologram is a lot like a couple of relatively simple devices for manipulating light.

Diffraction Gratings

Imagine that instead of the two slits Young used, there were thousands and thousands—all the same size and the same distance apart. Each slit acts as a point source of light and produces a series of wavelets that overlap with neighboring wavelets to form wavefronts at various angles (Fig. 8–14).

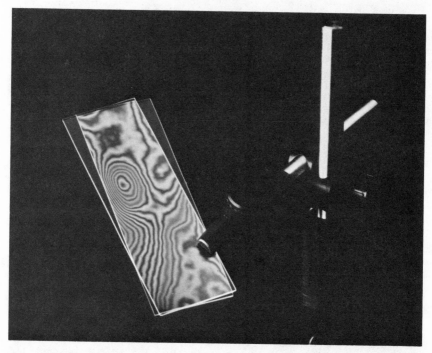

FIG. 8–13 Phase differences among light waves reflected from the back surface of one piece of glass and the front of another produce "Newton's rings." Constructive and destructive interference appear as bright and dark fringes. Monochromatic light is best for viewing Newton's rings, but if the surfaces are very close together, you can see the fringes any time. For example, a thin film of gasoline or oil on water produces familiar dark and bright (sometimes colored) swirls.

Newton's rings are used to test lenses while grinding. A perfectly curved glass surface laid atop a perfectly flat one produces rings that are perfectly circular.

If the light that illuminates a grating comes from a monochromatic point source, the bright interference fringes are replicas of the source. The grating has the effect of producing multiple images of the source.

But if the illuminating light is white, the fringe pattern contains sets of images for each wavelength, which are diffracted at different angles. These are arranged side by side and blend together, forming a spectrum.

Grating slit size is important. The finer they are, the more their separation approximates the wavelengths in white light, and the better the dispersion of colors. Early gratings were made of fine wires. But fine lines etched on a reflecting surface can substitute for slits, with the same effect. Today diffraction

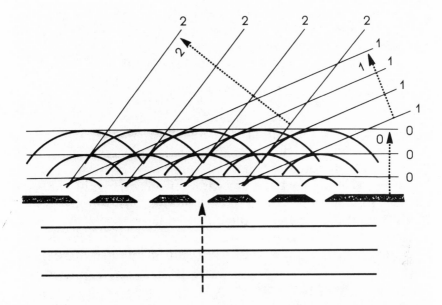

FIG. 8–14 A simple diffraction grating consists of a series of fine parallel slits very close together. Each slit acts as a point source when illuminated from behind. Lines drawn connecting the leading edges of wavelets expanding from the sources represent wavefronts—surfaces at which all wavelets are in phase.

Those wavefronts that are undiffracted, that is, parallel to the illuminating light, make up what is called the *zero-order beam* (labeled with zeroes). Other lines drawn to the right along surfaces of wavelets in phase indicate the first-order (ones) and second-order (twos) diffracted wavefronts to that side. Matching first- and second-order diffracted wavefronts (not shown) exist at the same angles to the left. Higher order diffracted wavefronts (also not shown) are weaker and harder to detect.

This figure as drawn represents the diffraction of monochromatic light. Illuminating the grating with white light produces similar sets of diffracted wavefronts, but at different angles depending on the wavelengths of the dispersed light. The result is a *spectrum*.

gratings are made by using a diamond to score as many as 1500 parallel lines per millimeter on glass. And they're also made without etching—holographically.

You can see how a diffraction grating works by holding a phonograph record up and looking across the grooves at a light. At eye level, the viewing angle is so shallow, the record grooves disperse light and put a rainbow sheen on the plastic.

A rainbow hologram generates spectral images in somewhat the same way a diffraction grating does. In addition, all holograms use diffraction to a large extent to redirect illuminating light. A device called a zone plate provides a good example of how light diffraction produces an image.

Bright Spots and Zone Plates

Fresnel entered a paper explaining his diffraction theory in a contest sponsored by the French Academy in 1818. Opponents of wave models of light attacked the essay. One who was especially critical pointed out that if Fresnel were right, light waves diffracted around the edge of a circular object should converge in one spot. There, constructive interference should form a bright spot in the center of the object's shadow.

The critic, a man named Poisson, meant his remarks as ridicule, not knowing the spot effect had already been discovered. Sure enough, when the experiment his remarks suggested was performed again, the bright spot reappeared. You can see it in Figure 8–4, where light diffracted by the very tip of the pin forms a roundish spot (labelled P). Perhaps it's fitting the phenomenon is known as Poisson's bright spot, in honor of his unintentional support of Fresnel's theory.

FIG. 8–15 A Fresnel zone plate is constructed so the opaque and transparent rings alternate from the center. The distance from each transparent ring to Poisson's bright spot—the zone plate's focal point—is one wavelength of the illuminating light farther away than the clear ring inside it. Therefore, light diffracted inward as it passes through the various clear rings of the zone plate reinforces itself by constructive interference at the focal point. A zone plate resembles a converging lens in this way.

At the same time, the successive dark rings—whose distances from the focal point are odd multiples of half-wavelengths—block diffracted light that would otherwise interfere destructively with the bright spot.

Poisson's spot is actually an image of the distant light source illuminating the round object that's casting the circular shadow. About fifty years after it was rediscovered, a British scientist named Lord Rayleigh constructed the design in Figure 8–15, which is called a *Fresnel zone plate*. When drawn properly, the concentric circles, all of which have the same area, get closer together the farther they are from the center. The design is made into a photographic transparency and set in monochromatic light. The zone plate then acts as both a *converging* lens to bring the light to a *real* focus on one side, and a *diverging* lens to produce a *virtual* focus on the other (Fig. 8–16). The real and virtual images are arranged along the axis of the zone plate. A hologram that forms images as the zone plate in Figure 8–16 does and as Dennis Gabor's did, is called an *on-axis hologram*.

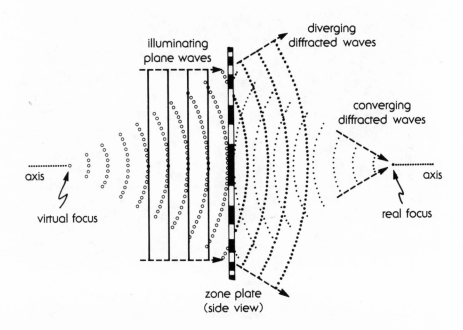

FIG. 8–16 When plane waves illuminate a Fresnel zone plate, its rings diffract light outward as well as inward. The converging waves of the first-order diffracted light, shown here, produce a real image at the zone plate's real focal point. The diverging first-order waves produce a virtual image, which appears to lie at the virtual focal point. Note that the two images lie on the zone plate's axis, an imaginary line drawn through its center.

A Fresnel zone plate also diffracts higher-order wavefronts (not shown) at wider angles.

Zone Plates and Holograms

Soon after Dennis Gabor announced his discovery of holographic principles, a scientist named Gordon Rogers made an interesting comparison. He suggested that Gabor's holograms formed complex images by diffraction in the same way that zone plates formed simple ones.

The simplest hologram of all, a hologram of a point of light, consists of an interference pattern that looks very much like a Fresnel zone plate. The hologram is called a *Gabor zone plate* because it's made by light wave interference rather than a drawing. Its concentric circles are not as sharply defined. But it works in similar fashion, diffracting light and forming images (Fig. 8–17).

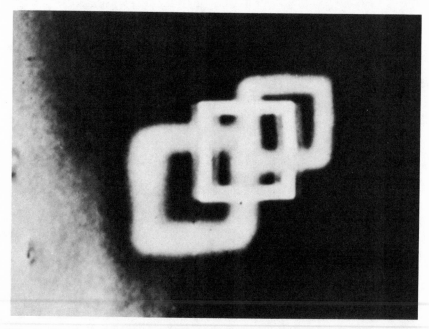

FIG. 8–17 A Gabor zone plate is an *on-axis hologram.* A Gabor zone plate formed these three images of a white square along the hologram's axis. The central image is the result of the zero-order (undiffracted) wavefront. The two first-order diffracted wavefronts form a diverging virtual image (on the left from this viewing angle) and the converging real image on the right.

A complex hologram mimics the zone plate's double-imaging action many times over. Although a hologram produces only first-order diffracted wavefronts, it does so for every point of the image of the holographed object.

Of course, as you've already seen under magnification (Fig. 3–5), most holograms look nothing like a zone plate. But as far as light waves are concerned, such a hologram's interference pattern acts much as if its tiny specks were parts of a zone plate of infinite complexity.

A mathematically inclined artist can draw the correct bull's eye pattern to make a photographic zone plate. But the intricate zone plate that is a hologram is a good deal more difficult to produce. Its pattern is a complicated arrangement of interference fringes, and these require a special kind of light that's far more uniform than the filtered sunlight Young used. This special kind of light didn't exist until a century and a half after Young's work—until 1960.

That was the year the laser was invented, the year that marked the beginning of real progress in practical holography.

THE LASER'S CALL TO ORDER

Sir George Cayley's work drew ridicule, so he preferred a dignified name for it: aerial navigation. Today it's a respectable worldwide industry by the name of flying. Cayley was ten years old when two Frenchmen made the first successful balloon ascension. From then on, aeronautics—the science of aircraft design—became Cayley's passion.

Cayley's accomplishments included the discovery that the low air pressure above a moving wing was the cause of its lifting power. This led to the realization that a curved wing had greater lift than a flat one. And, in perhaps his most glorious achievement just four years before he died, Cayley designed and built a controllable glider that carried his coachman on the world's first flight in a craft other than a balloon.

Cayley made many other contributions to aerial navigation. But "heavier-than-air-flight" couldn't make rapid progress until the invention of a method of propulsion better than a human body.

It took technology nearly a century to overtake Cayley's vision. His 1804 glider established some basic principles of lift and control that have been built into aircraft ever since. In 1903, the Wright brothers constructed a plane based on Cayley's principles. Then they flew it under the power of an internal combustion engine, another suggestion Cayley had made.

Dennis Gabor also had insight into laws of physics beyond the reach of his tools. Until technology caught up, Gabor, too, was restricted in how well he could demonstrate what he'd learned. As a result, Gabor's early holograms were as much like today's as Cayley's gliders resemble modern jets. Of course, Gabor's vision didn't leap a century. If he hadn't discovered the principles of holography in 1947, someone else would have soon. And unlike Cayley, Gabor lived to see the invention of the machine that would power his ideas. It was, of course, the laser.

The Limits of Disordered Light

Ordinary sunlight is a profusion of electromagnetic waves in a wide range of lengths. The disorder can be roughly compared to the surface of a lake in a gale—a jumble of random crests and troughs. For this reason such an assembly of wavelengths traveling in different directions is said to be incoherent, that is, without uniformity or harmony.

You've heard about a few devices designed to organize the confusion in white light. A lens, for example, focuses the light waves from each point of the object to a corresponding point on the film. Other tools, filters, narrow the bandwidth of white light and come closer to isolating a single wavelength.

Thomas Young's pinhole acted as a common point source for the white light it passed. The pinhole imposed a kind of order by making light waves form concentric wavefronts. You can see a similar order imposed on water waves as they enter an area protected by a breakwater.

As you recall, Dennis Gabor filtered the most monochromatic light he could find to make the interference fringes of the first holograms. But his holograms had to be tiny. The filtered light was still not coherent, or organized, enough to record more than his two-dimensional microphotographs.

In addition, Gabor's early holograms had to work like zone plates. They produced their real and virtual images in a straight line with the light source and the interference pattern. The images of his on-axis holograms overlapped (as in Fig. 8–17).

To overcome these limitations, holography awaited the development of a strong source of coherent light. The search took more than a decade. Understanding the difficulties involved calls for a look at how nature produces light—and how scientists discovered the secret.

Maxwell's mathematical description of light in the mid-nineteenth century was the most advanced explanation for many years. His equations are still useful for calculating light's behavior in some cases. Even so, scientists have had to come up with other theories to explain some of light's effects that neither Maxwell nor his contemporaries, such as Michael Faraday, could have known about.

Gustav Kirchhoff

Young and Fresnel confirmed the wavelike nature of light. Faraday and Maxwell observed and calculated its electromagnetic nature. It may have seemed as though exploration of the wave theory would lead straight to the entire truth about the real nature of light. But scientists soon discovered some disturbing results: Light had some effects the wave theory couldn't explain.

Gustav Kirchhoff (Fig. 9–1) was born in Germany a few years

FIG. 9–1 Gustav Robert Kirchhoff (1824–1887) personifies the dedication of the scientist. His spectroscopic studies included many hours spent observing sunlight through a special instrument as he drew the bright lines of its spectrum, the characteristic colors that revealed what it was made of. Kirchhoff's book *Researches on the Solar Spectrum* contains the following tragic footnote:

My drawing is intended to include that portion of the spectrum contained between the lines A and G. I must, however, confine myself at present to the publication of a part only of this, as the remainder requires a revision, which I am unfortunately unable to undertake, owing to my eyes being weakened by the continual observations which the subject rendered necessary.[11]

In effect, Kirchhoff was willing to trade his eyesight for a crack at knowledge of the mysteries of light.

before Maxwell and died a few years after him. A skilled mathematician, Kirchhoff improved some of Fresnel's calculations about light's ability to bend around objects. He also exchanged information with Maxwell about the electromagnetic effects Faraday had reported. And he studied the sun.

Some hot bodies, such as the wire in a light bulb, produce light of all visible wavelengths. When dispersed into a spectrum of emitted wavelengths, an *emission spectrum*, this light displays a continuous range of colors.

But scientists had long known that certain substances could produce certain isolated colors when heated. Table salt, for example, when burned turned the flame a characteristic yellow, indicating that the salt contained sodium. A prism, a specially shaped wedge of glass, could split up complex characteristic colors into component hues, sort of like unmixing paint. The results could be mapped in a series of thin lines representing the component colors in relation to the range of all possible colors.

Spectroscopy is the study of these separated colors. Kirchhoff was a spectroscopist who specialized in mapping and analyzing the characteristic color of the sun to identify some of the elements and compounds in it. The methods he pioneered even led to the discovery of helium in the sun's atmosphere before it was found on earth.

These and other spectroscopic findings raised difficult questions about the relationship between light and the matter that it comes from.

Atomic "Lamps"

Atoms produce light. More precisely, atomic and subatomic activity is the source of all electromagnetic radiation, including that of light. Longer wavelengths originate in the vibrations of atoms bound together in assemblies called molecules. Medium wavelengths come from changes in the orbits of the electrons around the atomic nucleus. Very short wavelengths radiate from the nucleus itself. In one way or another, atoms produce radiation from one end of the electromagnetic spectrum to the other.

But nineteenth century science was at a loss to explain how atoms did it. For one thing, Gustav Kirchhoff and others documented that individual chemical elements emitted light of certain specific wavelengths only. The element sodium, remember, releases light in two isolated yellow bands of the spectrum when heated. What limited the emission to those (and a few other, less prominent) lines? Why those and not others?

Some scientists tried to devise models of atomic structure that could physically account for the production of light as well as other radiation. The most widely accepted model of the time was patterned after the way the planets orbit our sun. So tiny electrons were thought to circle their relatively massive nucleus, emitting radiation all the time, the wavelength depending on the frequency of the orbit.

But the model of the atom as a tiny solar system didn't fit all the facts. For example, this model couldn't explain the nature of radiation produced by electron activity. If electrons truly radiated energy all the time, they'd lose energy constantly. If a planet lost energy, it would drop toward its sun in an ever-quickening spiral. *Orbital decay* should therefore cause electrons to speed up and radiate energy at shorter and shorter wavelengths. This means atoms of a single element should naturally emit radiation over a wide range of the spectrum as the orbits of their electrons decay. But atoms don't give off energy in all wavelengths.

Credit for the breakthrough in this theoretical logjam goes mainly to Max Planck. He found an explanation for the way energy is "packaged" that enabled others to explain the way atoms are built.

Max Planck

Maxwell's equations were an example of classical, well-established calculations and reasoning. But they couldn't explain how atoms *emit*, or give off, waves of electromagnetic radiation when heated. Many scientists, including Kirchhoff, had studied this problem by the time the German Max Planck (Fig. 9–2) tried his hand.

Planck's work turned the study of light on its ear. Classical wave theory assumed that radiation flowed in a continuous stream, like water from a garden hose. The formula Planck devised suggested that radiation was emitted only in certain quantities, as if the garden hose discharged its water in drops of certain sizes. He called a single "radiation drop" a *quantum* (plural *quanta*), from a Latin word meaning "how great."

Max Planck was the first of Gabor's eleven key figures to be eligible for a Nobel Prize. His discovery earned him the 1918

FIG. 9–2 Max Planck (1858-1947) was something of a reluctant hero. He was trained in the classical physics of his time, but his work caused the replacement of many classical theories. In his search for an answer to the problem of how atoms emit light, Planck devised a mathematical solution he believed to be only a convenient trick at the time. The conclusions this led to contradicted all of his training. In vain he tried to prove his own calculations were wrong. But this was not to be, for he had practically stumbled on one of the greatest scientific discoveries of all time—the quantum theory, which, with Einstein's theory of relativity, forms the foundation of modern physics.

Nobel Prize in Physics. The award recognized his contribution to the quantum theory of light, which soon evolved some startling ideas Planck himself found hard to accept.

Remember that up to that time, two major models dominated the thinking about light. Christian Huygens embodied the light-as-wave theory, while Isaac Newton was considered the champion of the corpuscular, or particle, theory.

During Planck's lifetime he witnessed the wave theory at its peak, then the return of the particle theory in a different form, and finally the union of the two. Although he was not entirely satisfied with this replacement of old ideas with the new ones, he was partly responsible.

Planck's Constant

Planck calculated how atoms could radiate energy in quantities that matched experimental measurements. He found a solution only after imagining that atoms might radiate energy in *specific* quantities—quanta—instead of *varying* amounts. Planck figured that a quantum for any specific electromagnetic wave equaled the frequency of that wave times a special number. The number has since come to be known as *Planck's constant*.

Planck's constant is an extremely small number, 6.626×10^{-34} (in units called *joules-seconds*). Such a tiny number has more influence on Planck's equation when the energy being calculated is associated with short radiation than with long. That's because a wave's frequency becomes a larger and larger number toward the short end of the spectrum. Therefore, short, high-frequency radiation consists of large quanta. And at the long end of the spectrum, low frequencies multiplied by the tiny constant equal small quanta.

In other words, as radiation's frequency increases, a quantum contains a greater amount of energy. So, for example, X-ray quanta are more energetic, and more harmful to life, than the quanta of radio waves.

Planck's quanta came in only one size for radiation of a specific frequency. There were quanta of different sizes for different frequencies, but for each frequency there was no fraction of a quantum. As long as a body emitted that type of light, the energy of its radiation totaled nothing but whole quanta.

Planck thought of his constant merely as a handy mathematical device that might lead to better and, from his viewpoint, more reasonable answers to questions about light. But the number turned out to be very useful, too useful to discard. Soon Albert Einstein was able to confirm the value of Planck's work by using his quantum idea to solve another problem.

Albert Einstein

Albert Einstein (Fig. 9–3) is perhaps best known for his theories of relativity, which described the nature of space and time in a revolutionary new way. But this work—recognized as his greatest contribution to science—doesn't directly apply to holography. For this reason, it must be overlooked in favor of less well-known ideas that advance the story at hand.

For example, light is both wave and particle, according to Einstein. This was the blending of Huygens's and Newton's points of view, although the details had changed quite a bit.

Einstein said light has wavelike characteristics as it travels through space or combines with other light. Yet it behaves like a stream of quanta-particles when it interacts with matter. Modern atomic theory resolves this apparent conflict between light's wave nature and its particle nature by accepting both models, depending on the circumstances. Incidentally, Einstein saw no

FIG. 9–3 Albert Einstein (1879–1955) is perhaps the most famous scientist of our time. Although nearly two generations have passed since his death, the name and face of Einstein are still synonymous with genius.

Other aspects of Einstein's life have faded from public memory. His favorite pastimes were playing the violin and sailing. And, although Einstein was a confirmed pacifist, he urged the United States government to build the atomic bomb to prevent Hitler's Germany from doing so. He then spent the rest of his life working to prevent further use of the atom for war.

need for an ether to explain how light waves propagate, nor have most physicists since.

Like Planck, Einstein received a Nobel Prize in Physics (1921), but not for his famous relativity theories, as many might think. Instead, Einstein's award came to him for work that laid the groundwork for the invention of the laser more than fifty years later.

The Photoelectric Effect

When certain metals are illuminated with the proper kind of light, their surface atoms emit electrons, which can be measured. Scientists before Planck knew that different metals required light of a certain frequency or higher before exhibiting this phenomenon, known as the photoelectric effect. And they knew that increasing the intensity of the light increased the number of electrons freed.

But they couldn't account for one major characteristic of those escaping electrons. None carried more energy than a certain maximum, which was distinctive for each metal. No matter how bright the illuminating light became, as long as its frequency remained the same, individual electrons leaving the metal's surface carried no more than a certain maximum energy. More energetic electrons didn't appear until the frequency of the incident light was increased (Fig. 9–4a, b, c).

Albert Einstein put Planck's work to good use in explaining the photoelectric effect. He proposed that the illuminating light arrived in tiny bundles of energy, later given the name photons.

Einstein figured the energy level of each photon was equal to the frequency of the light times Planck's constant. This, of

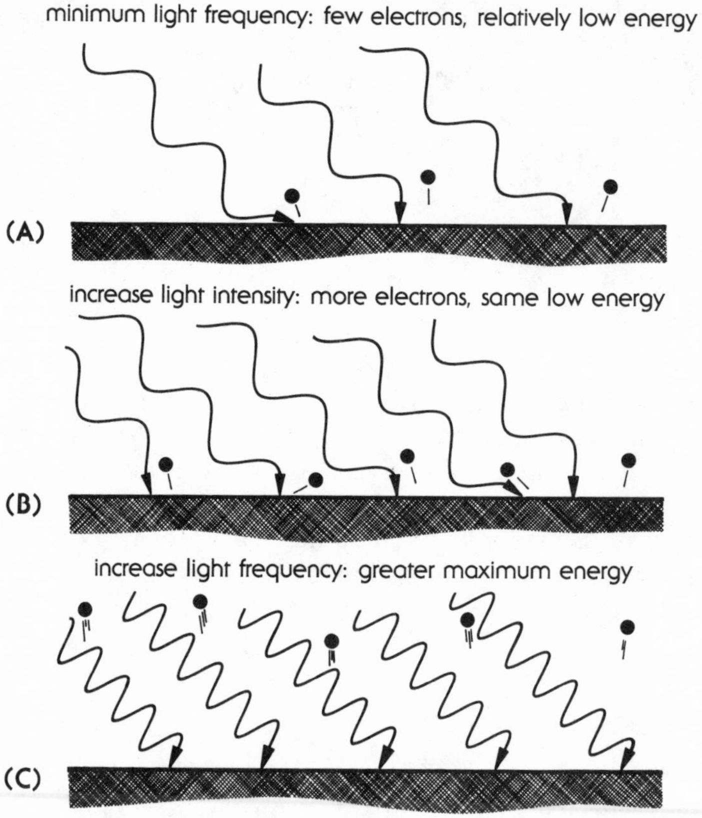

minimum light frequency: few electrons, relatively low energy

(A)

increase light intensity: more electrons, same low energy

(B)

increase light frequency: greater maximum energy

(C)

FIG. 9–4a, 9–4b, 9–4c The *photoelectric effect* displays the following peculiarities: Electrons of some materials can absorb photons associated with light of a certain minimum frequency. They then become excited enough to break free of the surface atoms with a certain maximum energy (4a).

Increasing the intensity of the same light delivers *more* photons, not larger ones. Therefore, the freed electrons are more numerous, not more energetic (4b). Only when the light's frequency is increased, providing larger photons, do the freed electrons have a higher maximum energy (4c).

course, was the same formula as Planck's equation for calculating the size of an electromagnetic wave's quantum. Einstein didn't simply duplicate Planck's work, however. He came to the same conclusion by different means, and thereby reinforced the importance of what Planck had done.

Einstein's photoelectric theory fit observations neatly. But there was no atomic model to explain either. Scientists struggled to develop a new model that would describe how atoms absorbed and emitted photons, light quanta. Niels Bohr had the first notable success.

Niels Bohr

Niels Bohr (Fig. 9–5) was born into a Danish family in which an interest in science was encouraged. His father was a professor of physiology at the University of Copenhagen, and his younger brother Harald became a famous mathematician.

Shortly after Bohr earned his doctorate degree, he moved to England to work with other physicists. The problem of how an atom was put together soon became the center of his studies.

At the time, Planck was not the only one who was having trouble visualizing a mechanical process that would account for the way atoms emitted light. Several scientists published papers containing experimental results and theories that helped Bohr develop his own line of reasoning. In time, he formed an especially fruitful relationship with Einstein, who frequently

FIG. 9–5 Niels Bohr (1885–1962) was respected for his humanitarian views—he promoted peaceful uses of the terrible atomic forces his own work helped unleash—and his all-around good humor.

Once a visitor to Bohr's summer home wondered about a horseshoe nailed above the door: Did that mean the great scientist was superstitious? No, replied Bohr, although he admitted he'd been told horseshoes also bring good luck to people who don't believe in them.

challenged Bohr's ideas, forcing him to rethink and improve them.

Bohr, for his part, influenced the thinking of many other physicists throughout his life. Perhaps his most stimulating idea came in 1913. That's when he succeeded in describing a hydrogen atom model that behaved according to the quantum theory.

The Bohr Atom

Niels Bohr improved the atomic model by contributing three key insights about the behavior of electrons. First, electrons aren't free to orbit a nucleus at any distance. They must revolve only at certain set distances, unique for each type of atom or molecule. An electron in each orbital position had a certain characteristic amount of energy.

Next, electrons don't absorb and emit radiation continuously as they revolve. This happens only when they shift from one set orbit to another.

Finally, an electron absorbs one quantum of radiation to jump to a higher orbit. And it emits a quantum of the same size to fall back again from there to its original level.

A diving tower next to a pool illustrates the various electron energy levels in the Bohr atom, if diving is permitted only from certain platforms at specific heights. Imagine identical dives from each of three levels. When the diver on the lowest platform cannonballs into the water, she creates a series of waves in the pool. The energy of these waves in connected to the height of the jump. Each time our model diver leaps from that platform, she generates waves that carry that certain characteristic energy.

The same diver creates more energetic waves when she cannonballs from greater heights. When Bohr's electrons fall from higher and higher orbits, they too produce waves—electromagnetic waves—of increased energy. And because the energy levels they jump and fall to are set by the nature of the atom, the sizes of the quanta they absorb and radiate are set as well.

The atomic model Bohr built produced, in theory, wavelengths that matched the spectral lines Kirchhoff and others had observed when elements and chemical compounds were heated. Atoms that emit quanta in the visible light range will produce only certain bands of color and not those wavelengths in between. After others had searched for formulas to describe the relationship of these many spectra, Bohr was able to account for the spectral lines of hydrogen, the simplest atom.

Bohr insisted his model of atomic structure was only a symbolic representation. He was convinced it would have to change to accommodate new information. Other scientists adapted the model to fit other elements, and gradually supported the theory that different atoms produce radiation throughout the spectrum. Bohr's atomic model eventually suggested a way to use certain materials to generate certain wavelengths of light on command—light in a narrow enough bandwidth to be worthy of the term monochromatic. The process by which this special light is now produced is a version of the way all light is made.

Fire at Will

You can become part of a model for the absorption and emission of energy by lying on your back on the ground with a ball in your hand. The ball represents an atom, and the ground on which you rest your outstretched hand is the energy level the atom occupies to begin with. If left alone, the atom tends to remain in its ground state, a position considered *stable*.

Adding energy causes an atom to jump to an energy level higher than its ground state. The form this energy jump takes—whether changes in the vibrations of atoms in a molecule, or changes in electron orbits, or changes in the atomic nucleus—are unimportant here. You duplicate the atom's overall increase in energy by throwing the ball into the air. The ball absorbs the energy of your throw and rises to a certain height. There it pauses very briefly before returning to ground level. At the peak of its journey, the ball represents an *excited atom*. Your throw represents the quantum of energy that raised it to that higher state (Fig. 9–6).

In human terms, an atom "prefers" a more stable lower energy level to a higher one. When an atom drops from an excited state, the quantum it releases is said to be the result of *spontaneous emission*, just as if the atom fired out the quantum of its own free will. In most cases, spontaneous emission takes place between 10^{-6} second and 10^{-8} second after an atom has reached an excited state.

In ordinary light sources, energy is absorbed in the form of collisions among subatomic particles or vibrations of molecular structure. For example, turning on a light switch causes electrons to flow through a tungsten thread in a lamp. The flowing

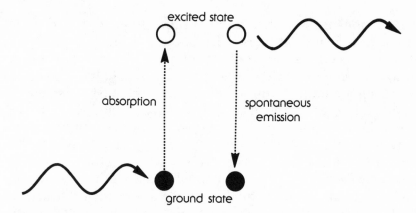

FIG. 9–6 An atom absorbs energy from collision with other particles such as electrons or photons. The added energy causes it to become excited to various degrees depending on the size of the quantum absorbed.

But the atom absorbs only those quanta that are the right size to lift it to the specific energy levels it's permitted by its nature to have. Then, like a flying ball, an excited atom almost immediately drops to its ground state, giving up as much energy in falling as it did in rising.

In other words, the particular quantum an atom absorbs in jumping to an excited level reappears when the atom returns to its starting point. And because the ground state is fairly stable, an atom will stay there until properly excited again.

electrons energize electrons in the tungsten atoms. As the tungsten atoms absorb energy from the electric current, they spontaneously emit a wide variety of photons. The filament begins to glow at many wavelengths—red, orange, yellow, blue. And you perceive the full range as white light.

In natural and most human-made light sources, photons are emitted spontaneously in a haphazard fashion. They cover a wide range of lengths, and the photons from individual atoms come singly, or in bursts called *wave trains*, which are short and disorganized.

A laser is a machine for producing long wave trains of a very narrow range of wavelengths. It does this by controlling all the atomic activities that emit photons.

Command Performance

To imagine the atomic activity that makes a laser possible, let's change the thrown-ball model slightly. This time you'll be lying on the ground under a tree. Now when you toss the ball skyward, it lodges in a branch at the very peak of its journey.

The ball's position is precarious. In real life, the slightest breeze might dislodge it. But let's imagine for this model that there is no breeze. You'll knock the ball from its unstable perch with another, thrown with just the same amount of energy you gave the first. The second ball then rises to the same height, collides with the first, and both fall together. By supplying the required energy in the toss of the second ball, you stimulate the first to fall to the ground.

The ball in the tree represents an excited atom. Of course, the ball remains caught on the branch far longer than the millionth of a second or so an atom would linger at an unstable energy level. But as long as the atom is there, it can be dislodged by the right photon "passing through."

Einstein calculated that a photon of just the proper size could stimulate an atom to fall from a higher level to the ground. The stimulating photon must contain the amount of energy equal to the energy difference between the two levels. In effect, the stimulating photon departs from the atom accompanied by an identical twin (Fig. 9–7).

It turns out to be a big advantage for stimulated emission that atoms aren't limited to absorbing and emitting energy between

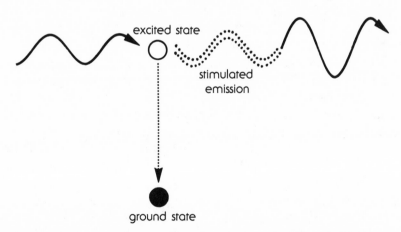

excited state

stimulated
emission

ground state

FIG. 9–7 While in an excited state, an atom can be knocked from its unstable perch. The only photon able to do this is one containing energy equal to the difference between the excited level and a lower one—in this case, the ground state. When this happens, the photon that stimulates the drop in energy level leaves the scene with an identical photon, the one that the atom absorbed to reach that level originally.

Because the two photons have the same amount of energy, they have the same wavelength. As a bonus, they also radiate in the same direction with their waves matched crest for crest. In other words, they are *in phase* and called *coherent*.

only the one excited level and the ground level at a time. If an atom absorbs enough energy, it may leapfrog over several energy levels. Then, instead of emitting a quantum with the same energy, it may emit a smaller photon—one that allows it to reside at an intermediate energy level. This would be like allowing the diver in the earlier example to hop between platforms as well as dive all the way into the pool.

In the ball model, this step behavior is like throwing a ball into a treetop and having it return to the ground in stages. It drops from branch to branch, pausing briefly at each one. It's possible to stimulate the emission of photons of intermediate sizes equal in energy to one or more of the transitions an atom can make as it returns to lower, more stable energy states.

With atoms having the proper kind of energy levels, it seemed possible to produce a great number of identical photons by means of stimulated emission. That's just what a laser does: It generates an enormous amount of light that's not only monochromatic, it's in phase as well, with all wave crests lined up side by side. Light in this highly organized state is called *coherent*.

Maser, Meet Laser

The word "laser" stands for light amplification by stimulated emission of radiation. To amplify is to increase or make stronger. A laser amplifies light by stimulating the emission of many photons of identical size.

The laser is an offspring of a device that produces microwaves by the same process—"microwave amplification by stimulated emission of radiation." In fact, the American who shares credit for discovering the basic principle of both devices, Charles Townes, originally called the laser an "optical maser." Townes helped build the first successful maser after years of frustrating work that led to a flash of insight. He claims the breakthrough came in a three-minute calculation on the back of an envelope. The calculation led to his sharing a Nobel Prize.

The first laser followed seven years after the first maser. Although both use stimulated emission, it proved more difficult using light waves, which are a million times shorter than microwaves.

There were two major obstacles. First, because atoms are more stable in the ground state than at higher energy levels, they tend to spend most of their time there. With most atoms in an unexcited state, any photons emitted from excited atoms would be unlikely to stimulate further emissions. In fact, emitted photons would easily be absorbed by "ground state" atoms. The goal was to reverse that relationship so that excited atoms outnumbered unexcited ones. Only then could atoms *lase*, the process of stimulated emission in which emitted photons "dislodge" others in a growing chain reaction.

The solution to this problem was to find an atom that could be excited first to a high energy level. From there it would quickly fall to a more stable energy level only partway back to the ground state. The pause at this intermediate level gives many other atoms the time to gather at their intermediate levels, too. This phenomenon is called *population inversion* because it tips the ratio of unexcited to excited atoms upside down.

Today many substances can be made to lase. The first was a ruby crystal (Fig. 9–8).

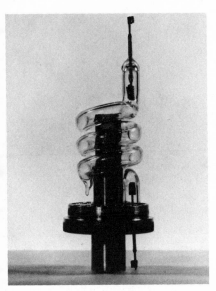

FIG. 9–8 The world's first laser consisted of a crystal of ruby one cm in diameter and two cm long. Ruby is made mostly of aluminum and oxygen combined in a molecule. It acquires its characteristic pink color from chromium scattered about the crystal. The chromium is in the form of an ion, which is an atom with an unusual number of electrons. The chromium ions are relatively few compared to the aluminum oxide molecules, but still number millions in a ruby this size.

Coiling around the ruby is a flash lamp filled with xenon gas. It emits a bright white light when an electric current passes through it.

A decade after the laser's invention, Dennis Gabor explained why he hadn't had a hand in the feat:

"In 1950, thinking of the desirability of a strong source of coherent light, I remembered that in 1921, as a young student in Berlin, I had heard from Einstein's own lips his wonderful derivation of Planck's law which postulated the existence of stimulated emission. I then had the idea of the pulsed laser: Take a suitable crystal, make a resonator of it by means of a highly reflecting coating, fill up the upper level by illuminating it through a small hole, and discharge it explosively by a ray of its own light. I offered the idea as a Ph.D. problem to my best student, but he declined it as too risky, and I could not gainsay it, as I could not be sure that we would find a suitable crystal."[12]

The xenon flash lamp surrounding the ruby excites the crystal's chromium ions by emitting a bright white light. Certain green and blue photons in the flash are the ones the ions absorb (Fig. 9–9).

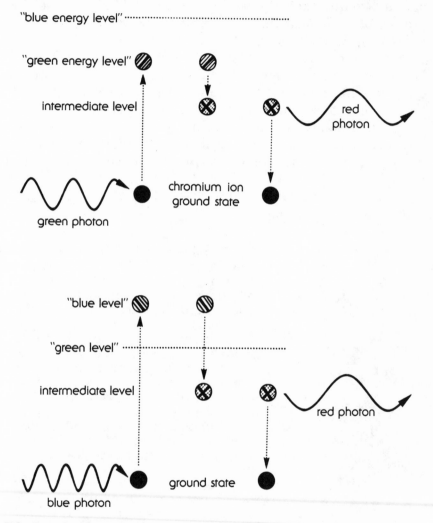

FIG. 9–9 A chromium ion in the laser's ruby is excited to one of two higher energy levels by photons of one or two wavelengths present in the xenon light. Quickly the excited ion drops from its peak levels by giving up heat. Whether they've absorbed the blue or green light when excited, the ions pause at the same in-between level. Because the pause is so much longer than the time spent at peak, the number of ions at the intermediate level soon surpasses those remaining in the ground state. Eventually ions begin to drop to the ground, emitting a photon from the red range of the spectrum, at about 694.3 nm. And laser action begins.

The excited chromium ions pause at the intermediate energy level about a thousand times longer than they did at the peak of excitement. This is long enough for most of the ions to assemble there. Soon a few ions begin to drop back to the ground state. As they do they emit a photon, which stimulates other intermediate ions to emit identical photons in turn. An irresistable chain reaction races through the crystal at the speed of light (Fig. 9–10).

This leads to the second major obstacle to developing the laser—controlling the photon stampede.

Resonance

When you have a string fastened at either end, such as a guitar string, wave motion is limited to certain wavelengths. When plucked, the string naturally tends toward waves that are whole number divisions of the string's length (Fig. 9–11).

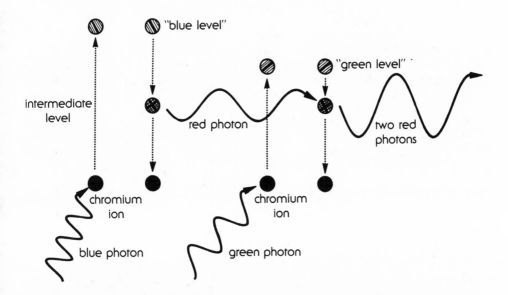

FIG. 9–10 Chromium ions arrive at the intermediate energy level by briefly absorbing blue or green light. A laser chain reaction is ready to take place once the majority of excited ions lose heat and reside at the in-between state. Suddenly a few ions emit red photons spontaneously. Some radiate away; other photons strike ions at the intermediate level and stimulate them to emit matching photons. These continue on their way in phase, perhaps stimulating further emissions which contribute to the rapidly growing stream of coherent light.

The string in Figure 9–11 also can be set vibrating by a series of properly timed impulses—taps, for instance. The waves these taps create grow more pronounced if the taps occur at frequencies associated with wavelengths equal to the string's length divided by whole numbers. Each tap then adds energy that reinforces the vibration. This is the principle of *resonance*, and it operates on many kinds of events that come in cycles.

For example, a playground swing responds to resonance when you thrust your legs forward at the peak of your forward arc. If your pumping action is poorly timed, you won't be reinforcing the swing's action. But if you pump at just the right times, the swing's motion increases steadily with each cycle.

A swing has only one frequency. But if you tap or pluck a fixed string at the proper times, those impulses that cause the string to oscillate with a wavelength equal to one-half (or one-third, or one-quarter, and so on) of its total length will reinforce those vibrations. All other tapping frequencies produce wavelengths that are not reinforced through resonance.

FIG. 9–11 A string stretched between two supports will vibrate when plucked. The wave that results can have a length equal to the distance between the supports or that distance divided by a whole number. Any nodes (marked by **n**'s in the ½ wavelength example) that form remain fixed, while the string on either side oscillates between crest and trough.

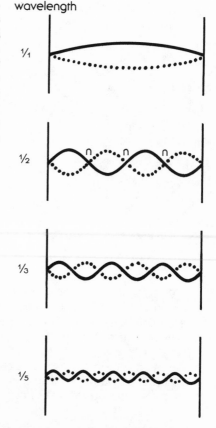

Resonance requires the *superimposition*, or overlapping, of waves of equal length, which, of course, have the same frequency. Water waves from two separate sources produce a standing wave pattern—such as the spoke pattern of the interfering waves in Figure 8–5. This means the wave crests, troughs, and nodes don't advance across the oscillating surface. Instead the wave motion varies from crest to trough and back again without seeming to move forward.

In the case of a fixed string, the original wave reflects back along the string after striking one fixed end. The reflected wave is exactly the same length as the incoming wave, so when they're superimposed, a standing wave pattern appears.

Superimposed waves in a standing pattern add their amplitudes, or heights, constructively. With continued resonance, the combined wave builds in strength.

Laser Resonance

More than 99 percent of the energy the xenon lamp discharged into the ruby crystal is lost in the form of heat and photons emitted in wayward directions. The remaining fraction of a percent contributes to the laser beam. This light consists of photons emitted directly down the laser's axis, the length of the ruby rod (Fig. 9–12).

Mirrors on the ends of the laser reflect the photons back and forth through the lasing material many times. The reflected photons cause more stimulated emission. Like the taps that increase the vibration of a fixed string, the growing number of reflected photons—all in phase—builds in strength through resonance. Resonance, the reinforcement of a few oscillation frequencies only, establishes the narrow bandwidth of laser light, making it very coherent, or orderly.

The resonating photons gain power through the stimulated emission of other photons in phase. In only a fraction of an instant a powerful beam of light bursts through the partially silvered mirror at one end of the ruby crystal. It emerges as a beam of light nature can't produce without human assistance.

Coherent Light

The difference between sunlight and laser light is enormous, as vast as the difference between the roar of an unruly crowd and the song of a highly trained vocalist. The crowd's noise might be deafening, but the single singer has the purity of tone to cause a glass to resonate until it shatters.

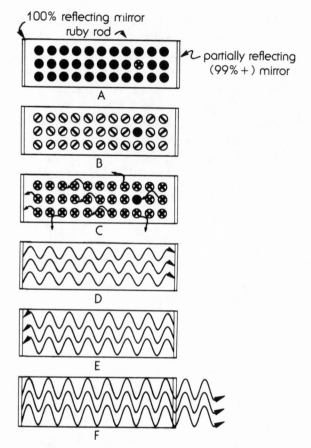

● chromium ion
in ground state

◐ ion excited by
blue photon

◑ ion excited by
green photon

✪ ion in
intermediate
state

100% reflecting mirror
ruby rod

partially reflecting
(99% +) mirror

A

B

C

D

E

F

FIG. 9–12 Each end of the crystal in a ruby laser is highly polished and silver coated to be reflective. One end reflects 100 percent of the incident light and the other more than 99 percent.

Before excitation by the flash lamp, most chromium ions exist in the ground state (**A**). When the ions absorb one of two wavelengths in the white flash, they jump to one of two higher energy levels (**B**).

Quickly the excited ions lose heat and drop to a more stable intermediate level, still higher than the ground state. They linger there long enough for nearly all the excited ions to join them. Soon some of the intermediate level ions emit photons spontaneously. Some of the emitted photons escape through the sides of the crystal. Some strike other intermediate ions, stimulating them to emit (**C**).

Photons that strike the silvered ends of the laser "head on" begin to reflect back and forth along the axis of the ruby rod (**D**). Photons that are even slightly off the perpendicular reflect closer and closer to the edge of the mirror and are lost after a few reflections.

Because the reflecting photons are in phase, the amplitude of their waves increases constantly, as more and more identical photons are stimulated to join them (**E**). Rapidly the combined waves of laser light become very powerful and pass through the less reflective end of the crystal (**F**). The emerging laser beam is highly concentrated and highly coherent.

The difference between sunlight and laser light is the difference between incoherence and coherence. Light from the sun is a haphazard collection of short wave trains of many wavelengths, impossible to keep in phase. In contrast, light from a laser contains long wave trains whose wavelengths hardly vary at all.

Laser light is created in a much tighter beam than incoherent light. If beams of each kind start out with the same diameter, the laser beam will diverge much less over a given distance. In one experiment a pair of lasers with only a few watts of power were aimed at the moon, where a camera aboard a spacecraft recorded their light. The resulting photo of the earth at night shows the two dots of laser light clearly, while the glow of whole cities, with their millions of watts of energy, is scattered and too faint to be seen.

There are two aspects to the coherence of laser light. First, the light is monochromatic, as you've already learned. But another way of looking at that is to say laser light is *temporally coherent*, that is, coherent over time. As time passes, laser light waves continue to oscillate at the same rate. So the light's wavelength measures the same at the beginning of the wave train as at the end (Fig. 9–13).

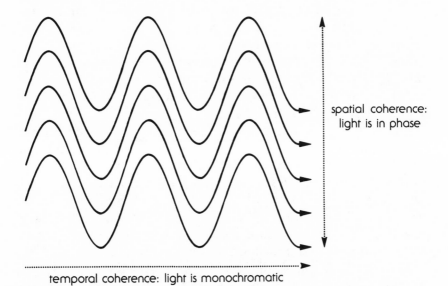

spatial coherence: light is in phase

temporal coherence: light is monochromatic

FIG. 9–13 Laser light is *temporally coherent*; its wavelength remains the same as the beam advances. The light is also *spatially coherent*; its individual waves are lined up with crests and troughs side by side. No natural source can produce light with these properties.

The other aspect of coherence is spatial, that is, coherence over space. While temporal coherence exists along the length of a laser beam, *spatial coherence* exists across the width of the beam. In this dimension, the laser light waves line up in phase with one another. From one side of the beam to the other, they oscillate in unison, with wave crests in phase like ranks of soldiers marching in parade.

Both types of coherence are crucial to holography. Light isn't suitable for making a hologram merely because it's monochromatic. And just because the light is in phase at first doesn't mean it'll stay in phase long enough to give the holographer room to work with it. It takes the extreme spatial and temporal coherence of the laser to make holography practical. From now on, you can take the term *coherent light* to mean light that has both spatial and temporal coherence.

Laser Holography

Shortly after it was demonstrated that a ruby crystal made a good lasing material, scientists succeeded in stimulating other substances to lase. The first gas laser consisted of a glass chamber filled with a mixture of helium (He) and neon (Ne) gases. Instead of using a flash of light to start the laser chain reaction, the HeNe laser is "pumped" to excitation levels by an electric current flowing through the gases, just like a neon sign.

A HeNe laser generates a continuous, unbroken beam, unlike the ruby laser's beam, which comes in a brief flash, or pulse. Both are suitable for holography, but the HeNe laser has become very popular because its price is within the budgets of schools and basement holographers.

Since the early successes, scientists have discovered numerous materials that can produce coherent light by stimulated emission. All operate on similar principles involving an *energy source, atomic excitation,* and a *resonating chamber.* The variations, however, are astounding. Some liquid lasers contain dyes that can be "tuned" to generate coherent light of different wavelengths. And semiconductor lasers are crystal lasers so small a dozen could fit on the nose on a Lincoln head penny!

Whatever the type—and who knows what new types will be developed in the future—lasers were the perfect solution to the problems Gabor faced in holography. They emitted light a million times purer than the best he had. Laser light was so much more coherent, it could produce a highly complex interference

FIG. 9–14 The laser was such a strong source of coherent light, holographers were at last able to record images with pronounced depth and parallax effects. This, one of the first off-axis holograms, produces a virtual image (shown here) and a real image that don't lie along the same line of sight.

pattern. This meant holographers were finally able to encode enough image information to make a hologram with full 3–D detail (Fig. 9–14).

PART 3

THE VIEW FROM INSIDE

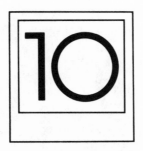

WHEN MESSAGE MEETS
MESSENGER

At the time of Columbus, the Incan civilization on the west coast of what is now South America was in some ways as advanced as those of Europe. Hundreds of kilometers of Incan roads rivaled those the Romans built. The stones of Incan buildings were fitted so precisely that, even though unmortared in that land of earthquakes, they still stand today. And the Incan system of government was a model of efficient complexity.

The emperor, the Inca, was a god, the son of the sun. Ordinary citizens paid a tax to the Inca in the form of labor. They built and maintained his roads, temples, and storehouses. They tended the Inca's fields and harvested his crops. All this effort required extensive recordkeeping, but the Incan language had no written form.

The solution to this bookkeeping problem was a device called a quipu (Fig. 10–1). No one today, not even the descendents of the Incas, can read a quipu, but it seems to have been a combination ledger, calculator, and history book.

The basic elements of the quipu—the string and the knot— make use of a principle common to many communication sys-

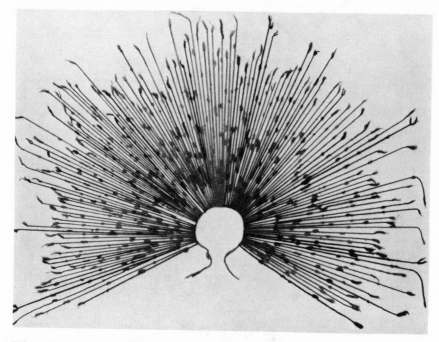

FIG. 10–1 The *quipu* was the Incan version of the personal computer. By tying various knots at intervals on the colored strings, an Incan administrator could record information about population, crops, war casualties, and so on. Individual quipus told a detailed story of the fortunes of a particular district of the empire. The knotted strings also may have worked like an abacus to perform basic calculations.

tems, including radio and holography. The knot is the message; the string is the messenger, or carrier. Each element is meaningless without the other. Together they convey information impossible for either alone.

When an Incan official knotted a quipu in a certain way, he impressed meaning on a string by altering its shape. This, in effect, is what happens when a vibrating drumhead impresses sound on the air that carries it. In radio, the merging of message and messenger is known as modulation. And the modulation of radio waves is similar to the process of altering coherent light waves to produce a hologram.

The Audio Message

As you saw in Figure 5–2, the diagram of a vibrating drumhead, sound consists of longitudinal waves of compressed (more dense) and rarefied (less dense) particles. The particles, usually molecules of air, make up the medium through which the sound travels. Christian Huygens learned this when he witnessed an experiment in which a pump drew air from a glass container with a noisemaker inside. As the air grew thinner and thinner, the sound gradually disappeared, even though Huygens could still see the noisemaker at work.

Sound travels at about 3,569 meters per second at sea level at 0° Celsius. It travels faster in water and faster yet in steel. But, of course, sound is a tortoise to light's hare.

As adequate as sound is for short-range conversation, it's not enough by itself for long-distance messages. Your favorite disk jockey speaks from a studio; you hear the words in your room. To cross the distance in between, the sound waves of the voice, which we'll call the audio message, must be converted to electromagnetic waves.

Radio Waves

Radio is an extension of voice communication. It enables us to get around the considerable limitations that restrict the usefulness of sound as a message carrier.

The radio band of the electromagnetic spectrum ranges in wavelength from about one meter to 10^5 m or more. Waves of this size are traditionally described in terms of frequency. Radio waves, in other words, range from about 3×10^8 cycles per second on the short end to about three cycles per second on the long.

A cycle per second was named a hertz (Hz) in honor of the man who demonstrated that the unseen waves implied by James Clerk Maxwell's equations actually existed. So radio waves range from 3×10^8 Hz to 3 Hz. Microwaves are sometimes included in the radio wave category, extending that spectrum to the threshold of infrared light at about 3×10^{11} Hz.

Radio waves have a tremendous advantage over sound waves for long-range communication. They can carry messages thousands of kilometers—over the horizon when bounced off reflecting layers of the atmosphere. Radio signals even can travel to spacecraft across the solar system.

But the radio spectrum doesn't operate as a communications tool with equal effectiveness from end to end. Generally, the lower the frequency of the radio wave, the less suitable it is for long-distance messages.

The human ear detects sound waves oscillating at rates from about 30 Hz to 18,000 Hz. Radio waves in that frequency range have limited "reach." That's why it's not possible to transmit sound waves as radio waves of the same frequency. The radio message must be "carried" to its destination.

Recipe for Radio Modulation

A sound wave's message consists of variations in the way it compresses and rarefies the particles of its medium—the molecules of whatever material it travels through. Variations in an electromagnetic field contain the same message if they follow a similar pattern.

And that's just what happens when low-frequency sound waves, a voice for instance, are converted to low-frequency radio waves. The meaning of the audio message then exists in a new form. While the audio message was a set of irregular longitudinal (lengthwise oscillating) sound waves, the electromagnetic message is a set of irregular transverse (crosswise oscillating) radio waves. The two forms of the message carry the same information because their irregularities match.

The electromagnetic version of the audio message can't be transmitted over long distances all by itself, however. What's needed is the addition of a set of high-frequency radio waves, which travel much farther. When the low-frequency radio message is superimposed on a set of coherent high-frequency radio waves, which we'll call a *carrier beam*, the latter carries the former along with it. This act of superimposition is called *radio modulation*, and its recipe looks like this:

Audio Message		
(sound waves)		

Radio Message	+	Carrier Beam	=	Radio Signal
(electromagnetic version of sound waves)		(coherent higher frequency e-m waves)		(superimposed, modulated waves)

Remember the quipu: The plain string carries a message once knots are added to it. A radio signal consists of high-frequency electromagnetic waves (the string) which carry a message in the form of irregularities in low-frequency waves (the knots).

The high-frequency portion of the radio signal is the carrier beam. The low-frequency portion that modulates it by "riding piggyback" is the radio message. Figure 10–2 illustrates one way a radio message modulates a carrier beam, by changing its amplitude.

The radio receiver in your home *demodulates* the radio signal by separating the radio message from the carrier beam. The radio speaker finishes the job by converting the isolated low-frequency radio waves back into the sound waves of the message you hear. *Demodulation*, reconverting the radio signal into an audio message, is the reverse of modulation. (*Holographic demodulation* is the subject of Chapter Twelve.)

Basic holography requires two sets of laser light waves. As with radio, one set—the *reference beam*—acts as a carrier. The other set—the *object beam*—is the message that modulates the carrier beam. There are two major differences between holographic modulation and the radio kind, however. One, laser

radio message A

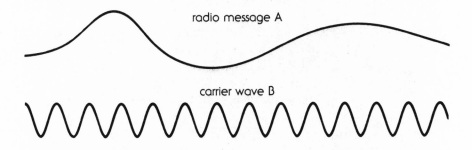

carrier wave B

radio signal A+B, after radio message has modulated carrier wave's amplitude

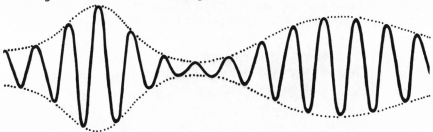

FIG. 10–2 To transmit an audio message such as a voice, sound waves are changed into electromagnetic waves of matching frequency (**A**). The irregular radio message is then superimposed on a high-frequency coherent carrier beam (**B**). The shape of the modulated carrier beam (radio signal **A** + **B**) contains the audio message like knots on a quipu string.

light waves are much, much shorter than radio waves. And two, both reference and object beams must be the same frequency for holographic modulation.

Let's begin our examination of holographic modulation with the message waves.

The Image is the Message

The words you're reading now are part of the image of the book you hold in your hands. The light reaching your eyes from the book looks nothing like the light as it came from its source, be it the sun or a lamp. The source's light carries an image of the source. The book alters the source's light so that after reflection it carries the book's image.

The book's image brings you a great deal of information about the book—for example, its color, its position, and the shapes of its letters and words. This information enables you to recognize the book, pick it up, and read it. The light waves that carry this information to you do so in three ways: by means of differences in wavelength (color), amplitude (brightness), and phase (direction and distance).

A single 2-D view of a book, such as you would get from a photograph, supplies only wavelength and amplitude information. This tells you about the book's outline shape, texture, and color (or in the case of a black-and-white photo, suggests color in variations of gray). Wavelength and amplitude enable you to distinguish the book from what's around it, and by comparison with its surroundings, reveal its size.

But without phase information—information about differences in the distances and directions the reflected light traveled to reach your eyes—there's no way to see the book's position in space or its true 3-D shape. You get this information with an actual image because binocular vision brings you more than one 2-D view of objects. A photograph can't show this information because it can't record the phase differences among the waves of image light. A photo can't supply a viewer with the whole message in an actual image.

Phase and Focus

Camera and eye have structures to focus image light. Lenses (camera), and lens and cornea (eye), ensure that light from each visible object point reaches only one point on film or retina. Both systems record sharp, faithful images of amplitude and wavelength information. But both allow phase information in the image wavefronts to go to waste.

An image comes to your eyes in wavefronts of light. In Huygens's model, a wavefront is the envelope formed by advancing wavelets. The wavelets for any one particular wavefront left their point sources at the same time, so they are in phase all across the wavefront.

The envelope's shape mimics the object's shape because the wavelets in a single wavefront keep the same foreground and background relationship as their sources on the object's surface. This holds true from every viewing angle.

But a camera or an eye takes only one point of view. And its focusing mechanisms collapse image light from many wavefronts onto a single plane. In the process, it treats light waves identically, whether they're from the same or different wavefronts (Fig. 10–3).

Because image detecting systems that focus light are limited to a single viewpoint, they must resort to parallax tricks to sug-

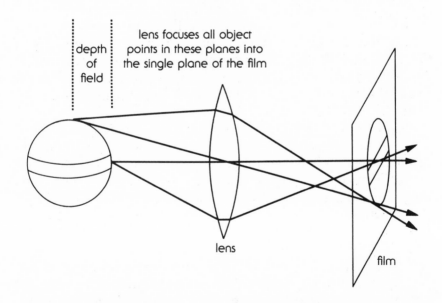

FIG. 10–3 The multiple lens system in a camera (symbolized here by a single converging lens) focuses light waves reflected from several planes onto the single plane of the film. Every visible portion of a 3-D object within the area labeled *depth of field* is then sharply focused. The camera doesn't recognize phase differences among light waves from near and far surfaces. Instead, it brings all within a certain volume to a sharp point. As a result, the 2-D image on the film is the only one the camera can record from this single point of view.

gest the phase information that was lost. The camera's trick, as you've seen, is stereo photography; the eye's is binocular vision. Both use the parallax effect as a substitute for information about phase differences among reflected light waves.

A hologram, on the other hand, yields an unlimited amount of phase information. Its almost unlimited viewing angles come from treating light waves differently, recording the phase relationships among them. To see how holographic modulation can preserve phase differences, let's consider how light strikes a film surface—first in a photograph, then in a hologram.

Intercepting Incoherent Light

Coherent light is often compared to a group of well-trained soldiers marching in step. At all times all right feet are in the same position, as are all left feet. And at every step, all of them advance the same distance. Incoherent light is then comparable to a group of people on the street. Even if they all begin in step, they take steps of different lengths at different times, and so they're soon very much out of step.

Incoherent light from the sun or a flashlamp will produce a photograph. During the fraction of a second it takes to expose the photographic film, it intercepts light waves of all visible lengths. If any two waves happen to arrive at the film plane in phase, they're out of phase an instant later because one completes its cycle faster than the other.

A typical photo exposure lasts a long time compared to a single cycle of an oscillating light wave. That means each point on the film absorbs many different wave trains. And that means any differences in phase among light waves striking neighboring points change from instant to instant (Fig. 10–4).

Photography can't record phase differences among light waves because they change during the exposure. As far as a photograph is concerned, phase differences don't exist. And as far as the viewer is concerned, a photograph is two-dimensional as a result. A hologram, on the other hand, has a means of "freezing" the phase differences among the light waves of image wavefronts.

Intercepting Coherent Light

Making a hologram involves dividing a laser beam in two to produce a pair of coherent beams with the same wavelength.

photographic film plane

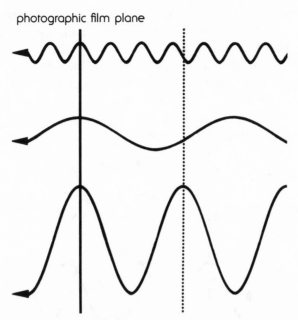

instant 1: light waves   instant 2: waves out of phase
in phase (all at crest)   (at different points in cycle)

FIG. 10—4 The incoherent light waves that strike photographic film at three neighboring points arrive at the same phase of their cycles. Because the waves have different lengths, however, the phase relationship changes from instant to instant. The film is unable to record the constantly changing phase differences during the course of an exposure. Even if it captured the initial relationship, the change of one oscillation later wipes out the information. The phase differences among waves of different lengths changes constantly, and so the phase relationships at any one instant are wasted information.

One—the carrier, or reference, beam—falls on the holographic film without striking anything that would affect its coherence.

The other part of the divided laser beam becomes the message, or object beam, after it strikes the object to be holographed. In the process of being reflected, message waves are changed in terms of phase; they lose spatial, but not temporal, coherence. The reflected waves form wavefronts with the characteristic shape of the object itself.

Then the film plane intercepts cross sections of the message as well as the carrier wavefronts. These wavefronts interfere in the plane of the film to form a standing wave pattern. The message waves meet the carrier waves at each film point in a complex way that doesn't change with time (Fig. 10–5).

Holographic exposures often last several seconds or more,

longer than typical photographic exposures. But because phase differences among light waves in a standing wave interference pattern at the film plane don't change over time, a hologram records this phase information as well as that of wavelength and amplitude. It's the additional phase information that enables a hologram to produce a view with depth.

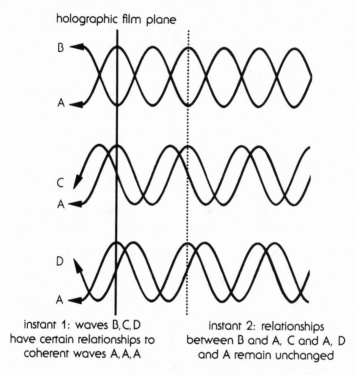

holographic film plane

instant 1: waves B, C, D have certain relationships to coherent waves A, A, A

instant 2: relationships between B and A, C and A, D and A remain unchanged

FIG. 10–5 During a holographic exposure, light of a single wavelength strikes the film in the form of two sets of wavefronts. One is the *carrier beam* and is spatially coherent. The other is the *message beam*, which changed its spatial but not temporal coherence when it was reflected from the object.

The two sets of wavefronts meet at the film and interfere in a standing wave pattern. No matter what the phase difference between any two interfering waves at the instant of contact with the film, it remains the same many cycles later. This also is true of neighboring pairs of interfering waves because the difference in phase between their combined amplitudes doesn't change from instant to instant either.

Once the film records the initial phase differences among waves, the standing waves "lock in" the relationship. Later wavefronts, which interfere in precisely the same way, reinforce the film record of phase information, instead of wiping it out.

It takes the very coherent light of a laser to produce the unchanging interference pattern recorded in a hologram.

The Whole Truth

Dennis Gabor coined the term *hologram*. The roots of this word and *holography* are Greek. "Holo" means whole or entire. "Gram" and "graph" refer to something written or drawn. By extension, the words mean the "whole message" and the act of recording it, respectively.

The terms are appropriate because a hologram is a record of all the image information in a wavefront—the wavelengths, amplitudes, and phases of the image light. More than any other visual record, holography captures the whole truth about an image.

When a message wave modulates a carrier wave during a holographic exposure, it imparts information about the distance and direction of the object from the film plane at various points. Carrier waves strike the film in phase; message waves are considerably less organized when they strike. The difference in the direction and distance each message wave travels causes it to interfere with a carrier wave at a unique phase of its cycle. A carrier wave at each point serves as a reference, or background against which to compare an object wave at that same point.

As you can imagine from Figure 10–5, the reference and object waves must be exactly the same length if the phase difference between them is to remain constant during an exposure. The holographer can't use two lasers of the same type to supply the two beams because lasers are unique. Each produces its own unique collection of wavelengths, which may be very, very similar, but never identical. Two beams coming from different lasers won't match with the precision needed for one to serve as a reference to the other.

The wavelengths of a single laser, its bandwidth, also change with time. A laser that has "warmed up" produces slightly different spectral lines than one that is "cold." And the wavelength and phase characteristics, the degree of coherence, of a single laser beam changes gradually with time.

So, by splitting the beam of a single laser in two, the holographer obtains reference and object waves that are identical from the start. As long as the two sets of waves travel roughly the same distance from laser to film, they'll remain matched closely enough to form a standing wave pattern, with the message (object) beam modulating the carrier (reference) beam and producing interference fringes. Each variation in interference between the two at various spots on the film tells some

slightly different about the location of each message wave's point source (Fig. 10–6).

Message waves that originate from different object points and strike the same film point also modulate carrier waves so as to tell something about the depth of the object (Fig. 10–7).

As always, don't imagine the wavy lines in the diagram are

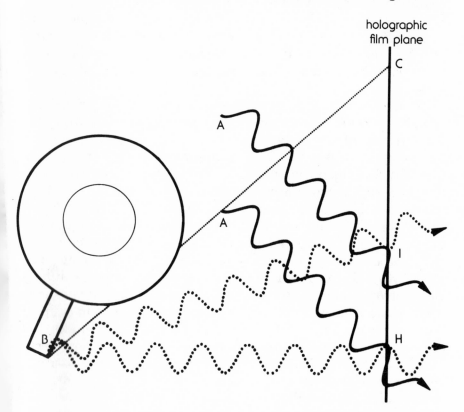

FIG. 10—6 Every unobstructed point on an object supplies image information to every point on the holographic film. Here you see two pathways by which point **B** on a cup reflects light to the film. The pathways differ in length. Therefore, light from **B** is at a wave crest when it reaches point **H**, and at a trough when it reaches **I**. At both points it interferes with waves from the reference beam, which is still spatially coherent.

Carrier waves **AH** and **AI** strike the film in phase. But **AH** interferes constructively with message light from **B** at point **H**. And **AI** interferes destructively with message light at **I**. If these were the only two pairs of waves to strike the film, it would be exposed at **H** and remain unexposed at **I**. (Waves from **B** that strike the film between **H** and **I** create carrier wave interference between the two extremes.)

The dotted line shows that the cup blocks light from **B** in the direction of point **C**. This means the image of the cup handle won't be visible from that point of the hologram, although it remains visible from points **H** and **I**. In this way, a hologram duplicates real-life experience.

physical reality. Figures 10–6 and 10–7 are symbolic representations of isolated carrier and message light waves. Actually each film point receives message light from every point on the object "visible" to it, as well as a great deal of carrier light. The overall effect of these innumerable waves is basically the same as that suggested in the figures, but vastly more complex.

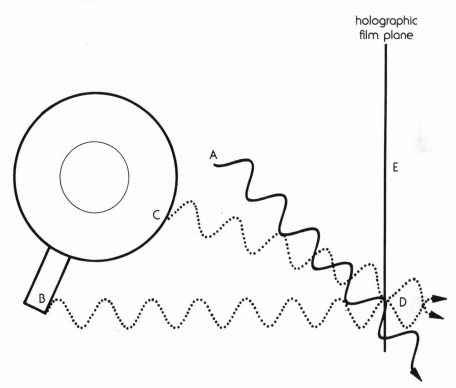

FIG. 10–7 The reference part of the laser beam also "locks in" the phase differences between light waves from two separate points on an object that reach the same point on the film. Light from points **B** and **C** travels different distances to the film at point **D**, and the two waves arrive out of phase. As a result, waves **B** and **A** interfere destructively while **C** and **A** interfere constructively. Therefore, **B** modulates **A** to have little effect on the film and **C** modulates **A** to expose it.

The combined effect of light from **B** and **C** is different at point **D** than it is at point **E**. The difference imparts important information about the relative positions of these and other object points at the holographic film plane. In effect, the hologram records the direction each light wave traveled from the cup to the film.

From this diagram, you might wonder why object waves from points **B** and **C** don't modulate each other as well. Actually, they do. But the holographer makes sure the object beam is only a fraction of the intensity of the reference beam. As a result, object wave-*reference* wave interference overpowers object wave-*object* wave interference, which doesn't appear as strongly in the fringe pattern.

The interference of carrier and message waves at a single spot on film is a complicated record of the unchanging combined phase differences of all those waves. The overall interference effects differ over the film plane because of differences in the angles between object and film surfaces. Therefore, the hologram receives information about an object as it appears from an infinite number of points of view. All that needs to be done is record the information.

The Next Step

Once the message wavefronts have interfered with the carrier wavefronts and modulated them, the image information they hold is ready for recording. Reconsider the recipe for encoding a hologram:

Object's 3-D Image + Light = Hologram

You can now think of the recipe as follows:

Object's 3-D Image +	Reference Beam =	Hologram
(message in e-m waves)	(coherent same-frequency e-m carrier waves)	(record of superimposed, modulated waves)

The waves of the object beam hold the image, the visual message. When superimposed on, or combined with, a reference beam, object waves modulate reference waves to carry the image's 3-D information. The interference pattern they form in the film is the record of that information about every visible object point.

Recording a hologram resembles the way a photograph is made. At least the photochemical reactions that take place in the film are the same. But as you might expect by now, there are also important differences, differences that contribute to a hologram's magic.

RECORDING AN
INTERFERENCE PATTERN

When Gabriel Lippmann made one of his beautiful color photos, he used black-and-white film. What's more, he always put the film in backwards!

In 1891, Lippmann discovered a way of recording an interference pattern by allowing light to pass through his film, strike a reflecting surface, and pass through the film again. When the reflected light waves became superimposed on the arriving light waves, they formed a standing wave pattern, something like the way the vibrating string formed unmoving nodes in Figure 9–11. The interference pattern had the ability to reflect viewing light in the same colors as the original scene. The quality of Lippmann's color photos was superb.

As you will learn, each of Lippmann's photographs was, in effect, a hologram of a 2-D scene. But Gabriel Lippmann made his discovery nine years before Dennis Gabor was born! So why, you might ask, doesn't Lippmann get credit for inventing holography?

161

Part of the reason for this apparent oversight was that Lippmann's technique had considerable disadvantages. It required long exposure times, for example, and the photo original couldn't make copies, as an ordinary photo negative can. Because the photographic image Lippmann recorded was still only two-dimensional, other photographers might not have thought the heightened color was worth the extra trouble. As a result, the Lippmann process never became widely used.

Holography in the early days was probably at least as difficult to master as Lippmann photography. But the holographic 3-D effect was worth the trouble, and so Gabor is now known as its father. Today some types of holograms act like an infinite number of Lippmann photographs rolled into one.

Quick Review

Let's re-examine a basic difference between photography and holography. Photography is a record of an image as seen from a single viewpoint. Holography is a record of an image as seen from many, many viewpoints.

A photographer uses lenses to focus incoherent light waves on film. The lenses direct light reflected from each visible spot on an object to a matching spot on the film, point for point. Phase differences among the reflected waves have no effect on the film. As long as the light comes from points within the depth of field of that particular lens arrangement, the waves are focused. The record of the single 2-D image is a photograph.

In contrast, making a hologram doesn't require lenses to focus image light (although lenses often are used for other reasons, as you'll see). Instead, light waves from each visible spot on the object strike the film everywhere they can reach in a straight-line path. Phase differences among these light waves carry depth information about the object to all parts of the holographic window. The record of these infinite 2-D views is a hologram.

A hologram is a record of the pattern of interference between laser reference and object beams. This code is the hologram's way of capturing the enormous amount of 3-D image information that comes to it. The most common method of recording the code is film similar to that used in photography. But because a hologram contains so much more information than a photo can, its film must have a greater storage capacity. And that's determined by its emulsion.

Exposure and Emulsion

Film, whether photographic or holographic, has the same basic structure. The two most important elements for this discussion are light-sensitive chemicals and a surface to spread them on. Typical surfaces are plastic, glass, or paper.

The light-sensitive chemical coating is called the film *emulsion*. Black-and-white emulsion contains silver compounds such as silver bromide, silver iodide, and silver chloride, which are sometimes grouped under the name *silver halides* or *silver salts*.

Silver halides have a useful instability. When a molecule in a grain of silver halide absorbs a photon, it breaks apart, leaving an atom of metallic silver, which is black. During a photographic exposure, millions of photons break down millions of silver halide molecules. Although this creates a great number of silver grains in the emulsion, the vast majority of silver halide grains are as yet unaffected (Fig. 11–1a).

Of course, photons don't strike the emulsion evenly. Bright areas of an object reflect more photons to the film than dark areas do. That means the atoms of silver these photons produce cluster in various areas of the film. The arrangement of silver atoms represents the object's *latent* or potential 2-D image. Development is the chemical process that transforms this latent image into a coded photographic negative.

Development

Dipping the exposed film into the proper chemical solution causes the breakdown of more silver halide grains. This happens in the vicinity of the silver atoms that make up the latent image. This effect is greatest wherever silver atoms from the original exposure are thickest. As a result, the latent image becomes about ten million times more pronounced (Fig. 11–1b).

The dark areas of the emulsion at this point are proportional to the bright areas of the object, and vice versa. The emulsion now carries a full range of areas from black to gray to white, depending on the distribution of silver in the latent image (Fig. 11–1c).

In the next steps, the emulsion is soaked in chemicals that stop development and then change all the remaining silver halide molecules into colorless compounds that are no longer sensitive to light. The film is washed after that to remove all chemicals remaining from previous steps. Finally the film is dried.

The result is a white-and-black photographic negative. As described earlier, the negative produces a positive 2-D print when light shines through it and is focused onto light-sensitive paper.

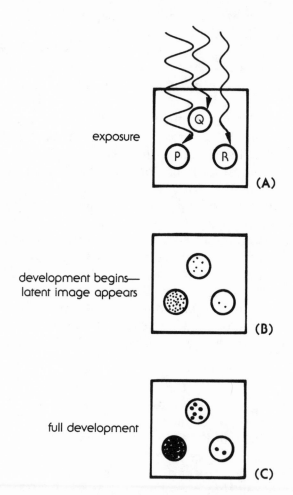

exposure (A)

development begins— latent image appears (B)

full development (C)

FIG. 11–1a, 11–1b, 11–1c Light falling on a film emulsion produces a *latent image* when a relatively few silver halide molecules in a grain of the compound absorb photons. The absorbed energy changes the molecules to atoms of metallic silver. In (1a), the silver halide grain P receives the most light.

The latent image isn't visible until the film is treated with chemicals during development. Then other metallic silver atoms form around the atoms of the latent image (1b).

As development proceeds, it amplifies the latent pattern so that grain **P** becomes visibly black, **Q** is gray, and **R** mostly clear (1c). Other chemicals stop development and make the amplified record of the latent image permanent.

General purpose black-and-white film is sensitive to visible light of all wavelengths, although its sensitivity is not equal across the spectrum. Holographic film need not be so widely sensitive in most cases because laser light is monochromatic. Of course, a holographer must choose a film whose sensitivity matches the laser's bandwidth.

The black-and-white film holographers use undergoes much the same photochemical changes as the film in your camera. But because a hologram must record more information, its emulsion is made with especially small silver halide grains.

Grain and Speed

Manufacturers can vary their emulsion recipes to make films for many conditions. Sometimes photographers need to make a photo in dim light; they need an emulsion that is extremely responsive to photons. The more photo-sensitive a film is, the more quickly it records a usable latent image. Highly responsive films are said to be "fast" because they require relatively short exposures.

Sports photographers and others who record moving objects need fast film to capture an image before movement blurs it. The advantages of speed are obvious, but speed has a big drawback. A faster emulsion has larger silver halide grains. And the larger the grains, the coarser the final photo detail. Grain size is a problem when a photo image is enlarged a lot. Then fast films have a "sandy" look because individual grains become noticeable.

That's why slow films are better than fast for work that calls for recording tiny detail. The smaller silver halide grains of slow film can record smaller variations in dark and bright. But even the slowest photographic film in common use has emulsion that's too coarse for holography. A hologram, after all, must be able to record details as tiny as the phase differences among light waves.

Fine Resolution

A film's *resolving power* is a measure of its ability to distinguish between details. Two side-by-side features appear as one when they're so small an emulsion can't record the separation between them.

Resolving power is expressed in lines per millimeter. An emulsion must have smaller grains to record more lines per millimeter, that is, smaller separations between details. A photographer's fine-grained film might have a resolving power of one hundred lines per millimeter. That's enough to make a photo that's acceptably sharp even when enlarged.

But to record phase differences among light waves, a film must have a resolving power of at least 1500 lines per millimeter. That means the emulsion can show 1500 distinct lines in a space about half as wide as the lead in a wooden pencil! Only then does it have the power to distinguish interference fringes.

Slices of Light

If photography had existed in 1800, Thomas Young could have recorded his now-famous interference fringes on film. And he would have had a simple hologram.

Recall the apparatus Young used (Fig. 8–9). The first slit acted as a line of stacked pinholes to force incoherent sunlight into concentric cylindrical wavefronts. The pair of slits in a second screen split the light from the first slit into two sets of identical cylindrical wavefronts. A final screen intercepted a cross section of these wavefronts as they interfered. This slice showed fringes in the form of bright and dark nearly parallel lines.

But Young's fringes are only one kind of cross section of interfering wavefronts. In this case, the slice consists of a small segment of a larger pattern formed when waves overlap at a narrow angle. If you imagine wavefronts interfering in three dimensions, you'll understand that other cross sections exist and can be recorded.

Start with spherical wavefronts interfering with plane waves. From one viewpoint, the two sets of wavefronts appear to interfere only at a few points (Fig. 11–2a). But from another point of view, looking straight at the screen, they appear as concentric circles (Fig. 11–2b).

The bull's-eye fringe pattern, when photographed and developed, makes what is known as a Gabor zone plate (Fig. 11–3), which is comparable to the mechanically drawn zone plate in Figure 8–15.

Other fringe patterns appear when spherical wavefronts interfere. Figures 11–4a,b and 11–5a,b show how the fringes multiply as the distance increases between the centers of the spheres.

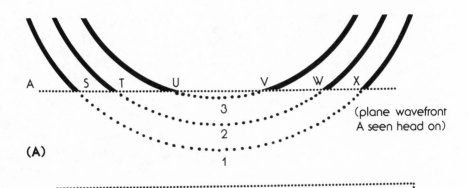

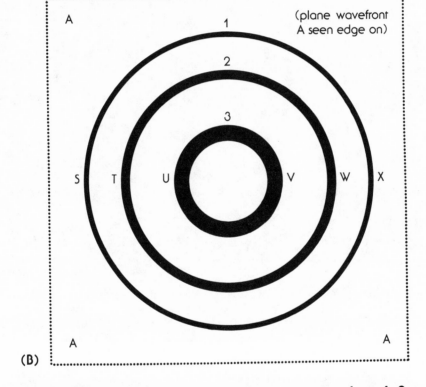

FIG. 11–2a, 11–2b Wavefront **A** is a plane wave; wavefronts **1**, **2**, and **3** are spherical. Viewed in the plane of the paper, the wave crests are represented by straight lines and arcs. At this instant and from this point of view, the spherical wavefronts interfere with the crest of plane wave **A** at only six points: **S**, **T**, **U**, **V**, **W**, and **X** (2a).

But all these wavefronts exist in three dimensions. Wavefront **A** is in contact with the film over its entire surface, and wavefronts **A**, **B**, and **C** are in the process of expanding like balloons. As Figure 11–2b shows in a different plane, wavefront **A** (from Fig. 11–2a) interferes with a circular slice of each spherical wavefront.

Wavefront **A** cuts across a larger slice of wavefront **1** than it does of wavefront **3** because **1** is ahead of **3**.

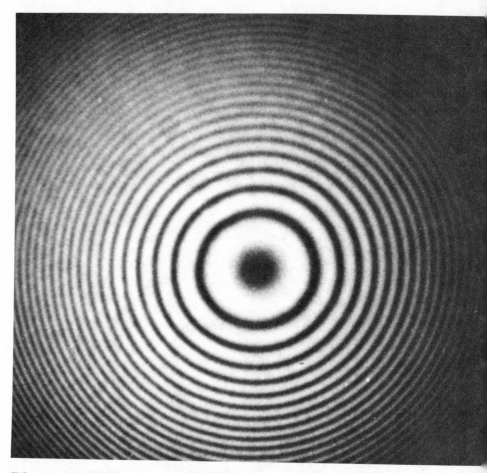

FIG. 11–3 A Gabor zone plate is the result of the interference of a plane wavefront with a series of concentric spherical waves, as diagrammed in Figure 11–2b. It resembles a mechanically drawn (Fresnel) zone plate, but its fringes are not as sharply defined as drawn lines can be. These fringes consist of areas of complete constructive interference blending into complete destructive interference. The Gabor version diffracts only first-order wavefronts. Still, a Gabor zone plate can produce real and virtual images just as the Fresnel version does.

FIG. 11–5 If the centers of the two sets of spherical wavefronts are ▶ moved farther apart, the points where they intersect more closer together. Constructive interference fringes are still hyperbolas, but are flatter hyperbolas. In three dimensions, the hyperboloids look more like stacked plates than nested bowls.

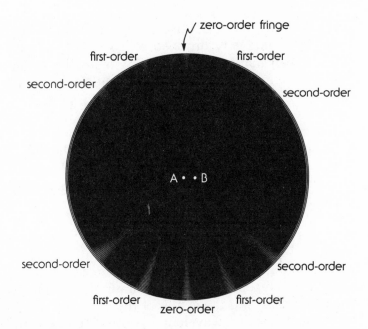

FIG. 11–4 Points **A** and **B** are the sources of two sets of spherical wavefronts. Constructive interference appears as a set of bright fringes in the shape of spokes on a wheel. Black areas show where the wavefronts overlap out of phase.

The middle, zero-order interference fringe is a bright constructive fringe that's straight and perpendicular to the axis line connecting **A** and **B**. Higher-order fringes to either side take curved shapes known as *hyperbolas*.

To visualize the fringes in three dimensions, imagine the hyperbolas spinning around axis **AB**, forming shapes like bowls nested one inside the next. The bowl shapes are called hyperboloids.

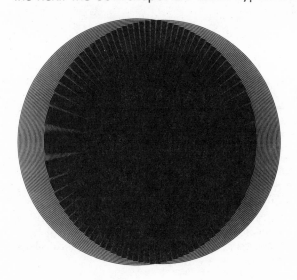

The patterns in these illustrations are ideal. In Young's experiment, light intensity dropped off so rapidly toward the edges of his screen that he observed only a small portion of the pattern. A larger view shows that what seemed to be parallel fringes were actually slightly curved (Fig. 11–6a).

Because these interference patterns, as well as emulsion itself, occupy 3-D space, it's possible to expose film to other portions of the full pattern. Imagine that the relatively thick emulsion intercepts the pattern in front of Young's screen. Then you can record fringes in the shape of slightly splayed ribbons (Fig. 11–6b).

Yet another cross section intercepts fringes that resemble stacked plates (Fig. 11–6c). These fringes, formed when interfering wavefronts approach each other at an angle of 180, are very close together. Recording them is a severe test of an emulsion's resolving power. The separation between the center of one dark fringe and the center of the bright fringe next to it can be as small as half a wavelength—only 316 nm or so in the case of light from a HeNe laser.

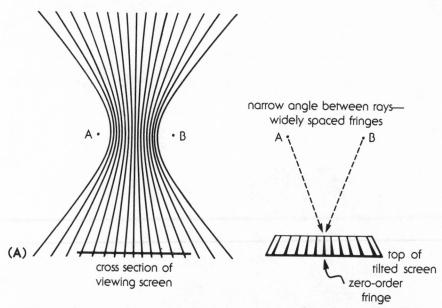

narrow angle between rays— widely spaced fringes

A   B

top of tilted screen

zero-order fringe

(A)

cross section of viewing screen

FIG. 11–6a The line cutting across the hyperbolic fringes represents a cross section of the viewing screen Thomas Young used to intercept the interference pattern in Figure 8–8. The parallel fringes run perpendicularly to the paper as suggested by the tilted view of the screen. In Young's experiment, the light from the two sources A and B met at a relatively narrow angle, as measured between light rays drawn from A and B. This produced fringes that were widely spaced.

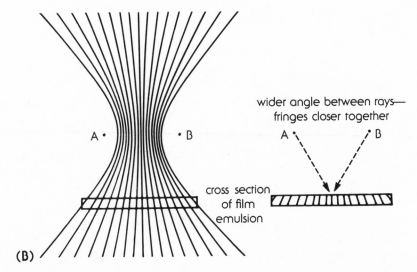

(B)

FIG. 11–6b The rectangles represent a cross section of film emulsion. In three dimensions, above and below the page, the relatively thick emulsion records individual fringes as thin ribbons. Note that the fringes tend to flatten out with respect to the surfaces of the film, the farther they are from the zero-order fringe in the center. Fringe separation also widens toward the edges of the film. Yet because the angle between light rays from the two sources is wider than in 6a, the fringes are closer together—more of them fit from left to right.

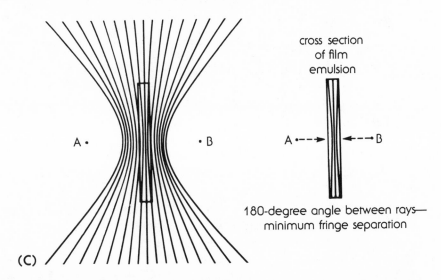

(C)

FIG. 11–6c Here the angle between the light sources is greatest—180°. The interfering wavefronts meet head on to form fringes in a series of sheets roughly parallel to the surfaces of the emulsion (and still perpendicular to the page). The fringe separation in this arrangement is the narrowest of all—as small as one-half wavelength of the light used.

Now let's see what more complex fringes demand of an emulsion's resolving power.

Fringes and Grain

The fringes of a Gabor zone plate are not perfectly sharp lines. The bright circles merge with the dark ones by passing through gray areas. These gray areas are the sign of phase differences between the extremes of completely constructive and completely destructive interference.

In addition, the simple fringe lines of a Gabor zone plate appear only when the object beam comes from a point source. The complex wavefront reflected from the many points of a 3-D object produces the tiny fringe specks in the enlarged holographic film you saw in Figure 3–5. The microscopic "salt-and-pepper" pattern of the holographic cipher is oriented along lines because each object point produces a unique set of fringes. But the overall pattern of overlapping fringes from many object points is far from sharply defined.

The finer the emulsion grain, remember, the more accurately a film can record small variations in phase difference. A fine-grain film is better able to separate the minute specks that make up the infinitely complex zone plate that is a fully 3-D hologram.

One manufacturer advertises film with an emulsion containing silver halide grains that average about 90 nm in diameter. This film has a proven resolving power of 3,000 lines per millimeter. An even slower emulsion from the same company carries an average grain size of 35 nm, capable of resolving 5,000 lines per millimeter!

Such fine-grained holographic films have a resolving power that's fifty or more times that of ordinary photographic emulsions. Such films are so slow they require high intensity pulsed lasers or extremely long exposures to a continuous wave laser to form a good latent image. So they're out of the question for snapshots. But this kind of resolving power is essential for distinguishing the separation between the tiniest holographic fringes.

As Figure 11–6c indicates, interference fringes are most compressed when coherent wavefronts meet head on. A typical emulsion is seven microns (7×10^{-6} meters) thick. When HeNe laser light from two point sources interferes in this way, perhaps only 15 or 16 fringes, formed half a wavelength apart, are recorded from front to back within the emulsion. If the film's grains are 90 nm across, the emulsion can devote about five grains to distinguishing one fringe from the next. But if the emulsion contains 35 nm grains, more than twice as many are available for recording the difference between fringes.

The same advantage is true of more complex holographic fringes: Smaller emulsion grains can record more information in the separation of fringe specks. As far as film is concerned, grain size is the single most important consideration for capturing the most image information possible.

When fringes are formed by interfering wavefronts from simple point sources of light, a tenfold improvement in resolving power might not be worth the expense. But when fringes are the result of a wavefront from an object infinitely more complex than a point source, any improvement in resolving power brings a wealth of additional image information.

At present, perhaps the world's finest grain film comes from Bulgaria. There scientists have succeeded in producing an emulsion that's able to resolve 10,000 lines per millimeter— that's 10,000 lines side by side in the width of a paper clip wire! As exciting as that news is for holographers, other recording materials also hold promise.

Variations

The extra-fine grain emulsions used in holography are based on time-tested recipes for photographic film. Film is easy to expose and develop. It also can be made sensitive to a wide spectrum. And it even works after its black silver grains are changed to transparent compounds. In fact, this "bleaching" step has become routine, making holograms with brighter images because more illuminating light can pass through them. That is, bleached holograms are more efficient image-makers than unbleached ones.

But there are other substances that make a permanent record of a holographic interference pattern. They include:

Dichromated gelatin (DCG)—So far DCG holograms are the most efficient of all, turning as much as 80 to 90 percent of the viewing light into an image. Holographers have to be willing to cook up a batch of DCG whenever they need it, though, so it's not widely used. DCG also is not usually sensitive to any colors other than blue-green, which excludes holographers who only have an HeNe laser on hand. Finally, these holograms must be sealed because humidity will ruin them. Still, the advantage of brightness is appealing (Fig. 11–7).

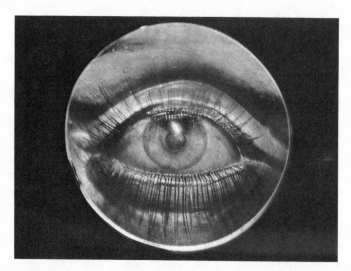

FIG. 11–7 The light-sensitive material in a DCG hologram is made from ordinary gelatin powder, ordinary tap water, and a small amount of ammonium dichromate. On exposure to light, the substance breaks down into a related compound that causes the gelatin to shrink when the water is removed. The holographic cipher is contained in the variations of shrinkage.

Photo polymer—Light-sensitive plastics in liquid form can produce holograms with the same efficiency as DCG. Photo polymers also can be made sensitive to many different wavelengths. To prepare for exposure, a glass plate is coated with the liquid, which is allowed to set. After a drying period, the photo polymer can be treated like a film emulsion. Holographic exposure causes fringe areas to become more dense, depending on the amount of light they receive. Later treatment makes the interference pattern permanent. The newer photo polymers are cheaper, more dependable, and easier to work with and keep than DCG, and will eventually replace it.

Thermoplastic and photoresist—Heat deforms thermoplastic material. Certain chemicals eat away photoresist material. Exposing these to light of different intensities determines the degree to which they'll be deformed or eaten away. Areas that receive more light due to constructive interference end up thinner than areas of destructive interference. These fringes have the same effect as those made with silver halide emulsion although the mechanism is slightly different. The main advantages of these methods is that the first is erasable and reusable (Fig. 11–8 a, b, c, d). The second makes mass-produced holograms possible (Fig. 11–9 a, b, c, d).

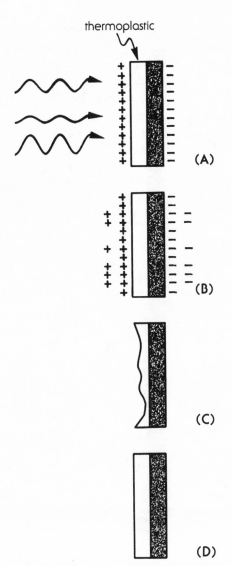

thermoplastic

(A)

(B)

(C)

(D)

FIG. 11–8*a*, **11–8***b*, **11–8***c*, **11–8***d* A *thermoplastic hologram* is made with a material that deforms when exposed to heat. The first step is to place uniform but opposite electric charges on the thermoplastic and the light-sensitive plate behind it (8*a*). Areas exposed to constructive interference receive a stronger electric charge (8*b*).

Now when the thermoplastic is heated, areas where the electric charge is greatest are squeezed more (8*c*). The irregularities in the thickness of the thermoplastic after development contain the holographic code. Controlled heating restores the thermoplastic to its regular shape, erasing the hologram, and preparing it for another exposure (8*d*).

This system has made possible a portable holographic camera that can produce a hologram ten seconds after the exposure. The lifetime of the thermoplastic in this particular system is 1,000 holograms.

All recording materials work because exposures to varying amounts of light cause varying degrees of physical change. Just as film emulsion turns gray or black or remains unchanged in response to constructive and destructive interference, for example, so do thermoplastics shrink or stay the same.

The kind of physical change a recording material undergoes determines how it forms a holographic image. This also means that different kinds of holograms are viewed differently.

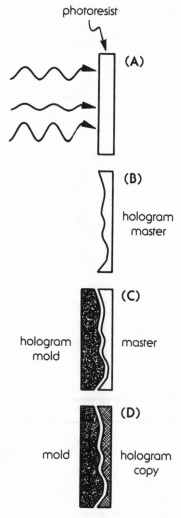

FIG. 11–9a, 11–9b, 11–9c, 11–9d Development of photoresist materials exposed to light results in a pattern of ridges corresponding to the interference fringes (9a, b). The uneven surface serves as a model to make a mold, which is coated with metal and used to press copies in much the same way phonograph records are made (9c, d).

12

VIEWING A HOLOGRAM

A perfect wave may have a lot to say to a surfer, but for communication a wave with an ideal and unchanging shape is meaningless. Only when a wave is altered can it carry a message. Like an Incan official tying knots in a quipu's string, the radio engineer and the holographer encode information by changing the shape of coherent electromagnetic waves.

This is the essence of modulation—adding meaning to a simple, regular wave by combining it with another whose irregularities represent information.

A radio signal and a hologram's interference pattern are made from the superimposition of two or more waves. The laser reference beam is like the radio carrier beam. The laser object beam encodes the reference beam in much the same way the radio message modulates its carrier beam. The hologram that results, as you've learned, is a record of an electromagnetic cipher. It has to be decoded to reveal its message.

Dennis Gabor called the process of decoding a hologram *wavefront reconstruction*. In effect, illuminating a hologram is like turning on a radio: The act frees the message by separating it from its carrier beam.

Recipe for Demodulation

Encoding or modulating an electromagnetic cipher means combining two sets of waves. In the case of radio modulation, as you recall from Chapter Ten, sound waves—for instance, voice or music—are first converted to electromagnetic waves with the same pattern of irregularities. This is the radio message, which is no longer in a form you can hear. The radio message is then superimposed on other electromagnetic waves that are coherent at a higher frequency. The recipe for radio modulation looks like this:

		(Modulation—Encoding)		
Radio Message	+	Carrier Beam	=	Radio Signal
(e-m version of sound waves)		(coherent, higher frequency e-m waves)		(superimposed, modulated waves)

Demodulation reverses the effect:

		(Demodulation—Decoding)		
Radio Signal	+	Carrier Beam	=	Radio Message
		(second set of coherent waves, 180° out of phase with first set)		

Your radio receiver at home extracts the sound from the radio signal. It does this by superimposing another electromagnetic beam—one identical to the original carrier beam—on the incoming radio signal. This demodulating beam is superimposed out of phase with the carrier beam, however, so that they cancel by destructive interference. What remains is the radio message, which your radio speakers convert from electromagnetic waves back into matching sound waves. Only then do you hear the voice or music from the radio station.

A hologram is a record of modulated electromagnetic waves—in this case, waves of light, not sound. As with radio (sound), though, one set of waves is the message, which you see as an image. Because the image is already electromagnetic, it needs no conversion before being superimposed on another set of electromagnetic waves, the coherent carrier beam. Unlike radio, the two beams must have the same frequency.

The image waves impose their message on the coherent carrier waves by modulating them. Holographic film "freezes" the interference pattern the superimposed waves make. The image exists in a form you can't recognize at that point. You must illuminate the hologram properly to demodulate the record of the superimposed image and carrier waves. This releases the image information once more.

Compare the recipes for holographic modulation and demodulation below with the recipes for radio encoding and decoding on the previous page:

(Modulation)

Object's 3-D Image	+	Reference Beam	=	Hologram
(message in e-m waves)		(coherent, same-frequency e-m carrier waves)		(record of superimposed, modulated waves)

(Demodulation)

Hologram	+	Reference Beam	=	Object's 3-D Image
		(viewing, or illuminating, light)		

From now on, we'll use the terms *reference beam* or *wave* to identify that portion of the laser light used as a carrier wave to make a hologram. We'll use the terms *viewing light* or *illuminating light* to identify that light, whether coherent or incoherent, used to demodulate a hologram and reconstruct an image.

In the simplest case, the hologram's image information reappears when coherent light shines on the interference pattern the same way the original reference beam did. The coherent viewing light goes into the hologram. What comes out is the object beam, the image of the holographed object.

When unaltered laser light is used both as a reference beam during the making of a hologram and as a reference beam for viewing—as in the simplest case—the relationship between them is clear. The two laser beams are coherent and strike the film from the same angle. The first coherent beam is modulated by the object light, and the film records the interference. The second coherent beam demodulates the film record by subtracting the effect of the first beam, and reconstructing object light for viewing.

But viewing light needn't always be coherent. White light from the sun or a small, bright lamp like a projector bulb is good enough for reconstructing an image from some holograms. Then incoherent viewing light also demodulates their interference patterns.

Holographic demodulation works by absorbing, refracting, reflecting, and diffracting light. Reflection and diffraction do most of the work in most holograms, however.

Decoding by Reflection

Let's return to a hologram of a single point to examine reflection demodulation. We'll use an approach first suggested by Dr. T.H. Jeong, of Lake Forest College. Remember that when two spherical wavefronts interfere, they form a family of hyperboloid fringes (shown in one plane in Figure 11–6a as a family of hyperbolas).

Each fringe of this pattern acts as a mirror. The zero-order fringe is a plane surface that reflects light from the center of one set of waves in a direction that makes it appear to come from the center of the other set (Fig. 12–1). And as Figure 12–1 also shows, the hyperbolic surfaces of the higher order fringes—the ones to either side of the central zero-order fringe—are just the right shape to do the same thing!

Reflecting fringes in this case make viewing light from source B seem to originate from point A no matter which fringe reflects the illuminating light. The angle of the reflected light creates the illusion that source A still exists exactly where it was when it created the fringes in the first place. This illusion, of course, is nothing more than a virtual image of A.

Figure 11–6b showed how an emulsion can record a portion of A and B's interference pattern of light as a set of ribbon-shaped fringes. Because these fringes are sections of hyperbolic surfaces, they reflect light the same way. From one side they

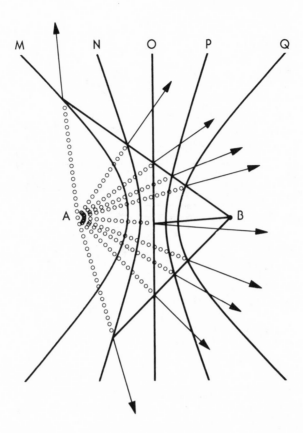

FIG. 12–1 Spherical wavefronts from point sources **A** and **B** interfere to form a straight-line zero-order fringe (**O**) and a family of higher-order hyperbolic fringes (**M, N, P, Q**) in the plane of the paper. When point **A** is removed, the fringes can produce **A**'s virtual image by reflecting **B**'s light along the solid lines back in the directions of the arrows. To observers on **B**'s side of the fringes, the reflected light seems to come from **A** along the paths of the dotted lines. No matter where the light from **B** strikes the hyperbolic fringe mirrors, its reflected rays *seem* to come from the absent source **A**.

form a *virtual* image of *A* (Fig. 12–2*a*) and from the other they reconstruct a *real* image (Fig. 12–2*b*).

Reflection demodulation is especially important in decoding holograms whose hyperbolic fringes are roughly parallel to the surface of the film, as in Figure 11–6*c*. Each fringe layer reflects only part of the illuminating light, allowing some through to other layers deep within the emulsion (Fig. 12–3*a, b*).

Reflection often works with diffraction to demodulate a hologram.

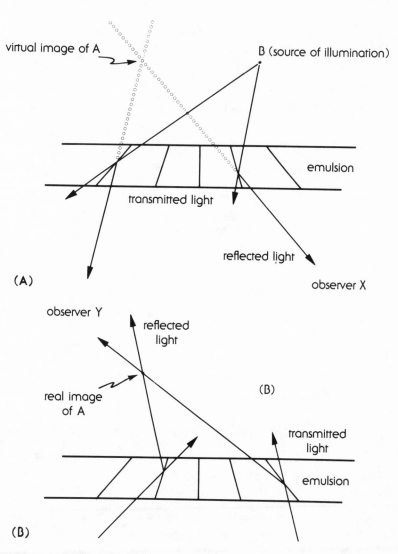

FIG. 12–2a, 12–2b A piece of film placed to record the various fringes from Figure 12–1 as a series of thin ribbons captures the hyperbolic mirror effect of a small section of the whole interference pattern. The ribbons behave the same way. When light similar to the original reference light strikes them from the position of the original point **B**, they reflect some of it in such a way as to produce a virtual image of **A** (2a) for observer **X**.

Because the path of the illuminating light is reversible, the hologram can be viewed in light that heads back toward point **B**. Then the reflecting fringes redirect it so it's focused in space—a real image for observer **Y** (2b).

In both cases, the partial mirrors of the fringes reflect some light and transmit the rest.

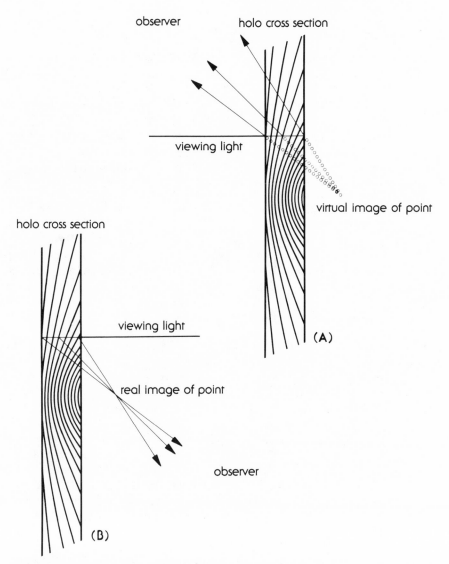

FIG. 12–3a, 12–3b Partially transparent fringes reflect some viewing light while allowing the rest to reach fringes deep within the emulsion. Because of the way equipment is set up for reflection holograms, the film records only the higher-order hyperbolic fringes on one side of the zero-order fringe. This allows the hologram to reconstruct both a virtual and a real image.

When viewing light strikes the hologram from the same side as the original reference beam, the fringes reconstruct a *virtual* image (3a).

When the viewing light comes from the opposite side, however, a *real* image forms (3b).

Reflection holograms are less sensitive than transmission holograms to the angle of the viewing light. It doesn't have to match the reference beam's original angle to demodulate the interference pattern.

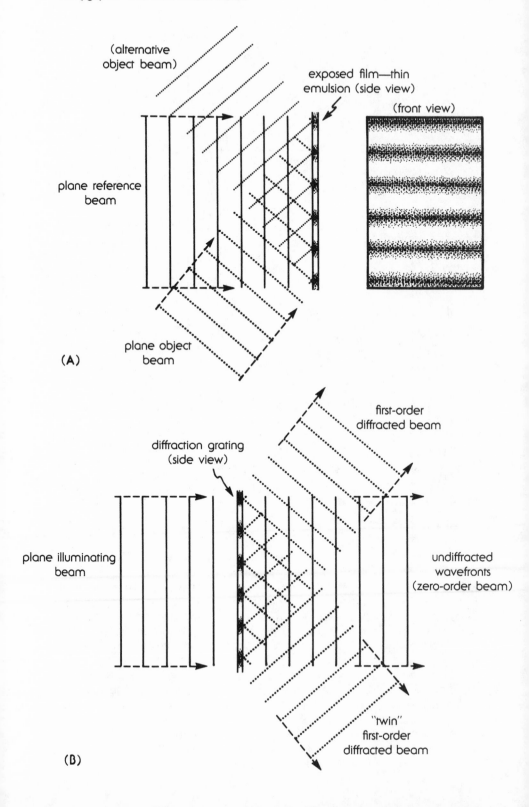

(alternative object beam)

exposed film—thin emulsion (side view)

(front view)

plane reference beam

plane object beam

(A)

diffraction grating (side view)

first-order diffracted beam

plane illuminating beam

undiffracted wavefronts (zero-order beam)

"twin" first-order diffracted beam

(B)

Decoding by Diffraction

A look at how diffraction demodulation works begins with a diffraction grating made of parallel interference fringes. Two beams of coherent plane waves interfering at an angle will make a grating of this type in a thin emulsion (Fig. 12–4a).

As Figure 12–4a illustrates, the same interference pattern results no matter which side of the reference beam the object beam is on, if the angle between them is the same. As a result, when a plane viewing beam strikes the grating from the same angle as the reference beam, it is diffracted in two directions (Fig. 12–4b), as if twin object beams had been used.

The same double diffraction effect produces a slightly different result when the modulating object beam has spherical wavefronts rather than plane ones. Then, instead of forming parallel fringes, the interference pattern takes the shape of a complete or partial Gabor zone plate (Fig. 12–5a). When demodulated, the hologram produces a pair of first-order beams by diffraction. This time they're not twins, however, because one *diverges* and the other *converges* (Fig. 12–5b).

These simplified examples of reflection and diffraction demodulation give us the means to visualize how holograms form images of 3-D objects. Visualize all points on an object contributing light to modulate part of the reference beam, as point P does in Figure 12–5a. The infinite number of overlapping hyperboloid and zone plate fringes produced by all points obscures the basic shape of each unique set.

Viewing light, acting on the whole complex collection of fringes, demodulates the sets for all object points at the same time. The net effect is the reconstruction of a virtual and a real image of each point—and two fully 3-D views (Fig. 12–6).

◀ **FIG. 12–4a, 12–4b** As long as reference and object beams consist of plane wavefronts, it doesn't matter whether the object beam comes from the top or bottom. Either way, the emulsion records equally spaced parallel fringes. These blend gradually from completely opaque to completely transparent (4a).

The developed film is a kind of diffraction grating. When illuminated by a beam like the reference beam, the grating, which might have been produced by either one of twin object beams, diffracts light in two directions—just as if both beams had been used (4b).

In human terms, because the grating couldn't "distinguish" which side of the reference beam the object beam came from, it diffracts light to reconstruct both.

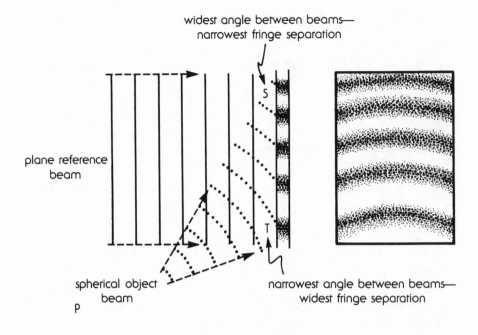

widest angle between beams—
narrowest fringe separation

plane reference
beam

S

T

spherical object
beam
P

narrowest angle between beams—
widest fringe separation

(A)

observer X

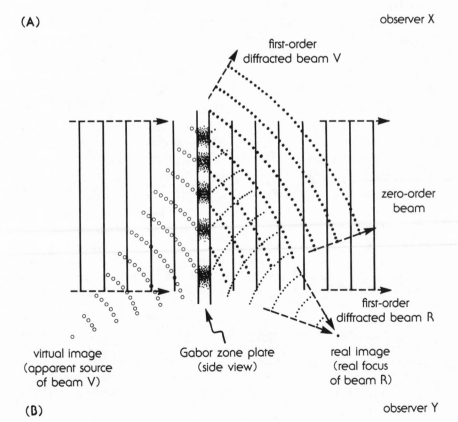

first-order
diffracted beam V

zero-order
beam

first-order
diffracted beam R

virtual image
(apparent source
of beam V)

Gabor zone plate
(side view)

real image
(real focus
of beam R)

(B)

observer Y

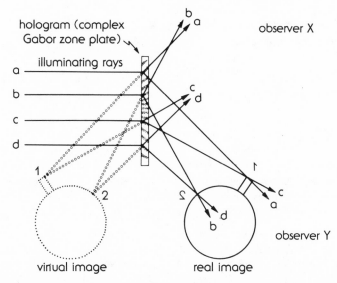

FIG. 12–6 A hologram can reconstruct a 3-D image because each point on the surface of a 3-D object contributes spherical wavefronts from its own unique location to form its own unique interference pattern. The result is a complex set of fringes made up of an infinite number of Gabor zone plates. Each of them is capable of diffracting light to reconstruct a real and a virtual image of its source. And if points **1**, **2**, and all their neighbors are reconstructed, the visual effect is the same as the sight of the actual object itself.

Notice the difference in the orientation of the two images: The *real* image, which observer **Y** sees, is a reversed version of the *virtual* image, which appears to observer **X**.

◀ **FIG. 12–5a, 12–5b** When an object beam comes from a single point, such as **P**, its spherical wavefronts interfere with a plane reference beam to produce an interference pattern of circular fringes—a Gabor zone plate. These fringes form closer together the farther they are from the object point because the angle between the reference and object beams increases from **T** to **S** (5a).

Recall that the narrower the opening, the wider the angle over which it diffracts light. Fringes that are closer together diffract demodulating light over a wider angle (that is, they cause it to *diverge*). The more widely spaced fringes diffract light over a narrower angle (that is, cause it to *converge*). The diverging light **V** reconstructs a virtual image of the point source for observer **X**. The converging light, **R**, reconstructs a real image for observer **Y**. Unlike a Fresnel zone plate, the Gabor kind diffracts only these two first-order wavefronts (5b).

As you can see, some light from the demodulating viewing beam continues unaffected after passing through the grating. That's why you have to stand in certain spots—in the paths of the first-order diffracted beams—if you want the best view of the holographed object. In the path of the zero-order beam, an object image is spoiled by an undiffracted image of the illuminating light source.

The appearance of both real and virtual images was to be expected, considering the similarity between a hologram and a diffraction grating or zone plate. But the difference in the appearance of the two images can be somewhat startling as far as 3-D objects are concerned.

The Deceptive Sight

A holographic virtual image is an exact replica of the object it was made from. It resembles the object from every viewing angle. And as an observer shifts position she sees a normal parallax effect—that is, background portions of the virtual image move more relative to foreground portions.

But everything is inside out in a holographic real image. What appears as foreground in the virtual image is background in the real image and vice versa (Fig. 12–7).

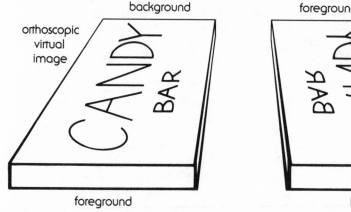
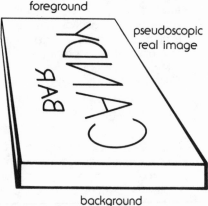

FIG. 12–7 At first sight, the holographic real image appears to be simply a mirror image. But a closer inspection reveals an effect called *contour reversal*, meaning its outlines have been switched back to front. A real image is a virtual image turned inside out, so that what was once foreground is now background and vice versa.

A camera lens focused on the orthoscopic "C" in candy would have to be pulled back to focus the "Y." But the same lens focused on the pseudoscopic "C" must be moved forward to focus the "Y."

The human eye reacts by making its lens thicker or thinner. When the eye focuses on the pseudoscopic "Y," it tells the brain the "Y" is closer than the "C." The brain is confused, though, because perspective clues—such as the fact the pseudoscopic "Y" is smaller than the "C"—tell it the "Y" must be farther away. This visual contradiction is what makes inside-out, pseudoscopic images so startling.

In addition, parallax is reversed in a real image. As an observer shifts position, she sees the nearest portions of the scene (the background originally) move more, compared to portions farther away. This is the opposite of what we're used to.

And what's most disturbing to a new viewer, objects in a real image have a kind of hollow look, as if seen inside out.

The appearance of the real image is logical, once the arrangement of the hologram and its images is examined. Yet at first sight, the inside-out effect seems to defy logic. Because the virtual image appears normal, it's called *orthoscopic*, meaning "correctly seen." The deceptive real image is *pseudoscopic*, or "false-appearing." It isn't magic either, just another aspect of physical laws at work in a holographic image.

All holograms have the ability to form real and virtual images. The ways they use reflection, diffraction, and other effects to decode interference patterns enables us to classify holograms.

Through Thick and Thin

As you've seen, the angle at which the object and reference beams interfere determines fringe size and arrangement. An angle of less than 20° produces relatively large fringes that are widely spaced. This was the case with Thomas Young's experiment and Dennis Gabor's first holograms. Such a narrow angle between reference and object beams forms fringes that lie roughly perpendicular to the plane of the film. When illuminated for decoding, a given light wave will be diffracted by only a few fringes (Fig. 12–8a). Such a hologram is known as a plane hologram because the interference pattern doesn't vary much across the thickness of the emulsion. The pattern's effect is almost entirely a surface effect. A plane hologram most resembles a 2-D zone plate or diffraction grating.

Holograms made with an angle of 20° to 180° between reference and object beams produces much narrower, more closely spaced fringes. These fringes form at an angle across the emulsion, making an interference pattern that is different from front to back of the film. They are likely to reflect and diffract passing light waves in complex ways (Fig. 12–8b). These are called *volume holograms* because the fringe effects act throughout the emulsion's thickness. A volume hologram most resembles the hyperboloid fringe model.

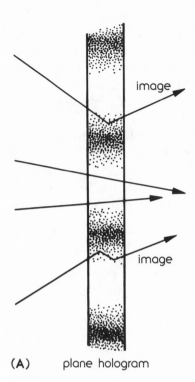

FIG. 12–8a A hologram whose fringes are oriented at nearly right angles to the surface acts as though it were two-dimensional—a single plane. There are only a few angles over which viewing light can enter and encounter the fringes properly to produce an image. If the viewing light isn't carefully aligned, it enters the emulsion and is either absorbed or undiffracted, and no image is formed.

image

image

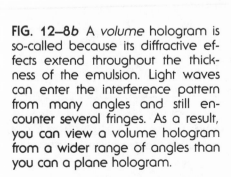

(A)   plane hologram

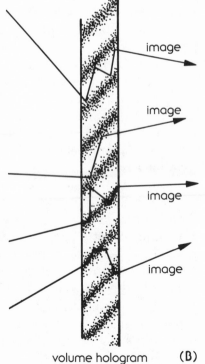

image

image

image

image

FIG. 12–8b A *volume* hologram is so-called because its diffractive effects extend throughout the thickness of the emulsion. Light waves can enter the interference pattern from many angles and still encounter several fringes. As a result, you can view a volume hologram from a wider range of angles than you can a plane hologram.

volume hologram   **(B)**

Volume holograms are able to record much more information than plane holograms because they can contain more numerous and more detailed fringes. This makes them ideal for recording a full 3-D effect. Another major advantage of using a wide angle between reference and object beams to make a volume hologram is that you can record more than one scene with the same piece of film (Fig. 12–9a, b).

The material that records the fringes also affects the holographic image.

Clearing the Record

All holograms absorb, reflect, refract, and diffract light to some degree, although typically one or two effects dominate. A hologram containing opaque silver grains, for example, will absorb

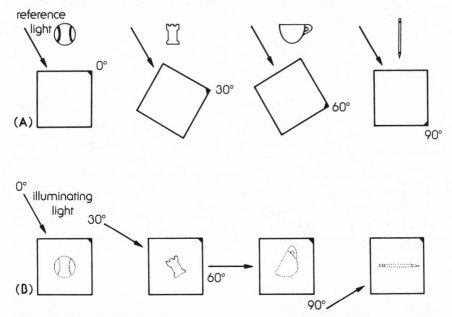

FIG. 12–9a, 12–9b A volume hologram can record more than one interference pattern in separate sets of fine fringes. Between exposures, the holographer rotates the film with respect to the reference beam (9a). This causes each interference pattern to form with a different orientation in the emulsion. Each interference pattern requires separate illumination.

To view all virtual images without rotating the hologram requires changing the direction of the illuminating light so it matches the original angle of the reference beam for each exposure. The proper angle of the viewing light for one pattern is wrong for the others and so only one image forms at a time (9b).

a considerable amount of light. Holograms that store image information in variations of opacity are called *absorption holograms*. When they're illuminated, they absorb some of the viewing light and reflect or diffract the rest into images.

Obviously the more viewing light a hologram soaks up the less there is for image formation. So absorption holograms are much less efficient than those that are more transparent. Holograms recorded with dichromated gelatin (DCG) are a good example of the transparent kind, known as *phase holograms*. DCG holograms are highly efficient, turning perhaps 90 percent of the illuminating light into an image.

A phase hologram stores image information mostly in variations of refractive index—the measure of how much a transparent medium affects light's speed and, therefore, its path. Such a hologram acts like a collection of tiny, dissimilar lenses. Light passing through is bent at the proper angles to reconstruct an object's various image points.

A silver halide absorption hologram can become a phase hologram by bleaching the emulsion during development. This, you'll recall, changes the opaque silver grains into transparent silver salts, which keep the same positions. So where the dark metal was densest, the clear salts are the same, and the fringe pattern is preserved. The way the opaque silver fringes diffract and *absorb* light to reconstruct an image is identical to the way the bleached fringes diffract and *refract* it.

A transparent bleached emulsion wastes less light than an unbleached one. That's why a phase hologram reconstructs a brighter image than its absorption counterpart.

Bleach a photographic negative and you destroy it. Bleach a hologram and you can make it better.

Noise and Color

Reflection and diffraction—like absorption—can detract from as well as contribute to holographic image quality. While excessive absorption produces a dim image, the side effects of reflected and diffracted light can be just as troublesome.

Besides reflecting light toward a viewer, a film emulsion or other recording material also reflects light in various directions within itself. This effect, called *scattering*, depends on an emulsion's grain. Larger grains reflect more light in unwanted directions, adding "nonsense" interference to the holographic pattern.

A hologram's internal reflections can obscure image information when scattering is significant. Holographers speak of scattering as "noise" that "drowns out" an image. Recall that the holographic recipe described the image information as a message. Quality holograms have a high ratio of message to scattering—or "signal-to-noise" ratio. When this ratio is high, scattering is insignificant and most reflection is put to use.

Diffraction in a hologram also can cause problems because of *dispersion*, the separation of light into spectral colors. Before ways were found to avoid dispersion problems, all holograms could be viewed only in transmitted monochromatic light (Fig. 12–10).

Transmission Holos

One kind of hologram forms an image that you see in light from a source behind you. The other kind forms an image when you look through the hologram toward the light source. This second

FIG. 12–10 Illuminating this transmission hologram with monochromatic light produces a single sharp image, as in Figure 1–3. But light from a mercury vapor lamp consists of several distinct spectral lines, so that the interference pattern diffracts each wavelength at a slightly different angle. As you see here, a collection of slightly displaced images results. Blurring would be even worse in white light.

kind of image is made of transmitted light. The fringes of a transmission hologram redirect light passing through mainly by diffraction or refraction.

Ordinary transmission holograms are limited to viewing in monochromatic light because of their tendency to disperse white viewing light into a fuzzy collection of many-colored images. If all holograms were like this, the magic of holography would be limited to those with a laser handy. The next chapter will describe the rainbow hologram, a transmission type that's viewable in wh te light. But another kind of hologram solves the white light problem by filtering out most wavelengths.

Reflection Holos

Emmett Leith and Juris Upatneiks deserve credit for developing the volume transmission hologram in the early 1960s. At about the same time, Y.N. Denisyuk invented the *white light reflection hologram* in the Soviet Union—or reinvented it, if you consider Gabriel Lippmann's contribution.

As you have read, transmission holograms come in all types: The *absorption* kind are relatively opaque, while the *phase* type are relatively transparent. *Plane* transmission holograms consist of relatively thin interference patterns, while *volume* transmission holograms work by means of relatively thick arrangements of interference fringes.

Reflection holograms, on the other hand, are always the volume, or thick type. And the images of absorption reflection holograms are usually so dim, the phase, or transparent type is preferred.

Viewing a reflection hologram is a matter of looking from the same side as the illuminating light. The fringes diffract as well as reflect the viewing light. But the only light waves that are reinforced to form an image are those whose wavelength is twice the distance between fringes (Fig. 12–11a, b). The effects of all other wavelengths are filtered out by destructive interference.

Usually a reflection hologram reconstructs an image in the same color as the original laser light because the fringe spacing is half that wavelength. But a hologram's emulsion can shrink during development. This reduces the distance between fringes and causes them to selectively reinforce a shorter wavelength of the white viewing light. Thus the viewer of a reflection hologram made with the red light of an HeNe laser might see a

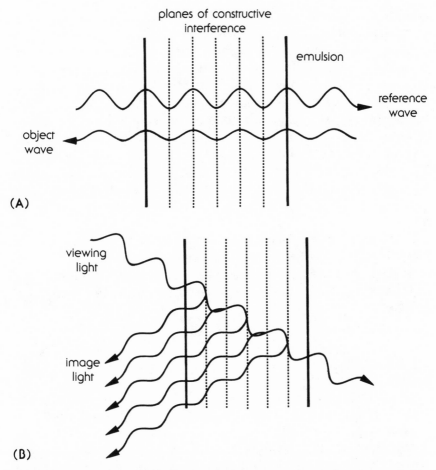

planes of constructive
interference

emulsion

reference
wave

object
wave

(A)

viewing
light

image
light

(B)

FIG. 12–11a, 12–11b Reflection holograms are made when a reference beam comes "face to face" with an object beam. Modern holographers use reference and object beams of laser light. Gabriel Lippmann's object beam came from the scene outside his camera. Lippmann's reference beam consisted of that part of the object beam that passed through his film and reflected back to interfere with incoming·light (11a).

The holographic fringes that the interfering wavefronts produce lie roughly parallel to the surface of the emulsion. These fringes act as reflecting layers for viewing light. A reflection hologram is a volume hologram, so you can illuminate it from various angles and still produce an acceptable image (11b).

Fringe separation in this kind of hologram is such that incoming light waves whose length is twice that of the distance between fringes are reflected and reinforce each other. Because this distance might shrink with development, white light can reconstruct an image in a color different than that of the laser light from which it was made. Light of longer or shorter wavelengths is absorbed in the emulsion or has its effects canceled by destructive interference.

greenish image. Chemicals that prevent emulsion shrinkage can control this effect.

White light reflection holograms brought the magic out of the laboratory. Their only viewing restriction is the relative size of the viewing light source. The more the source of illumination resembles a point of light, the sharper the image appears. Spotlights and slide projector bulbs produce good, clear images. So does sunlight on a cloudless day. The sun, as big as it is, makes a good point source because it's so far away.

Frosted incandescent bulbs, fluorescent lamps, and the sun on a hazy day are poor sources. Their diffuse light strikes a hologram's fringes from many angles. The result is a blurred image.

Diffuse light isn't necessarily bad for holography. One way of using it is worth mentioning here because it shows the relationship that's needed between the modulating beam and the demodulating beam. It also gives another meaning to the term holographic cipher.

Secret Code

What you've read so far suggests that the light waves of the reference beam and the illuminating, or viewing, beam must be completely in phase to make and view a transmission hologram. Actually, this is more a matter of convenience than necessity. What's important is that the reference and viewing beams for a transmission hologram must be as nearly identical in shape as possible. The easiest way to ensure this is to use a spatially coherent reference beam, that is, one whose waves are lined up in phase. Then any laser's light—which, of course, is also spatially coherent—will reconstruct an image.

But suppose you threw a spatially coherent reference beam out of phase by passing it through a piece of frosted glass. When it emerged it would be diffuse, meaning it would have lost its spatial coherence—its waves would be out of step with one another. But the beam's temporal coherence would be preserved—its waves would still be of equal length. In other words, the emerging light would remain monochromatic and, although its waves were out of phase, they would remain out of phase in a way that wouldn't change over time.

Such a reference beam would be fully capable of serving as a carrier beam to "lock in" the phase relationships among object waves. The interference pattern they would form, like all others, couldn't be decoded except by an identical viewing beam. In this case, however, the proper viewing beam wouldn't be so easily obtained. No laser could do the trick unless its spatially coherent waves were altered in exactly the same way the carrier waves had been. As a result, no one could reconstruct the image you recorded unless he or she had a piece of frosted glass exactly like the one you used to make the hologram.

This technique would appeal to anyone wanting to send a truly secret message. It's a case of the holographic cipher acting as a cipher, and another example of how versatile holograms can be.

Holographic Variety

The holograms described so far are some of the basic types. You've seen simplified diagrams of how the holographic code works to reconstruct images. More elaborate holograms operate on much the same principles. To apply them, the holographer uses surprisingly simple tools, some expensive, some home-made. A look at the basic equipment will help explain some of the more advanced holograms. It will also lead directly to descriptions of how people are using and planning to use holography.

TOOLS AND SETUPS

"Ready?"

Sure. The room goes black.

You can't see the holographer, but your eyes follow his voice anyway, as he moves to the far side of the table. He talks as he works, telling you he's feeling for the filmholder, he's placing the film in it, yes, everything seems to be right.

The holographer has already taken light readings, checked and double-checked each portion of the split laser beam with his meter. Now he's about to expose the film to the meeting of message and messenger, and make a hologram.

"We'll expose for fifteen seconds, but it'll take sixty or more for the table to settle down. Any last words?"

Nope. Let's go.

"OK. Remember not to move or talk until after the exposure, which will be about a minute and a half from—now."

It's black and silent as you wait for air currents to die down and the table on which the hologram will be made to stop shaking. Even the film the holographer handled moves slightly for a while as it cools from the heat of his hands. In a minute it will have reached room temperature, the table will have calmed, and the air will have stopped drifting from the activity of preparation.

Until then there could be no hologram. The laser's reference and object beams must not move during an exposure. If any part of the holographic setup shifts as little as a fraction of the laser light's wavelength in that time, areas of constructive and destructive interference will shift. And the interference pattern holding the object's image will disappear.

It doesn't take much to disturb the delicate relationship between the beams. The sound waves of simple conversation can cause the air through which the light passes to change its density. The resulting changes in refractive index can make passing light shimmer like the horizon above a hot highway—on a smaller scale certainly, but more than enough to ruin a hologram.

So you wait with the holographer without speaking, and the minute passes ever so slowly.

Suddenly you see red. You can't detect the beam paths from the HeNe laser, but they light up dust in the air, the equipment, and the object being holographed.

You mentally count the seconds as the light waves unite in the film emulsion, and you stare at the eerie red scene.

Black again. It's done; the holographic message has been encoded. Now all you have to do is wait through the film processing to see if the exposure was correct and if you were sufficiently still.

Table the Motion

The vibrations of our surroundings are considerable. The ordinary movement of a footstep in the next room, a furnace turning on, or a door closing causes vibration, the number one enemy of holographers. The best methods of combating it are cushioning, mass, and "absorbent" construction.

Air is a good cushion. A large, dense mass resists vibration through inertia; when it's at rest, it tends to stay at rest as long as forces acting on it don't become too great. Industry and government labs usually contain the best equipment available. Their *vibration isolation* tables consist of a steel skin about ¼-inch thick, surrounding a honeycomb structure made of aluminum. This rests on pneumatic supports that operate something like the shock absorbers on a car (Fig. 13–1). The table's honeycomb core absorbs shocks that get past the legs.

Independent holographers make up for lack of funds with characteristic resourcefulness. They set up their studios in basements, which are much quieter than upper floors. They often work in the dead of night, when traffic is less on nearby streets. And instead of spending thousands of dollars on a top-of-the-line honeycomb table, they put their money into much cheaper mass and cushioning.

A homemade *sandbox* table consists of about a ton of clean sand atop a cinder block base. This is cushioned with carpet scraps and partially inflated inner tubes. It's not as effective at dampening vibrations as a lab table, but patient and light-footed holographers can make it work. They fasten their optical equipment to plastic plumbing pipe, which they shove deep into the sand.

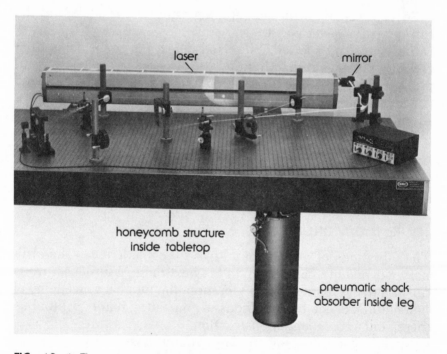

FIG. 13–1 The pneumatic shock absorbers in the legs of this vibration isolation table support a steel working surface covering an aluminum honeycomb inside. The air-cushioned mass soaks up most disturbances coming up from the floor. For extremely delicate work, the holographer may attach a plastic box to the tabletop to stop disturbances from air currents or sounds. The holographer can fasten optical equipment to the table's surface with bolts or magnetic mounts.

Despite this ingenuity, do-it-yourself holographers tend to whisper and tiptoe, especially if they're working with low-power lasers.

The Laser

Many kinds of lasers are suitable for holography. Holographers base their choices mainly on price, power, wavelength, and type of beam.

Lasers range in price from $300 or so up to many thousands. Basement holographers prefer the inexpensive HeNe laser, which can produce good quality holograms in experienced hands.

HeNe lasers are measured in milliwatts (10^{-3} watts) of power. Compared to your 100-watt reading lamp, a HeNe laser's ½-mw to 50-mw output may seem feeble. But remember, the laser beam is highly concentrated, while the reading lamp's is spread over a large area.

The brilliant colors of laser beams can be very beautiful. But if you're ever in a laser's presence, BE AWARE: Staring into a laser beam of even one-half mw can damage your eyes. Beams spread by lenses are safer, but even then laser light of 50 mw or less can burn the retina and ruin vision. And more powerful lasers, mostly found in research or industry labs, are a fire hazard as well as a threat to vision.

As laser power increases, holographic exposure time decreases. More power also means more flexibility for the holographer in planning setups. But more power requires more care. Respect any laser in operation. Never look into the business end of a laser, and don't let the beam reflect in your direction. Some experienced holographers even take the precaution of removing jewelry to prevent accidental reflections.

A laser's wavelength is important when the holographer wants an image of a certain color. It's possible to make a multiple-exposure reflection hologram of the same scene using a red, a green, and a blue laser. When viewed in white light, such a hologram will reconstruct identical images in each of the three wavelengths, which the brain combines to see in natural color.

As you recall, certain lasers produce continuous beams, while others emit light in brief pulses. *Continuous-wave lasers* include the less expensive, low-powered models widely used by independent holographers. *Pulsed lasers* generate more light for an exposure brief enough to *freeze* all motion. This makes pulsed lasers ideal for those times when a vibration table isn't available or when the subject is constantly moving, as in portrait holography.

Mirrors

Reflecting surfaces are currently a must for holographers, who often need to change directions of reference and object beams several times between laser and film. Ordinary household mirrors won't work, however, because their reflective coatings have been applied to the back surface of the glass. A holographic mirror reflects light from its front surface (Fig. 13–2).

The most commonly used mirrors are flat (or plane) mirrors. They simply redirect light along a desired path. The first mirror in Figure 13–1, for example, enables the holographer to transfer the laser's beam to any part of the table without moving the laser itself.

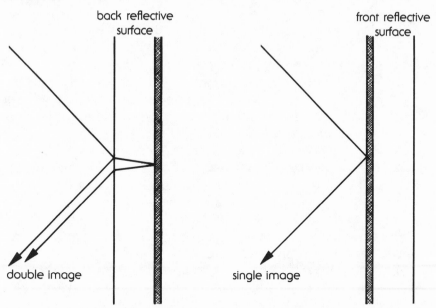

back reflective surface

front reflective surface

double image

single image

FIG. 13–2 The reflective coating of a household mirror is applied to its rear surface. This protects the coating from scratches, but adds a troublesome double reflection. You can see the double image caused by partial reflection from the two surfaces by looking closely in your bathroom mirror.

A mirror whose coating is applied to its front surface reflects a single image. Holographers handle their mirrors carefully by the edges to avoid smearing or scratching the coating, which is usually a thin layer of aluminum.

A concave mirror is sometimes needed for more advanced holography. Known as a *collimating* mirror, it reshapes a spherical wavefront into a plane one. To collimate means to make straight. A mirror of this type reflects a diverging beam so that its sides become parallel. After collimating, a conical beam (with spherical wavefronts) becomes a cylindrical beam (with plane wavefronts).

Lenses

Holography has been called "lensless photography" because lenses aren't needed to focus an image for the film, as in a camera. Holographers do use lenses, though. An unspread laser beam is far too narrow to illuminate anything but the smallest objects. The most useful lens is a simple diverging one similar to the endpiece of a microscope. This widens the object beam so its light reaches the whole visible surface of the subject to be holographed.

Lenses are necessary for some of the holographic applications mentioned in Chapter 15. But understanding why requires knowledge of advanced math.

Beamsplitter

As the name suggests, a beamsplitter is a device for dividing the light from the laser into reference and object beams. It does this by transmitting a portion of the incident light and reflecting most of the rest (Fig. 13–3). The amount of light it absorbs is so small it can be ignored.

The ratio of transmitted to reflected light distinguishes beamsplitters. A 90:10 beamsplitter, for example, transmits 90 percent of the incident light while reflecting 10 percent. This ratio is the same over the entire surface of some beamsplitters. With others, the coating varies from high transmission in one area to high reflectivity in another.

A variable beamsplitter allows the holographer to divide laser light into beams of many different intensities. This flexibility is useful because different kinds of holograms call for a reference beam that's anywhere from one-and-a-half to eight times stronger than the object beam. This ratio between beam strengths ensures that the interference between object and reference waves obscures interference between object waves and other object waves.

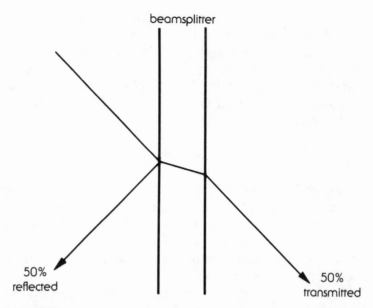

FIG. 13–3 A *beamsplitter* works by transmitting a portion of the incident light and reflecting the rest. It's basically a mirror whose aluminum reflecting layer is only thick enough to reflect some percentage of light less than 100 percent. To get reference and object beams of various intensities, holographers rely on several beamsplitters. Or they get a *variable beamsplitter,* which ranges from high reflectivity on one end to low reflectivity on the other.

Pinhole

In Chapter Nine, you learned that coherence is a relative term. As pure and as organized as laser light is, however, it can be thrown out of phase not only by space and time, but also by impurities in the media through which it travels. And holography, which usually depends on the modulation of an unchanging reference beam, is easily spoiled by anything that detracts from the light's coherence.

Thomas Young and Dennis Gabor both used pinholes to improve the coherence of the light they worked with. But because their light was less than ideal to begin with, the improvement was limited. Today's holographers still find pinholes useful for preserving and restoring the high coherence of laser light.

The reference and object beams encounter many impurities on their ways from laser to film. Dust in the air and scratches on mirror and lens surfaces scatter some of the light waves. This stray light creates noise in a hologram, and a pinhole can remove much of it.

Modern pinholes are much better than the slits Young made in a screen. For one thing, their edges are sharp and their diameters are measured precisely; they're not really made by anything as crude as a pinprick.

In addition, a quality pinhole works with a converging lens. This pinhole-lens assembly is called a *spatial filter* because it screens out the light not focused to the correct position in space.

Certain other devices make holography easier. Basement holographers often make do with common household items and a great deal of imagination. Now that you've been introduced to the most basic equipment, you're ready to see how it fits together to produce the most basic kinds of holograms.

"Single-Beam" Transmission Holos

Recall that the angle between the reference and object beams as they strike the holographic film affects the size of the interference fringes they form. The larger fringes result when the beams meet at a narrow angle, as they did in Gabor's early holograms (Fig. 13–4).

The larger the fringes, the less image information they contain. As you can see in the interference patterns at the tops of Figures 4–3a and b, the fringes are so coarse you can almost detect the individual letters they represent. Notice, too, that the images reconstructed from each hologram are rather poor in detail.

Gabor was forced to use a setup that produced reference and object beams at a very narrow angle to each other because he had no strong source of coherent light. The arrangement produced both a real and a virtual image along the same line of sight—through the center of the hologram, along its axis, the way the zone plate in Figure 8–16 does. Viewing these on = axis holograms was somewhat frustrating because the real and virtual images overlapped and obscured each other, as the squares do in Figure 8–17.

Once holographers were able to use the laser's strong, coherent light, they were able to increase the angle between the reference and object beams as they interfered. Widening the angle produced finer fringes, which recorded more image information. What's more, separating the reference and object beams also separated the real and virtual images. No longer did they

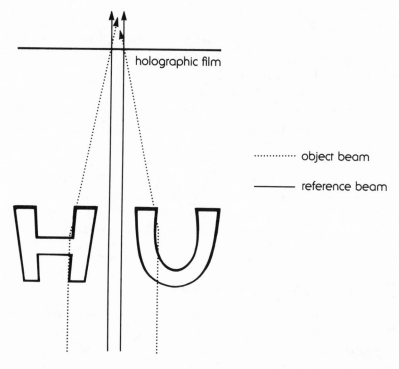

holographic film

.... object beam

——————— reference beam

FIG. 13—4 To make the first hologram, Dennis Gabor shone filtered light from a mercury lamp through a photographic transparency bearing microscopic names, and onto a piece of film. The edges of individual letters diffracted light passing closely by (shown here as dotted rays). This diffracted light became the object beam for the hologram when it interfered with the undiffracted light, which acted as the reference beam.

Because the reference and object beams met at a very narrow angle, they formed very large, widely spaced fringes. As a result, Gabor's holograms reconstructed rather poor real and virtual images that overlapped along the same line of sight.

appear along the axis, or centerline, of the hologram. No longer did they obscure each other.

Emmett Leith and Juris Upatnieks separated the real and virtual images in the early 60s. Using the newly invented laser, they were able to arrange a single beam so that part fell directly on the film while part struck the film after bouncing off the object (Fig. 13–5). The angle between them was much larger than Gabor was able to achieve.

The real and virtual images this kind of hologram formed didn't fall along the same line of sight. Instead, they fell to one side of the hologram's axis, or centerline, like the cups in Figure 12–6. An observer saw one image or the other, but never both at the same time.

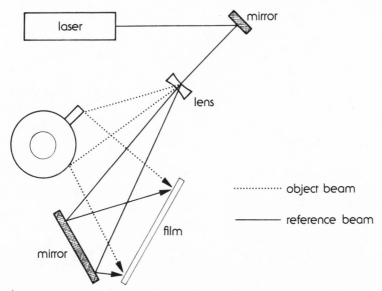

FIG. 13–5 The diverging lens in a single beam transmission setup spreads the laser beam wide enough to cover object and mirror. The *reference* beam is that portion of this cone of light that passes the object and strikes the film by way of the mirror. The *object* beam is that light the object reflects to the film.

Dr. T. H. Jeong modified the single-beam transmission setup by surrounding an object with a cylinder of film. He spread the reference beam wide to fall on the inside of the cylinder. Light from the center of the beam reflected from the object, acting as an object beam when it, too, struck the film. Jeong's 360° hologram reconstructed a virtual image, which could be seen from all sides, as if the cylindrical hologram contained it.

Leith and Upatnieks later improved the quality of their off-axis holography by splitting the laser beam.

Split-Beam Transmission Holos

Split-beam holography uses one or more beamsplitters to divide the light leaving the laser into two or more parts. Mirrors then direct these portions to the film along widely separated paths (Fig. 13–6). Separating the beams gives the holographer greater control over the angle at which they meet. It also allows for adjusting the relative strengths of the reference and object beams.

The distance the reference and object beams travel should be as nearly equal as possible. That's because even laser light suffers wavelength changes over time. The difference in wavelength is much less than for incoherent light, of course. But if either the object or reference beam traveled too much farther than the other before reaching the film, the wavelength of the longer beam would have altered more so that a stable interference pattern couldn't form.

Coherence length is a measurement of the greatest allowable difference in length between the reference and object beams. An interference pattern is possible only if the difference between the two beams is less than the light source's coherence length.

Gabor's mercury light had a coherence length of less than a millimeter. Even if his light had been strong enough to split into two widely separated beams to make finer interference fringes, it would have been nearly impossible to keep the beam lengths within a millimeter of each other. This isn't a problem for today's holographers, whose lasers have coherence lengths of several meters or more.

Notice that in all setups for transmission holograms the reference and object beams enter the film emulsion from the same side. When the beams enter the emulsion from opposite sides, they make a reflection hologram.

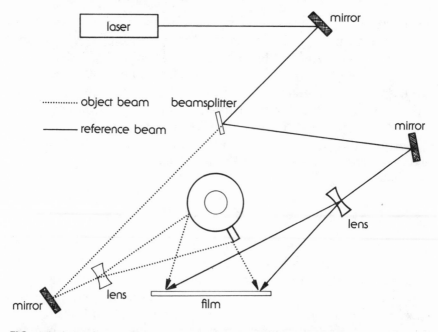

FIG. 13–6 Multiple-beam setups like this one for a transmission hologram divide the laser's light before spreading it. Here, the beamsplitter creates the reference beam, which travels unobstructed to the film as always, and the object beam, which bounces off the object first.

Split-Beam Reflection Holos

Y.N. Denisyuk of the Soviet Union made the first reflection holograms, which are viewable in ordinary white light. Figure 13–7 is an advanced version of Denisyuk's original setup.

The setup in Figure 13–7 is similar to the split-beam transmission hologram setup (Fig. 13–6). The main difference here is that the object rests on the opposite side of the film. Light reflected from this position enters the emulsion at a 180° angle with the reference beam. The head-on collision between the reference and object beams forms the standing waves that produce reflecting fringes, like the ones in Figure 12–11a and b.

Of course, the film used here must be transparent from both directions. This is in contrast to the film for transmission holog-

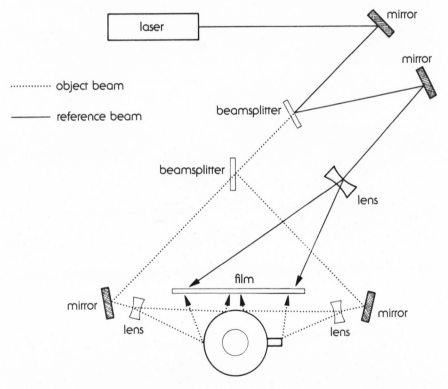

FIG. 13–7 Moving the subject of the hologram from the reference side of the film to the opposite side and adjusting some of the optical equipment will turn a transmission setup into a reflection setup. This diagram also includes a second beamsplitter that divides the object beam so that it falls on the object from two sides. This way the object is more evenly lit, and more information is reflected to the emulsion from parts of the object that would otherwise be in shadow.

raphy and everyday photography, which has an opaque backing to absorb light that might scatter inside the emulsion and produce unwanted, "nonsense" fringes.

Denisyuk's original reflection hologram setup was much simpler than this split-beam version.

"Single-Beam" Reflection Holos

Interference patterns were the secret of Gabriel Lippmann's extraordinary color photographs of nearly a century ago. Lippmann modified a conventional camera to accept a glass photographic plate so its emulsion rested against a sheet of liquid mercury. When he exposed the plate, light from the object passed through the lens and the film coating. The mercury's surface reflected this light back toward its source. The reflected light re-entered the emulsion, where it met incoming object waves and interfered with them. This produced fringes that reflected viewing light in wavelengths that matched the object's original colors.

Figure 13–8 illustrates the type of setup Denisyuk first used. With this arrangement, the object itself takes the place of the

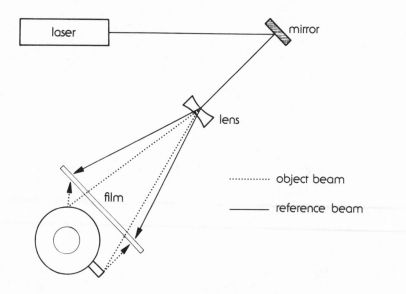

FIG. 13–8 This is the hologram Gabriel Lippmann might have made if he'd had a laser. No beamsplitter is necessary because the transparent film allows enough light from the reference beam through to reflect off the object and return to the emulsion. The reflected object waves then interfere with waves coming directly from the laser.

mercury mirror in the back of Lippmann's camera. The object is lit by the portion of the reference beam that passes through the transparent emulsion. The object reflects light back into the emulsion, where it interacts with the reference waves to create a Lippmann interference pattern.

The reflected object light represents an "older" part of the laser beam, waves that left the laser before the reference waves they interfere with. Therefore, the path of the object beam is always longer than that of the reference beam, and the object waves have undergone more oscillations. For this reason, the object to be holographed can't be farther from the film than one-half the coherence length of the laser. That's the distance over which the laser's beam maintains spatial coherence, with its wave crests in phase in one plane.

A Hologram of a Hologram

If you can make a hologram of image waves from an actual object, there's no reason you can't make a hologram of holographic image waves. As you recall, a hologram can generate a virtual image, which assumes the same position as the object holographed. The virtual image is an illusion, however, the result of diffracted diverging wavefronts.

A hologram's real image, in contrast, consists of wavefronts that converge in space. Although you can't detect light where a virtual image appears to be, you *can* detect light where a real image is. By placing film inside the real image in the presence of a reference beam, you can make a hologram of a hologram (Fig. 13–9).

The image formed by the copy hologram in Figure 13–9 is reconstructed on both sides of the film at the same time. The hologram lies on a plane through the middle of the image. As a result, this hologram of a hologram is called an *image plane hologram*.

The image plane technique is also used in even more advanced holography.

Rainbow Holos

Perhaps the most popular holograms are those whose images change color as you move your head up and down. The spectral colors give this type of image plane hologram the name *rainbow*.

Dr. Stephen A. Benton invented the rainbow hologram, also

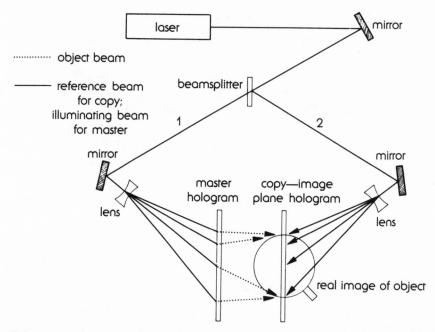

FIG. 13–9 The beamsplitter in an image plane setup divides the laser light into two reference beams. Beam **2** goes right to the copy film. Beam **1** goes to the master transmission hologram, where it reconstructs a real image in the same space the copy film occupies. This image becomes the object beam for the second hologram. The copy hologram will stand in the image plane when illuminated, that is, the image will form on either side of the film.

known as the *white light transmission hologram* because it's viewable in white light. A *laser-viewable* transmission hologram disperses white light into many images, one for each wavelength in the illuminating light. That's because each fringe diffracts each wavelength at a slightly different angle. The result is many overlapping images in many colors—a spectral smear (Fig. 13–10a).

A white light transmission hologram, in contrast, eliminates this colorful blurring. To make a rainbow copy of a laser-viewable transmission hologram, the holographer uses only the real image that is reconstructed by a narrow portion of the master (Fig. 13–10b). The copy—which is an image plane hologram—records a much smaller, and therefore simpler, set of images than the master did. When illuminated by white light, the copy still disperses light, but without the confusing overlap of images of the master (Fig. 13–10c).

The transmission master image must be viewed in monochromatic light for best results, which are monochromatic as well. You can view the rainbow copy in white light, which makes

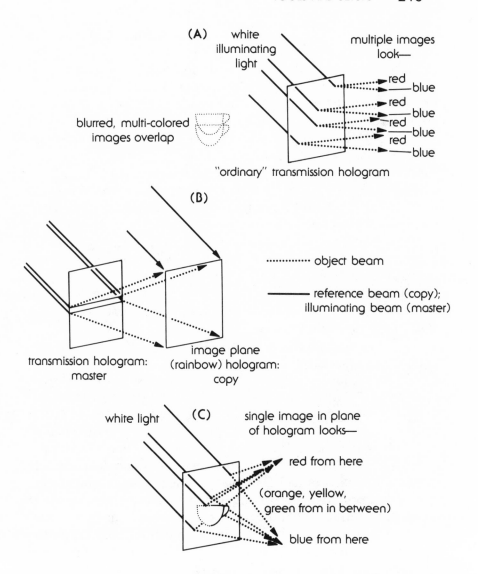

FIG. 13–10a, 13–10b, 13–10c In white light, the fringes of a transmission hologram diffract each wavelength at a different angle, dispersing the colors of the spectrum (only blue and red shown here). The viewer sees a colorful blur because the spectral images of neighboring fringes overlap (10a).

The rainbow technique eliminates the spectral overlap by reducing the number of neighboring fringes. Only a narrow slit of the master is illuminated, so the copy film resides in the plane of a much simpler holographic image from only a portion of the interference pattern (10b).

The fringes of a rainbow hologram still disperse white light into colors, but the colored images don't overlap (10c). And as the viewer raises and lowers her head, she sees a single image in the various colors of the rainbow.

multi-colored images. But there's an additional difference between the two.

The master image displayed both horizontal and vertical parallax, meaning you could see a difference in the view by moving your head from side to side or up and down. The rainbow
copy, on the other hand, exhibits only horizontal parallax. Its
vertical parallax was lost when the master image was reduced
to only a narrow horizontal slit.

Fortunately, the parallax human observers use to see 3-D lies
along the same line as their binocular vision—that is, in the
horizontal plane. And the rainbow hologram still provides each
eye with a different view in this direction. So while this type
of image plane hologram sacrifices vertical parallax, in return it
gains the ability to transform white light into a scene of many
colors, which change as you move your head.

So far, we've discussed holographic still life images only. But
the image plane technique can be used to reconstruct the illusion of motion, too.

Holographic Stereogram

Holographic movies have been made and will be discussed in
Part IV. In the meantime, let's look at a special kind of stereogram. It's akin to the dual photographs so popular in Lincoln's
day, but with a true 3-D effect and the appearance of motion.

A photographic stereogram produces a single 3-D view by
presenting a different 2-D image to each eye. A holographic
stereogram provides a changing 3-D view with hundreds of different 2-D images. A *holographic stereogram* goes by other
names, including *multiplex* (meaning multiple) *hologram*, and
integral hologram. It's a series of holograms made from a special series of photographs (Fig. 13–11a, b, c).

The holographic stereogram is a kind of rainbow hologram,
so it's viewable in white light, and it produces a spectrum of
images. The 3-D effect occurs because a viewer's eyes see the
image through different strip holograms some distance apart.
Each strip presents a slightly different 2-D image, which the
brain combines into a 3-D view.

What's more, as the holographic stereogram rotates or the
viewer walks around it, holograms of different movie frames
come into view (Fig. 1–7a, b). The ever-changing pair of 2-D images presents the same change in subject position the movie recorded, so someone watching thinks of the change as motion.
Of course, the speed of the stereographic movie depends on the

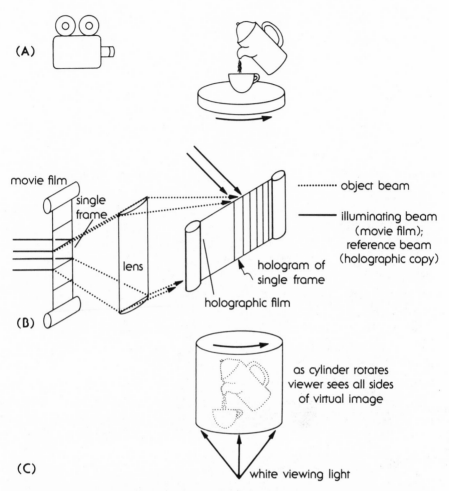

FIG. 13–11a, 13–11b, 13–11c A holographic stereogram begins as an ordinary movie. The holographer films a subject as it rotates on a turntable before a stationary camera (11a). The subject can move; the finished stereogram will preserve the motion.

After development, the real image of each movie frame is projected by the coherent light of an object beam onto a narrow strip of a roll of holographic film. There it interferes with a reference beam to make a narrow hologram (11b). The holographic film advances just enough between exposures to present an unexposed strip of emulsion for recording the next movie frame as a 2-D hologram. If done properly, the borders between holograms are unnoticeable.

The result is a long roll of film containing thin holograms of successive movie frames. Thin photo transparencies of similar shape would produce only squeezed images too narrow to recognize. Each thin hologram, however, can diffract viewing light over a wide enough angle to present an undistorted image to the eye. A viewer with binocular vision detects the images from a pair of different holograms (of two different movie frames) at one time (11c). Each pair of 2-D images gives a different 3-D view of the subject.

speed of its rotation or the walking speed of the viewer, just as projector speed determines a movie's fast, regular, or slow motion.

What Good is a Hologram?

A hologram's ability to mold light into a 3-D record makes a dazzling display of its images. A holographic image reproduces an image of its source out of thin air. Versions of the image can be made in colors far more brilliant than any rainbow, and even suggest movement.

But a hologram is more than just a light show, as stimulating as that may be. Just as important if not more so are its ability to store and reconstruct tremendous amounts of information, and its ability to detect differences in shape of a few hundred nanometers. These have improved our ability to record and communicate, and to measure our world and our work.

So what good is a hologram? It's already proved itself a useful tool for the artist, the engineer, the mapmaker, the advertiser, the teacher, and the librarian. It promises more to these and many others, to scientists and non-scientists alike, to governments and citizens, to businesspeople, and consumers, in short, to you.

But the story of those—the real and as-yet imagined uses of holography—is the reason for Part IV.

PART 4

HOLOGRAPHY AT WORK

HOLOGRAMS ALL
AROUND YOU

There are limits to how small we can see. In theory the best lens can't distinguish between details closer together than one-half the wavelength of light used. Even with ultraviolet light, this theoretical limit of resolution is about 100 nm.

Again, in theory, the limit might be reduced with the use of even shorter electromagnetic radiation—X-rays, for example. Unfortunately, X-rays are so short it's very difficult to refract them; therefore, X-ray lenses are rare and expensive.

But there is an alternative. And it's indirectly related to Albert Einstein's theory of the dual nature of light. He proposed that light acts as if it were a wave under some circumstances, and as if it were a particle under others.

The idea that light waves had particle characteristics led a man named Louis de Broglie to suggest the opposite might also be true, that particles had some characteristics of waves. This theory of *matter waves* has held up, although wave behavior is detectable only with very small particles—not elephants but electrons.

The discovery of electron waves, 100 thousand times shorter than visible light, opened up the possibility of an electron microscope. But conventional lenses were once more out of the question: Electrons were particles, after all, and couldn't be refracted in the usual sense.

The solution came about almost by accident. One man who studied the paths of electrons in magnetic fields showed some of his results to another scientist. The second man realized that the way the fields acted on the electrons resembled the way a lens refracts light.

Soon this effect was put to use. The first electron microscope, using magnetic lenses to focus on electron beam, had the power of an ordinary magnifying glass. Within four years, an improved version compared favorably with an ordinary light microscope. And in just another four years, the electron microscope was one hundred times more powerful than its visible light counterpart.

At that point, the electron microscope could resolve details down to 8×10^{-10}m (0.8 nm). Photographic enlargements of the electron images revealed never-before-seen details of bacteria and viruses. This was tantalizingly close to the resolving power that would reveal atomic structure itself, about 1.5×10^{-10}m. What was even more frustrating were the calculations that showed the best the electron microscope could ever hope to achieve was a resolution of 3×10^{-10}m—only half the resolving power needed to "see" atoms.

That's where things stood in 1948, when Dennis Gabor wrote a now-famous article.

A New Microscopic Principle

Gabor was an expert in electron microscopy. He was well aware of the instrument's limitations. More than once he said the best electron lens compared to the one he wanted was no better than a raindrop compared to the best glass lens in the world.

There were two main problems with the electron lens, and decreasing the effects of one increased the effects of the other. With the electron lens opened wide, a magnified image was distorted, curved in a way similar to an image seen through a drop of water. But when the lens opening was smaller to reduce this spherical distortion, the image was blurred for another reason, diffraction of the electron beam. Like waves, the electrons changed course as they passed through the narrow opening of the lens.

The solution finally came to Gabor while he sat on a bench at his tennis club on Easter morning, 1947. He suddenly thought it might be possible to record a poor electron image and improve it with visible light techniques. If he could capture all the electron image information, the whole message as it were, the procedure might stand a chance.

To do that, he'd have to record not only the intensity differences among the electron waves of the image, but their phase differences as well. And that meant adding a *coherent background* of reference waves to the image waves. After development, the interference record would reconstruct the image wavefront when illuminated with another coherent reference beam.

Gabor's article, "A New Microscopic Principle," appeared in *Nature* magazine[3]. The paper described his method of wavefront reconstruction in little more than a thousand words. And it contained photographs of the world's first hologram, that tiny image of the names Huygens, Young, and Fresnel.

Electron Hologram

Gabor guessed that his technique might some day provide magnifications of 100,000 times, even before photographic enlargement! That's the ratio between the length of the electron waves he'd use to make the hologram and the light waves he'd use to reconstruct its image. Gabor ended his article by promising to begin work on the *electron interference microscope* immediately.

But the invention was not to be his. As he pointed out in his 1971 Nobel address, there were too many other problems twenty years before, in the early 1950s. Most troublesome was the lack of a strong electron beam in a narrow bandwidth, an "electron laser," so to speak. Also the electron microscope of that time suffered from vibration and stray magnetic fields. Gabor told his Nobel audience of the many noteworthy achievements in optical holography, successes he couldn't have dreamed of before the laser. And he expressed hope he'd live to see the fruits of his original goal—*electron holography*.

He did. Within three years, L.S. Bartell and C.L. Ritz of the University of Michigan produced an electron hologram. Their "trick," as Gabor called it, gave a resolving power of better than 1×10^{-10}m, enough to record the holographic image of an atom (Fig. 14–1).

FIG. 14–1 The holographic image of neon atoms in this photo has been magnified about 200 million times! To make it, the holographer shone a beam of electrons through neon gas. The atomic nuclei and electrons diffracted the electron waves to produce an interference pattern. This bright spot is a photographic enlargement of the image the electron hologram formed. What you see is the blurred motion of orbiting electrons.

The image is *not* that of a single neon atom. Rather, it's the product of overlapping images of many atoms. The technique places the identical images exactly atop one another. Electron microscopy, which reveals details less than a hundredth of a nanometer apart, has a greater resolving power than any other method.

When L.S. Bartell told Dennis Gabor about the first holographic images of atoms, he wrote: "The pictures are crude, distorted representations of the atoms, but it is rather agreeable, nevertheless, to get such a direct look at them by means of your suggestion!"[13]

This is how André Gabor described the irony of the accomplishment:

What originally induced Dennis Gabor to make his great invention was the desire to improve the resolution of the electron microscope. Owing to the technical difficulties encountered by the research laboratory to which the development was entrusted, the work was soon abandoned, and it was only about thirty years later that Professor Bartell of the University of Michigan brought it to the point where pictures of individual atoms can be obtained. When I congratulated Bartell on this momentous achievement, he replied that it was all there in my brother's first paper on holography—all that was needed was the careful interpretation of his work.[14]

Today holography is in more widespread use, with more far-reaching consequences, in areas other than electron microscopy. The most logical use was for display—as an alternative to photography.

Holographic Advertising

If you have something to sell, it's important to make your offer as appealing as possible. You have only a few seconds to catch someone's eye and you have plenty of competitors trying to do the same thing. When it comes to advertising, the right picture can create ten thousand sales.

Perhaps the most famous holographic ad was a window display at a New York jewelry store. Passersby were startled to see a disembodied hand dangling a bracelet out over the sidewalk (Fig. 14–2).

FIG. 14–2 This holographic real image projected twelve inches over the sidewalk in front of Cartier's jewelry store in New York in 1972. Passersby who reached for the $100,000 worth of diamonds discovered their hands passed right through. Some New Yorkers were as astonished as their predecessors had been at their first sight of a photograph more than a century before.

FIG. 14–3 Hallmark introduced the holographic greeting card in 1984. Holographic pendants, jewelry, and other novelties had already been available for years.

Since then, advertisers have made use of holograms in many forms. Manufacturers have gone to trade shows with holograms of their products, which take up less room and are cheaper to transport. Holographic stereograms can be especially useful for showing how a product, such as a tennis racket, performs.

Holograms also have appeared on the covers of magazines and company annual reports. They've been included as gifts with packages of candy and cereal. And they've become products in themselves (Fig. 14–3).

The cost of making a high quality hologram or copying large numbers of them has kept all but a few companies from trying holographic advertising. But expenses are coming down steadily as techniques improve. It's a safe bet you'll be seeing more and more holograms used as ads in the near future.

Holographic Art

The artistic side of holography developed in three stages. Right after the laser arrived, holographers chose subjects mainly for their ability to produce bright images. White, simple objects were popular. And from the looks of many early holograms, the pioneers often raided their children's toyboxes. Many game pieces, alphabet blocks, dolls and figurines posed for holographers during the 1960s.

Once holography became routine, holographers looked for more interesting and more challenging objects. They began to set up scenes with an eye to pleasing or to whimsical arrangements. Those with pulsed lasers worked with human subjects and produced portraits of many famous people.

At some point, holographic artists began to think of holography as much more than "new and improved" photography. Instead of recording the ordinary sights available to photographers, these artists began to make use of the magical qualities of holograms to reveal the world of imagination. Gone were the days when an observer could call a chess piece a "traditional" subject for holography.

Holographic art is now startling as often as it is beautiful. Artists and art lovers alike are attracted to the rainbow hologram, whose pure spectral colors are more brilliant than any paint or dye. The images are often so far removed from everyday experience, the viewer stops thinking for a time. That's what today's holographic artists seem to be after when they talk about the reality of dreams and other universes. They seem to be saying: Here's something you never saw before. What do you make of it? (Fig. 14–4).

FIG. 14–4 The holographic artist is a sculptor of light: "Faces" by Nemeth & Balogh, Bulgaria.

Holographic Archives

The hologram's ability to record images faithfully and thoroughly makes it an excellent visual storehouse. It's already possible to view holographic museum exhibits in some parts of the world. The governments of Bulgaria and the Soviet Union, for example, have decided to record some of their national treasures in the form of holograms (Fig. 14–5).

The advantages of holographic exhibits are several: Relatively inexpensive holograms can go on display while the priceless objects they represent remain safe from theft, vandalism, and the damaging effects of rough handling, humidity, and so on. Holograms are cheaper to transport, so residents of out-of-the-way towns and villages can see examples of their heritage as easily as the residents of major cities. Several copies can go on exhibit at the same time, increasing the viewing audience tremendously. And, above all, the holograms offer viewers just as much visual detail as they could get from the actual artifacts.

The faithfulness of holographic images make them ideal for textbook illustrations. Holograms of the human skeleton and

FIG. 14–5 Catherine the Great, who wore some of this jewelry, ruled Russia from 1762 to 1796. The Soviet government holographically recorded this symbol of times before the communist revolution.

muscle structure would be a valuable addition to medical books, for example. Perhaps some day soon, you'll have a chance to open your schoolbooks and study in 3-D.

Although display is the most obvious application, the hologram has proved itself of equal or greater value as a measuring tool.

Interferometry

"Measure twice, cut once" is good advice for carpenters. But even the most careful craftsperson isn't likely to need a higher degree of precision than that available with a plain old carpenter's rule or measuring tape.

This isn't true for many scientists and engineers, however. Their tasks often require accurate measurements of length far smaller than the eye's ability to distinguish between two marks on a stick. Some machine parts must be measured to a tolerance of less than the thickness of one of the marks itself. And for scientists who examine nature on a molecular scale, measuring in thousandths of a meter can be as crude as trying to measure with a meter stick how much your hair grows in a day!

Measuring small distances calls for small units of measurements—such as the wavelength of light. In the visible range, this means precision expressed in billionths of a meter.

The tool of measurement by light wave is the *interferometer*. As the name suggests, it measures interference. It does so by detecting changes in interference fringes. Remember that the distance between neighboring dark (or neighboring light) fringes in an interference pattern is half the wavelength of light used. Therefore, an interferometer is sensitive to distance differences on the order of a mere few hundred nanometers (10^{-7}m)!

Thomas Young's double-slit experiment produced a parallel fringe pattern. The zero-order fringe was bright because the wavefronts from each slit traveled exactly the same distance to the screen. Because they started out in phase, they met in phase and interfered constructively.

But if one of the wavefronts had been made to travel one-half wavelength farther, the interference pattern on the screen would have reversed itself. Destructive interference would have made the zero-order fringe dark.

Had Young conducted such an experiment, his primitive interferometer would have easily been the most precise measuring device in the world then. Today's interferometers are far more elaborate, of course. And the handiest of all is the kind that's a hologram.

Double-Exposure Interferometry

As you know, most holograms are made using a reference beam that's spatially coherent—with all waves in phase in a single plane. But you know, too, that the reference beam doesn't have to be in phase, merely temporally coherent—with all waves of equal length. This means a temporally coherent reference beam can interfere with a temporally coherent object beam to make a hologram.

What is also true is that two temporally coherent object beams can interfere to form a useful fringe pattern as well.

If the object wavefronts are identical and overlap exactly, they reinforce each other everywhere. They appear to be one brighter but otherwise unchanged image.

And if the overlapping object wavefronts are completely different, their waves interfere at random. Each separate image degrades the other in helter-skelter fashion and both are obscured.

But suppose the object wavefronts are just a little bit dissimilar. Then dark fringes form on the combined image in a regular—and meaningful—way (Fig. 14–6).

Figure 14–6 is a *holographic interferogram*—a map of how a soda pop can reacts to a certain kind of stress. If you wanted to build a better can, you might study this double-exposure hologram to decide where to strengthen its walls.

Some tire manufacturers use this technique to test their products for flaws. The tire is holographed at two different air pressures. Widely spaced fringes in the double exposure show where the tire wall has expanded gradually. Fringes that appear closer together reveal drastic expansion, a weak spot or "bubble" in the rubber. The closely spaced fringes look like bull's eyes that fittingly encircle weak spots, where the chances of bursting are greatest.

Before tires could be examined holographically, the best way to test for flaws was to increase the air pressure until the tire exploded. Needless to say, this test made studying the evidence difficult. Now engineers can pinpoint flaws without an explosion. Holographic nondestructive testing like this yields much more information.

FIG. 14–6 This hologram has recorded the image of a soda can twice. The first time, the can wore a rubber band, which squeezed it slightly. After the holographer cut the rubber band for the second exposure, the can resumed its undistorted shape. The illuminated hologram reconstructs virtual images from each exposure, which overlap. Dark fringes show wherever the rubber band had squeezed the can a distance equal to a half-wavelength or multiple half-wavelengths of the laser's light. The two images cancel each other out along those lines.

Holographic interferometry is useful whenever tiny changes in a surface need measuring. Interferograms of parts such as helicopter rotors and automobile clutch plates reveal weaknesses in joints and bonded layers. They even help scientists design better artificial replacement parts for the human body (Fig. 14–7a, b, c).

Double-exposure holograms can measure changes that are too rapid or transparent to observe easily any other way. For example, you might make a hologram of empty air and double expose it the instant a bullet passes through the same space. The way the bullet displaces the air forms a fringe pattern like a boat's wake. Engineers can test an airplane wing's shape in this same way (Fig. 14–8).

Similarly, you might double expose a bit of rocket fuel before and after igniting it. Then the fringe pattern maps the shape of the heated layers of air above the burning fuel.

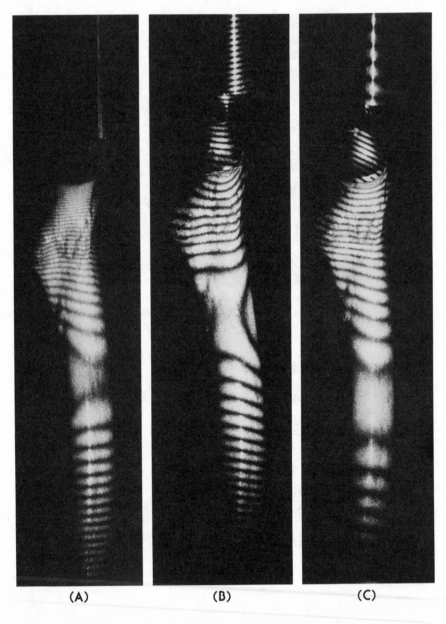

(A)   (B)   (C)

FIG. 14–7a, 14–7b, 14–7c Double-exposure holograms of a normal leg bone (7a) and the same bone with artificial joints of two different metals attached show how all react to the same stress. Researchers looked for the interference fringes of one replacement joint to resemble the fringes on the intact bone more closely. They decided the artificial joint made of titanium (7b) made a better match than the one made of chrome cobalt (7c). The interferograms make unnecessary the old method of laboriously testing each sample point by point with a strain gauge.

FIG. 14–8 Interference fringes reveal how air flows around a wing. Changes in the wing's design will change the airflow, as differences in the fringes of another double-exposure interferogram would show.

Double-exposure holograms are just right for testing some products and observing some phenomena. But for others, a single-exposure interferogram is better.

Single-Exposure Interferometry

Think of a vibrating surface. If the force disturbing it is regular, its vibrations are, too, because the surface's edges confine the vibrations, and standing waves form. Some points don't move; they're at the nodes, or mid-points, of the standing waves. Some points oscillate a great deal, and others oscillate to a lesser degree.

The surface points that don't vibrate reflect light from one position; they will be faithfully reproduced in the holographic image. The oscillating points, however, reflect most of their light from two positions—at the crests and troughs of their cycles. Lightwaves from vibrating points whose crests and troughs are multiples of a full wavelength apart will reinforce each other. Light waves from points whose extremes of oscillation are multiples of a half-wavelength apart will cancel each other out.

When illuminated, this kind of interferogram reconstructs images of both extremes of vibration, which interfere with each other to form fringes. The pattern of dark lines over the combined image shows all points where the surface was displaced by multiple half-wavelengths. This is *time-average holographic interferometry* (Fig. 14–9a,b).

The third kind of holographic interferogram works like the double-exposure type except that the second image, the distorted one, is never recorded. Suppose you wanted to test an

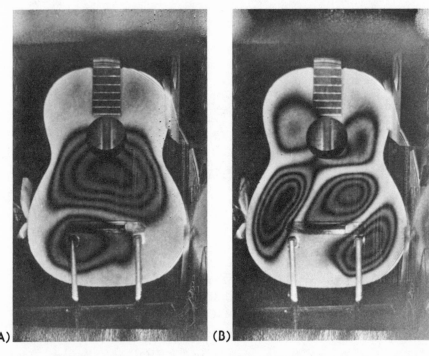

(A)   (B)

FIG. 14–9a, 14–9b Time-average holograms show how the surface of a guitar vibrates when it's made to oscillate at 310 Hz (9a) and 495 Hz (9b).

airplane wing for flaws in the bonding that holds its layers together.

First, you'd secure the wing and make a transmission hologram of it. Then you'd leave the wing in position while you developed the holographic film and bleached it to be transparent. Finally, you'd illuminate the wing with the same laser object beam you used to make the hologram in the first place.

By looking through the hologram at the wing, you'd cause the holographic virtual image to overlap light reflected from the wing itself. The two images would interfere. As long as the wing remained unstressed, its surface wouldn't change from the shape the hologram recorded. But as soon as you applied stress, fringes would form along lines of equal displacement. The fringes would show where the distorted wing differed from its unstressed holographic image. As with the double-exposure hologram, bull's eye patterns would indicate bulging flaws.

The advantage of *real-time holographic interferometry* is that it's possible to test objects quickly. In the case of airplane wings, some of which are tested holographically now, one worker watches through the hologram, while another holds a heat gun near the wing. As the wing's surface heats, weak spots expand more than properly bonded areas. Patch bonds correct the weaknesses and make a flawless wing.

What Next?

Holographic displays and interferograms are the most common uses of the magic of holography. They're by no means the only ones, however.

Current research in many areas promises to bring the holographer other jobs. Guessing what they might be and when can be great fun, even though some applications are better bets for routine use than others. The last chapter samples a field that's growing so fast that a young person's eventual career specialty might not have been thought of yet.

PRACTICE AND PROMISE

*C*assandra woke up to a rainbow shining in her basement room. She had no window below ground level, of course. The daylight came through a periscope from a holographic solar collector outside. The stationary hologram redirected dispersed sunlight to the periscope port no matter what the sun's position in the sky. All day long her basement room was full of color.

It was a school day. Before Cass dressed, she got out a new pair of eyeglasses. She couldn't wear contacts, and she much preferred her glasses to the old-fashioned kind her mother wore. Instead of heavy glass or bulky plastic lenses, her holographic lenses were nothing more than a rigid sheet of film. . . .

HOEs

As you saw in the image of the magnifying glass in Figures 1–5a and b, a hologram of a lens acts just like a lens. And as you learned in Chapter Twelve, a hologram's interference fringes can act as mirrors. Holograms designed to do the work of lenses and mirrors are known as *holographic optical elements* (HOEs).

HOEs offer tremendous savings in weight because they consist of a thin layer of emulsion on a plastic base. For example, it would be possible to construct a holographic lens many times bigger than the practical limit for a conventional one made of glass or plastic.

The hologram of a lens or mirror behaves exactly like the original, with one major exception. A simple HOE gives best results when used with light of the same wavelength as the laser light it was made from. This isn't necessarily undesirable. Aircraft companies have developed a HOE mirror for an airplane's windshield. It was made with laser light that's the same wavelength as the flight information displayed on a TV screen behind the pilot's head. The HOE mirror therefore reflects the TV picture to the pilot while remaining transparent to the scene outside (Fig. 15–1).

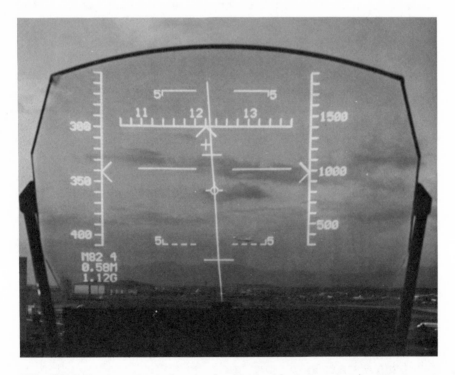

FIG. 15–1 In the past, pilots had to lower their eyes to the instrument panel to read important flight information. Now HOEs allow them to get this information off the windshield. This hologram reflects only the wavelength of the green messages that appear on a TV screen behind the pilot. All other wavelengths pass through the *head-up display* (HUD), giving the pilot an unobstructed view of the sky and ground outside.

Several holographic lenses can be combined to diffract or reflect several wavelengths or correct other focusing limitations conventional lenses may have. Cass's eyeglasses will probably have to be some sort of thin "HOE sandwich" to work in white light.

HOEs also can be combined with conventional lenses for an increase in power without an increase in space or weight. Suppose you coated both sides of a glass lens and recorded interference patterns in them. Then you'd have a three-for-one advantage in weight and size over glass lenses with the same focusing abilities.

HOEs have the potential to replace glass elements in cameras and binoculars as well as eyeglasses. Many grocery stores now use lasers aimed by HOEs to read the bar identification code on packaged purchases. The scanners contain a rapidly spinning disk made up of many wedge-shaped HOEs. They redirect the laser's beam in many directions so the checkout clerk doesn't have to worry about aligning each package carefully. There's always one HOE in line to send the beam to a package at the right angle.

A solar collector operates like the multiple-hologram HOE in a supermarket scanner, only over a much wider angle. To direct light onto a periscope port so it travels into Cass's room, a mirror would have to be constantly readjusted by motor as the earth turns under the sun during the day and presents a more northern or southern face with the seasons. A holographic solar collector, in contrast, can direct light to the same spot from many angles without any moving parts. The complex hologram it's made of acts like a wide-angle lens to diffract sunlight to the same spot no matter how the sun's position changes. It also acts like a prism to disperse that light into a spectrum.

HOEs will be more easily and cheaply mass-produced than conventional lenses. Copies will be *pressed* from a master in much the same way phonograph records are made. This, more than any other fact, will bring HOEs into the home.

During her free study period, Cass went to the school library. She asked for the encyclopedia at the desk and received a thin envelope from the librarian. Cass pulled out the single sheet of film that was volume E–F, and inserted it in a laser projector. The page she needed was in column three, row seventeen. Quickly she pointed the laser's beam at the tiny hologram there, which contained the chart she needed for her science paper. The information appeared on a viewing screen. . . .

Holo Files

This is the age of information. Every day a new mountain of data is added to the mountain range already in storage. The problem is more than simply finding a place to keep all the facts; it's also finding information once it's been stored.

Paper records are extremely bulky and difficult to dig through. Converting paper records to magnetic ones in the form of tapes or disks helps. But magnetic records are sensitive to storage conditions. Heat, humidity, and stray magnetic fields can ruin them quickly. Even under the best circumstances, magnetic files need re-recording every decade or so.

A better solution is to miniaturize documents photographically. It's now possible to reduce thousands of pages to fit a postage stamp-sized piece of film, a *microfiche*. At such an extreme, however, a few specks of dust on the film during an exposure can wipe out a lot of information, especially if it's in the form of the 1's and 0's of computer code.

A holographic filing system is immune to this kind of damage. Remember that a hologram stores information redundantly—recording each bit of data over its entire interference pattern. A few dust specks here and there can't wipe out such a widespread record completely.

In one Japanese holographic file, a hologram 5 mm square records the contents of a single 8½-inch x 11-inch page. A sheet of film the size of a paperback book cover holds 400 of these tiny holograms—the contents of a hefty paperback book! The whole file consists of 700 such sheets. And most impressive of all, you can call up and view any one of those 280,000 pages on a high resolution TV screen in less than a second (Fig. 15–2)!

Holographic files would be attractive to any organization, such as an insurance company or library, that keeps records in large numbers. For example, a British organization is converting thousands of dental records into holograms. Up to now, the best records were plaster molds. But holographing the molds reduces the storage space to a fraction without sacrificing any information. The holograms are life-size records, whose 3-D images allow a dentist to measure individual teeth as precisely as the plaster models did.

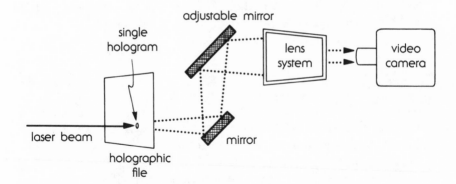

FIG. 15–2 In this simplified diagram, mirrors direct a *collimated* laser beam to one specific hologram in an array of holograms on file. The hologram diffracts the beam to reconstruct a page of information. Mirrors and a special lens system prepare the holographic image for a video camera, which sends it to a TV monitor for high-resolution display.

The improvements of holographic recordkeeping might have disadvantages, of course. Any citizen concerned with privacy will have cause for concern if government and business files become as efficient as they are big.

Cass saw her friend Tracey in the hall between classes. Five weeks after his car accident, his nose was still bandaged. The wound he got from the steering wheel had healed, so he no longer needed to have it taped. It was misshapen, though, and she knew he wore the bandage as a mask.

But today Tracey was in good spirits. "Look at this," he called, waving a piece of plastic in the air. There in a hologram was her friend, his nose restored.

She turned the film in the sunlight to look at both profiles, which seemed a bit unfamiliar. "Where'd you get it?"

"My plastic surgeon designed a new nose for me on her computer. How does it look in the hologram?"

"Not bad," she said. . . .

Holos by Computer

So far, you've become familiar with the hologram as a tool for separating an image from its object. There's also a need for images of nonexistent objects. Your thoughts, which are mental images, have no actual objects as sources. You reconstruct them from memory of physical reality rather than the things themselves.

Generating holograms from a computer's memory is another way of producing images of objects that have no physical existence. These images might show design engineers how a yet-to-be-built part would look, or show flight controllers the relative positions of airplanes many miles away, or create lenses and other HOEs too expensive to make from plastic or glass.

One type of computer-generated hologram begins as a computer program that tells the machine how to make a stereographic drawing. The computer calculates how an imaginary object should look from all sides according to instructions. It then draws a series of 2-D pictures that show how the object would look in three dimensions. These drawings become the basis of a holographic stereogram when they're made into a series of narrow 2-D holograms placed side by side to form a cylinder. When viewed, separate holograms reconstruct different 2-D images for each eye. The brain combines these to perceive a 3-D view of the computer's creation. Different views of the imaginary object are available from other viewing positions.

Another technique uses a computer to calculate the interference fringes point by point. When printed on film, the pattern reconstructs a particular image. It's far easier to calculate a simple pattern like a zone plate, of course, than to design the fringes that would reveal how a person's nose will look after plastic surgery. Such a complex hologram would require so many bits of information that it would challenge even a computer's memory and speed. (Fig. 15–3).

FIG. 15–3 A computer calculated the location and angle for the laser beams that created the fringe spacing needed to produce this holographic image of objects that never existed. Even now, more advanced computer programs can construct more complicated images in 3-D, even without using a laser to make the recording.

Even so, scientists are working on shortcuts to allow a computer to draw complicated interference patterns. Many people believe this area of holography shows the greatest promise of all, for a computer's memory is just a human's in another form. And if computers can give form to human thoughts holographically, there may be no limit to the jobs they can do.

All that work wasted, Cass thought. Just because she hadn't double-checked the camera before taking the pictures for her science project. Now the report was due in three days, and all the proof she had was a handful of fuzzy photos. There wasn't enough time to repeat the whole experiment. But she'd have to do that unless Uncle Frank was right. He said he'd sharpen her photos holographically in his lab. She hoped it would work. It was her only chance. . . .

Image Deblurring

A blurred photograph contains much of the image information to be found in a sharply focused version. It's just not in a form that eye and brain can easily interpret. Computers have improved poor images by decoding them, most notably those of the planets sent back by visiting spacecraft. But specially prepared holograms can do the same thing a computer does (Fig. 15–4a, b).

The secret of holographic deblurring is to determine, as closely as possible, how a single image point has been blurred. In some cases, this is known precisely. One technique of electron microscopy, for example, requires the image be blurred on purpose to overcome certain limitations of the instrument.

But when the reason for the blurring is less clear, the holographer must study the image for clues to the movement or defocusing responsible. When the subject of the photo is familiar, he compares recognizable image edges and features with the way they should look. If the object is unfamiliar, however, it might take quite a bit of trial and error to figure out just how the blurring occurred.

To deblur a photo, the holographer needs a transparency of a point that's blurred the same way as the image points were. He combines this with a hologram in a special arrangement of lenses to make a filter. When the photo is illuminated with laser light, the filter decodes the information in its blurred image.

The more closely the blurring of the copied point matches the blurring of points in the image, the more improvement the filter

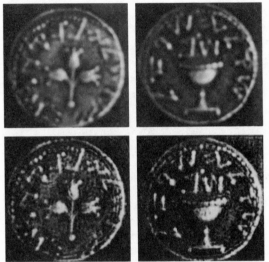

FIG. 15–4 An unknown camera problem caused these photos of rare coins from A.D. 66–70 to be blurred (4a). There was no chance for the U.S. scientists to return to the Middle East for another try, so researchers made a holographic filter to remove the blurred effect (4b).

causes. In the case of strange objects, the holographer may have to try to mimic the blurring many times before constructing a filter that does the trick.

Cass settled into her desk. The electric lights overhead made her squint at first. This history class could use a little rainbow sunshine from her room, she thought.

Her eyes quickly adjusted to the even illumination, however, and she forgot about it. You couldn't tell just by looking that its source was a human-made sun, a fusion reactor.

Or that holography played a part in making it possible . . .

Dynamic Holograms

A holographic optical element (HOE), as you've learned, can act like an ordinary mirror. Its holographic interference pattern is "static," or unchanging, and mimics the action of a regular mirror. Diverging light continues to diverge after ordinary reflection, for example.

But a mirror consisting of a "dynamic," or ever-changing, holographic interference pattern creates a reflected beam that's a near-twin of the incident (incoming) beam. Light reflected from such a mirror is identical to incident light—except for traveling in the opposite direction and having the opposite phase. Diverging light converges after this kind of reflection, turning right back the way it came, *as if the beam were traveling backward in time.*

The incident beam and the reflected beam are called "conjugates" because of this similar yet opposite relationship. The special hologram that creates the second, opposite-phase beam from the first beam is known as a "phase-conjugate mirror."

Phase-conjugated light is a reversed version of an original beam. Remember that the optical principle of reversibility means that a beam follows the same path no matter which direction it travels. You couldn't see yourself in a phase-conjugate mirror because the only reversed image light reaching your eyes would be image light that came from your eyes originally. Reversed image light from your chin, for example, would return to your chin unseen.

A phase-conjugate mirror is made from certain substances that have the ability to instantly record the changing interference pattern of an out-of-phase object beam and a coherent reference beam. A second reference beam instantly reconstructs a reversed object beam no matter what the shape of the incident wavefront.

A dynamic hologram puts reversibility to good use. Suppose a piece of frosted glass distorts an incident beam on its way to a phase-conjugate mirror. Then the reflected beam that travels backwards through the glass is just the right shape to become "undistorted." In other words, optical phase conjugation reverses wave distortions caused during the forward trip through a medium. For example, it can restore coherence to a laser beam that has been thrown out of phase, *while sending the beam right back where it came from.* Scientists hope to use this property to build a tiny "sun" to run a nuclear power plant by fusion.

Fusion power promises to be "clean," with none of the potentially dangerous by-products of today's fission reactors. Fission releases energy by splitting a heavy atom into lighter ones. Fusion works in the opposite way—by combining two light atoms into a single heavier atom.

Forcing hydrogen atoms together to tap fusion energy requires a temperature and pressure similar to that at the sun's core. Laser beams will supply the heat and force needed to fuse the atomic nuclei—if they can be made to hit their target. With dynamic holography, laser light can't miss. Here's how:

The target in a fusion reactor is a bubble of hydrogen gas far smaller than the head of a pin. Hitting such a tiny spot with high-power laser beams about as wide is nearly impossible, so scientists will cover the bubble with the widened beams of low-power lasers. The small portion of each beam reflected from the hydrogen bubble passes through an amplifying chamber, where it is strengthened by stimulated emission. This single pass distorts the beam, making it incoherent. But the distortion is undone when the amplified light strikes a phase-conjugate mirror and is reversed. The reversed beam travels backward through the amplifying chamber, gaining even more power as its waves are "undistorted" back into phase. Finally the reversed beam—tightly focused, highly coherent, and very powerful—returns to the bubble with the precision and the energy to fuse the hydrogen atoms.

The ability of holographic phase-conjugate mirrors to restore order to garbled electromagnetic waves also has value for communications. For example, dynamic holograms could "undo" the distortion of signals returning through the atmosphere to track satellites. And they could reassemble the proper relationship of different wavelengths (and speeds) of electromagnetic waves transmitted by optical fiber. By the time phase-conjugate mirrors make nuclear fusion a reality, they will surely be put to many other uses as well.

There in front of Cass was the route Hannibal took in crossing the Alps with his elephant army. She studied the photograph closely as her history teacher went on about the hardships of the surprise attack. The photo in her textbook showed the rugged terrain in detail. It was a photograph of a hologram taken from an airplane using not visible light, but microwaves ...

Radar Holography

There's no doubt aerial photography has been one of the mapmaker's greatest tools. First balloons, then airplanes, and now orbiting satellites have allowed cartographers to step farther and farther back for a wider and wider view of our world.

Despite the increasingly more accurate pictures mapmakers have obtained by means of aerial photography, the technique has limitations. Conventional photography makes use of light in the visible and infrared ranges. At night, its subjects are restricted to sources, such as cities and volcanoes, that emit radiation at those wavelengths. There's plenty of reflected visible and infrared radiation in reflected sunlight, of course. But the daytime atmosphere absorbs a great deal even when clear. And if it's cloudy, you can forget about aerial photography entirely.

Radar isn't subject to these limitations. Sunlight isn't needed for an image because the radar equipment sends out its own beam to illuminate the ground. And clouds are no obstacle because they're quite transparent to the microwave radiation radar uses.

Microwaves ranging from one centimeter to 30 cm are about a million times longer than visible light waves. Although they pass right through water vapor, they're short enough to resolve enough detail for mapmakers and others. Their resolving power is greatest, however, when the radar system uses the largest possible sensor. A radio sensor is commonly known as an antenna.

One scientist has calculated that to detect details as small as 20 m across from a satellite 250 kilometers (km) high using 20 cm microwaves, you'd need an antenna 2 km in diameter. One that large is clearly impractical.

Researchers found a holographic solution to this problem in the 1950s with the invention of side-looking radar. They mounted an antenna underneath an airplane and directed a fan-shaped beam of microwaves to the side of the flight path. The beam was so wide by the time it hit the ground, an object might be covered for several seconds. During that time, the object reflected microwaves back to the antenna aboard the moving aircraft. And, in effect, the antenna became as long as the distance it traveled with the plane while receiving that object's reflections. Using side-looking radar with an antenna attached to a satellite, an object might remain in the beam path long enough for the satellite to travel fifteen kilometers. The satellite's antenna, then, behaved as though it were fifteen kilometers long!

The record a side-looking radar system makes is like a hologram because part of the signal reflected from a point on the ground acts as an object beam when it's superimposed on another part of the same reflected signal, which acts as a reference beam. This allows the system to record amplitude and phase—the "whole message"—of the microwaves reflected from the Earth's surface. A high-speed computer interprets the phase and amplitude information into an image that can be recorded on film, producing a photograph of what the radar "saw" (Fig. 15–5). Although side-looking radar doesn't produce a hologram, it records holographic information about the shape of the ground below.

Some scientists are especially interested in radar holography because of the ability of microwaves to penetrate covers that are

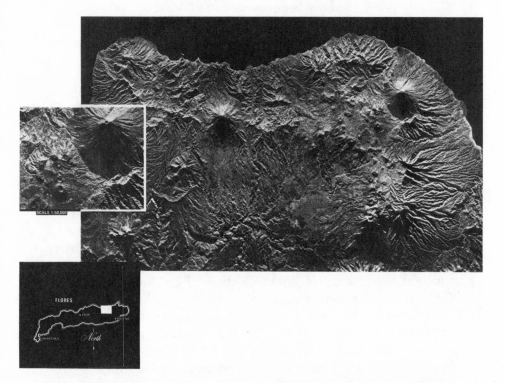

FIG. 15–5 Side-looking radar recorded this view of rugged Flores Island, in the Indian Ocean, from 40,000 feet. The island was completely covered by clouds at the time. The ocean water and mountain shadows appear totally black because they reflected no microwaves back to the antenna aboard the airplane.

opaque to other radiation. Oceanographers will use the method to study subsurface currents. Geologists will look below desert sands for ancient riverbeds and rock structures, and archaeologists will be looking over their shoulders for signs of sand-covered ancient cities.

Radar holography is well-suited to mapping terrain often covered by clouds. One of the first projects using side-looking radar mapped rain forests in the Amazon River Basin. In the future, you may see maps made from radar holograms of the now-hidden face of Venus.

The doctor had promised Cassandra she'd be holographed and on her way in half an hour. She was glad they'd finally get a good look inside her stomach because it still hurt now and then. But she didn't know quite what to expect.

The doctor was right, of course. The procedure required little more than a bit of local anesthetic to prepare the way for two slender glass optical fibers. One was connected to a low-power laser and carried light to illuminate her stomach wall. The other carried a reflected image back out to the film, where it interfered with a reference beam. The result was a hologram of her insides she hoped would reveal the cause of her pain. . . .

Fiber Holoptics

Holography is steadily becoming easier and more popular. At first, you needed an expensive research lab to make a hologram. Then, you could make one in your basement or classroom. In the future, holographers and students will send reference and object beams through thin strands of glass. These optical fibers, as thin as a few millionths of a meter, make excellent guides for laser light because of internal reflection (Fig. 15–6).

Optical fibers, whether used singly or in bundles, present distinct advantages to holographers. First, by transmitting laser light along pathways of glass rather than air, they eliminate the scattering effects of airborne dust.

Second, with a special single-strand optical fiber, the holographer has to anchor only each end. One that's done, movement

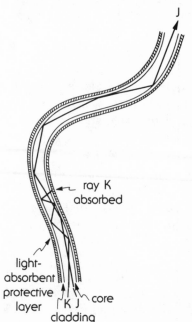

ray K
absorbed

light-
absorbent
protective
layer
K J core
cladding

FIG. 15–6 A single-strand optical fiber consists of two types of glass. The core has a slightly higher refractive index than the cladding that surrounds it. Light ray **J** strikes the cladding at a shallow angle, is reflected along a zig-zag or spiral path and remains in the core until reaching the end of the fiber.

Because of the sharp bend, however, light ray **K** strikes the cladding at an angle that's too steep to result in reflection. Ray **K** escapes the core to be absorbed by a protective outer layer.

Light that's coherent when it enters an optical fiber is still coherent when it emerges. A coherent beam that's split and sent down identical fibers of equal length emerges as two coherent beams.

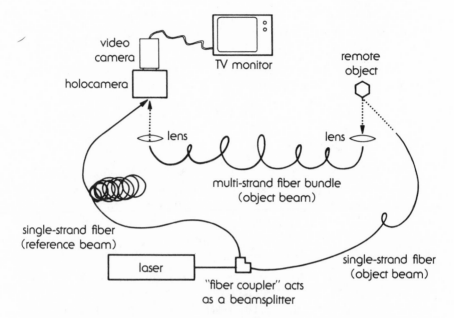

FIG. 15–7 Optical fibers allow holographers to record holograms of distant or hard-to-reach objects. A single-strand glass fiber carries part of the laser beam to the object. A multi-strand fiber bundle brings a reflected image—the object beam—back to a holocamera. There it interferes with the reference beam to make a thermoplastic hologram. A video camera carries the reconstructed holographic image to a TV monitor for viewing.

elsewhere along the fiber will not affect the beams (Fig. 15–7).

And third, the lengths of the reference and object fibers can be adjusted so that any setup will more easily satisfy the laser's coherence length requirements. This will allow the holographing of objects that are difficult to remove to the studio, or even difficult to reach.

A natural combination would be to combine fiber optics with the portable holographic camera, or *holocamera*. The holocamera's ability to make erasable thermoplastic holograms quickly, coupled with the fiber's ability to put laser beams anywhere with precision, could have many uses. For example, a repair crew could examine disabled machinery in the field—or even at the bottom of the ocean. Engineers could make holographic interferograms of structures such as bridge supports without taking them apart. And paramedics could get a quick 3-D look at how victims are pinned in wreckage so they can more easily and safely set them free.

Cass got home before her parents, so the door was locked. She placed the tip of one finger on a glass plate near the knob and waited. In a matter of seconds, a laser scanned her finger-print and compared its image with holographic images on file. The door opened automatically once the machine recognized a match and identified her as a family member. . . .

Pattern Recognition

One way to imagine how an optical system can recognize shapes is to think of assembling a jigsaw puzzle. Let's say you're looking for a certain piece to fit a hole formed by sur-rounding pieces. You know exactly what shape the missing piece has and, before you go looking for it, you memorize its shape. As you search, you concentrate on the features of the hole you have in mind. Your eyes scan pieces, one by one. But you discard them as soon as you realize their features don't match the mental image of the hole. Finally, in a flash of recog-nition, you find the twin.

This method of locating a puzzle piece is akin to pattern rec-ognition by holography. Instead of using a mental image as your guide, however, the holographic technique compares test shapes to a special optical filter. The filter is basically a holo-gram of the target shape. In the scientist's vocabulary, a poor match between test shape and hologram is a *cross correlation*. A perfect match is an *autocorrelation*.

The search consists of superimposing the hologram's image on a test image by means of a special lens arrangement like the one used for image deblurring. A cross correlation between the two yields visual noise. But an autocorrelation shows up as a spot of light, a flash of recognition known as a *correlation peak* (Fig. 15–8a, b, c).

Holographic pattern recognition might prove useful wherever it was necessary to locate one shape in a field of many. Suppose you wanted to find information about a topic in the holographic filing system described earlier. Then you might prepare a holo-graphic correlation filter to detect a key word or phrase in the image of each page on file. The system might be set to display each page containing an autocorrelation on a video screen for follow-up inspection.

Similar systems might search not only fingerprint files, but also microscope slides looking for signs of cancer among healthy cells, or aerial photographs looking for enemy weapons. The more distinctive the target shape is compared to its sur-

PROFESSOR
ASSOCIATE PROFESSOR
PROFESSOR AND HEAD
SECRETARY TO HEAD
PROFESSOR

(A)

PROFESSOR

(B)

FIG. 15–8a, 15–8b, 15–8c *Holographic pattern recognition* makes it possible to search for one word in a group of words. When the test image (8a) is superimposed on a holographic image of the target word (8b) using a certain arrangement of lenses, bright spots of light appear in a dark field. The spots indicate wherever the matchup, or *correlation*, between test image features and target word features is at a peak—in other words, wherever the word appears on the page.

Figure 15–8c shows these correlation peaks on a special 3-D camera display. The view is from the back, with the top of the list of words in the test image toward you.

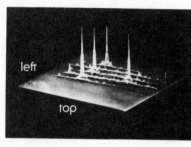

(C)

roundings the better the results. Partial correlations can yield false peaks. So, for example, camouflage might hide a tank from a holographic system. And in a way, similarities among letters—such as those between a *Q* and an *O*—are a form of camouflage and a possible source of confusion.

Holographic pattern recognition and image deblurring use special properties of lenses and holograms to do jobs that might be done by long strings of computer calculations. For this reason, their work is thought of as *optical computing*. As they're improved, optical computers might become as important as the electronic kind.

Cass settled into her seat just as the movie began. The credits appeared to zoom right off the screen toward her face. She'd seen photos of the old 3-D movies her parents had gone to. The audience had to wear funny cardboard spectacles to separate the stereo image for each eye. It was a good thing the holo-

graphic screen made the specs unnecessary. How could anyone enjoy the old 3-D effect while looking so silly?

Just then the hero of the movie entered the old abandoned house, and Cass almost reached up to brush the cobwebs away. . . .

Holo Movies and TV

The Soviet Union unveiled the world's first true holographic movie in 1976. It projected onto a holographic screen the multiple 2-D images of a young woman approaching the viewer with a handful of flowers. During its forty-five-second run, observers could stretch in their seats to peer behind the bouquet to see her face.

The images' narrow viewing angle restricted the audience to only four people. The screen that focused the images for each viewer was made by exposing a large photographic plate four times to a pair of laser beams. One beam for each exposure came from the point where the projector would stand. The other beam came from the point where a seated observer's head would be. The developed plate then acted as a multiple mirror to reflect the holographic image from the projector to each seat.

In his 1971 Nobel lecture, Dennis Gabor had suggested a similar system for a possible audience of two hundred. So far, it hasn't been built.

It's more likely you'll see holographic movies before you'll see holographic TV, however. The main problem of true 3-D cinema is constructing a screen to provide many viewers with separate image pairs. Holographic television must contend with the bigger problem of handling the enormous amount of image information contained in even a single hologram.

A typical TV set uses an electron beam to construct a 2-D image out of perhaps a quarter million black-and-white or colored dots. Gabor estimated that ninety *billion* dots would be needed to resolve the multiple 2-D images an average hologram provides!

An even greater problem exists in transmitting that picture. Whether the electromagnetic signal comes by wire or microwaves, that ninety billion bits of information might take hours to bring just one hologram's image to your living room. Holographic TV will probably remain a dream until a way is found to reduce the sheer amount of information in a hologram without sacrificing too much image quality.

Still, it's an appealing dream. Imagine what it would be like to sit smack dab in the middle of a Western. How would a cattle stampede look from that point of view?

Cass had lots of homework to do, so she went downstairs right after dinner. The sun was down by then and her room was dark. First Cass turned a spotlight on a window-sized hologram on the wall. Instantly a tree-lined mountain stream appeared. She relaxed before the view for a moment, shifting in her chair slightly to get a better look at the water through the trees.

Then she turned on her desk lamp and sat down to work next to the sight of a distant meadow in her basement room.

What About You?

The list of uses of holography currently under study goes on and on. Holograms have characteristics that are attractive to scientists in many fields. As X-ray holography becomes a reality, for example, it could provide a 3-D view of the inside of inanimate objects, or maybe even the human body.

Holograms don't require electromagnetic waves. Sound also can form interference patterns. *Acoustic holography* is beginning to offer images of underwater objects with greater precision than today's sonar equipment—and a totally harmless view of living, intact human organs.

Scientists are working on other, unrelated procedures that might prove better than holography for certain jobs. But it seems likely that holograms will find permanent places in many labs and homes of the future.

If the magic of holography inspires you to read further, use the list of books for further reading as a guide. You might become sidetracked by subjects connected with holography and optics. But if you remain fascinated by the magic, and work at it, who knows? You might be able to fashion a career out of thin air.

APPENDIX I

SOME PLACES TO VIEW HOLOGRAMS

The following list is incomplete. If you don't live near any of these places, you may hear about a traveling exhibition or permanent display coming to a nearby museum. You might also contact the physics or art departments of colleges in the area, to ask if there are holograms available for public viewing.

The Exploratorium
Marina Blvd. & Lyon
San Francisco, CA 94123

Fine Arts Research and
    Holographic Center
1134 W. Washington Blvd.
Chicago, IL 60607

The Holographic Film Co., Inc.
361 W. Broadway
New York, NY 10013

Holos Gallery
1792 Haight St.
San Francisco, CA 94117

Museum of Holography
11 Mercer St.
New York, NY 10013

Sapan Holographics
240 E. 26th St.
New York, NY 10010

Museum of Science
Science Park
Boston, MA

SCIENTIFIC NOTATION

A. Our number system is based on ten. A numeral's position tells how many of each multiple of ten to consider. In the example below, there are 4 hundreds, 3 tens, 2 ones, 7 tenths, and 9 hundredths:

$$432.79$$

B. A decimal point separates the ones digit from the tenths digit. When there are no units to the right of the decimal point, it is usually dropped:

$$78.00 = 78(.)$$

C. Moving the decimal point one place to the right multiplies a digit's value by ten:

$$.2 \times 10 = 2(.)$$
$$2 \times 10 = 20$$
$$20 \times 10 = 200$$

D. "One hundred," "100," and "10 × 10" are three ways to write the same number. So is "10^2." The superscript "2" tells how many times to multiply the number ten by itself to arrive at its actual value.

$$10^2 = (1) \times 10 \times 10 = 100$$
$$10^3 = 10 \times 10 \times 10 = 1,000$$

E. Multiplying a number by 10^2 has the effect of shifting its decimal point two places to the right. Of course, it's then necessary to fill up any open places to the left of the decimal point with zeroes:

$$7 \times 10^2 = 700$$
$$2.14 \times 10^3 = 2,140$$
$$.10004 \times 10^5 = 10,004$$

F. By the same reasoning, moving the decimal point one place to the *left* divides a digit's value by ten:

$$200(.) \div 10 = 20$$
$$20 \div 10 - 2$$
$$2 \div 10 = .2$$

G. "One one-hundredth," ".01," and "$\frac{1}{100}$" describe the same quantity. So does 10^{-2}. The superscript "$^{-2}$" tells how many times to divide by ten to arrive at real value:

$$10^{-2} = \frac{1}{10 \times 10} = .01$$

$$10^{-4} = \frac{1}{10 \times 10 \times 10 \times 10} = .0001$$

H. Multiplying a number by 10^{-2} has the effect of shifting its decimal point two places to the left. Once again, it's necessary to fill up empty places with zeroes. This time, however, the empty spaces will appear to the right of the decimal point:

$$5.3 \times 10^{-2} = .053$$
$$1.16 \times 10^{-4} = .000116$$
$$8,702 \times 10^{-7} = .0008702$$

I. In general, to change scientific notation to everyday numbers when the *superscript is positive*, move the decimal point that many places *to the right*. Add zeroes to open places if needed:

$$7 \times 10^{14} \text{ cycles per second} = 700,000,000,000,000 \text{ cycles/s}$$
$$1.86282 \times 10^5 \text{ miles per second} = 186,282 \text{ mi/s}$$

When the *superscript is negative*, move the decimal point that many places *to the left*:

$$10^{-6} \text{ seconds} = 1 \times 10^{-6}\text{s} = .000001 \text{ s}$$
$$6.328 \times 10^{-9} \text{ meters} = .000000006328 \text{ m}$$

J. In general, to change everyday numbers *greater than one* to scientific notation, move the decimal point to the left and place it *between the first and second digits on the left*. Count the number of places the decimal point jumped. That number is the *positive* superscript:

$$280{,}000 \text{ pages} = 2.8 \times 10^{-5} \text{ pp.}$$
$$299{,}792{,}500 \text{ meters per second} = 2.997925 \times 10^{-8} \text{ m/s}$$

For everyday numbers *less than one*, move the decimal point to the right and place it *on the right of the first digit other than zero*. Count the number of places the decimal point jumped. That number is the *negative* superscript:

$$.000001 \text{ seconds} = 1 \times 10^{-6} \text{ s} = 10^{-6} \text{ s}$$
$$.0000000000000000000000000000000663 \text{ joules-seconds} =$$
$$6.63 \times 10^{-34} \text{ joules-s}$$

NOTES

1. E. Leith, "Some Highlights in the History of Display Holography," *Proceedings of the International Symposium on Display Holography*, ed. by T.H. Jeong, 1982 vol. 1, p.3.

2. André Gabor, "In Memorium: Dennis Gabor, 1900–1979," *New Hungarian Quarterly*, Winter 1984, No. 96.

3. Dennis Gabor, "A New Microscopic Principle," *Nature*, 1948, vol. 164, pp. 777–8.

4. André Gabor, correspondence, April, 1984.

5. *Aspects of Quantum Theory*, Salam and Wigner, eds., Cambridge University Press, 1972, p. 59.

6. Ambrose Bierce, "The Damned Thing," in *Can Such Things Be?*, p. 147; reprinted with permission of Citadel Press.

7. James Clerk Maxwell, "Preface to the First Edition," *A Treatise on Electricity and Magnetism*, 1873.

8. IBID.

9. Isaac Newton, *Optics*, Book I: Part 1, Proposition 1, Theorem 1, Experiment 2.

10. IBID., Book III: Part 1, Question 3.

11. Gustav Kirchhoff, *Researches on the Solar Spectrum and the Spectra of the Chemical Elements*, 1863.

12. Dennis Gabor, "Holography, 1948–1971," *Science*, 28 July 1972, vol. 177, p. 313.

13. L.S. Bartell, correspondence, April, 1974.

14. André Gabor, "In Memorium, Dennis Gabor."

GLOSSARY

A

absorption—the act of taking up energy; atoms become more energetic when they absorb light

absorption hologram—one that takes up selected parts of the viewing light so that the rest can go into making the image

acoustic hologram—one made up of a sound wave interference pattern

AM radio—amplitude-modulation radio; a radio signal whose message exists in variations of carrier wave intensity (contrast with **FM radio**)

amplify—to increase, make stronger

amplitude—a measure of the maximum displacement of a wave or vibrating particle; the height of a wave crest or depth of a trough, as measured from the wave cycle's mid-point

antenna—a metal device for sending and receiving electromagnetic signals; a radio wave sensor

atom—the smallest bit of matter that has the characteristics of an element

autocorrelation—in pattern recognition, a perfect or nearly perfect match between two sets of features

axis—a straight line dividing an object or group of objects into similar parts; a line about which a body rotates or can be imagined to rotate

B

bandwidth—a measure of wavelengths included in a portion of the spectrum

beam—a collection of light rays moving in the same direction

beamsplitter—a partially transparent mirror that divides a light beam by reflecting some of it and transmitting the rest

Benton, Stephen—inventor of the rainbow, or white light transmission hologram

bleaching—an extra step in film development in which opaque silver atoms are converted to transparent compounds

Bohr atom—the first model of atomic structure to represent the mechanism by which atoms absorb and emit quanta

C

carrier wave—the coherent electromagnetic wave that's superimposed with a message wave for transmission; in holography, the laser reference beam acts as a carrier wave for recording phase differences among object waves

centi- —prefix meaning one-hundredth

chromatic aberration—a lens distortion caused by a difference in refractive index for various wavelengths; such a lens disperses white light into colors—a prism does this very well

cipher—in this book, a synonym for code

cm—centimeter(s)

code—a method of converting a message into another form according to certain rules; the holographic code is a record of the interference of reference and object beams

coherence—a property of waves that oscillate in unison because their lengths and phases are identical (see spatial coherence, temporal coherence)

coherence length—the difference in the distances over which two or more parts of a laser beam can travel and still remain spatially coherent

collimate—to make parallel

collimating mirror (or lens)—a optical device for producing a laser beam of plane wavefronts and parallel sides

color—the name given to a certain visible light wavelength or range of wavelengths

compound—a chemical combination of two or more atoms or ions; matter made up of molecules

compress—to make more dense or compact; to push the particles of a gas closer together

computer-generated hologram—a hologram of a non-existent or absent object, made by calculating a multiple stereogram or plotting and printing the fringes of an interference pattern

concave—having a surface curved like the inside of a sphere

concentric—having the same center, such as circles or spheres one inside the next

conjugate—near-twin, one that's identical except for an opposite relationship

continuous wave laser—a device for producing an uninter-
rupted beam of coherent light

contour reversal—the inversion of foreground and background
in a typical holographic real image, turning its surface inside
out

converge—to approach a common point; a converging light
beam becomes steadily narrower

convex—having a surface curved like the outside of a sphere

cornea—the hard, refractive outer surface of the eyeball, covering the lens

corpuscles—Newton's particles of light

correlation—a relationship between quantities or things

correlation peak—a spot of light indicating a similarity between two sets of features, produced by a holographic pattern
recognition system

crest—the high point of a wave, the point of maximum positive
energy value

cross correlation—in pattern recognition, the absence of a similarity between two sets of features

current—electrons oscillating in or flowing through a conductor

cycle—one complete journey through all phases of an oscillation

D

decode/decipher—to apply the rules needed to change a code
back to the original message

demodulate—to separate a message wave from a carrier wave

Denisyuk, Y.N.—inventor of the white-light reflection hologram

development (film)—the process of amplifying the latent image
in an exposed emulsion

dichromated gelatin (DCG) hologram—a hologram that uses a
mixture of gelatin, water, and ammonium dichromate as an
emulsion

diffraction—the bending of light waves as they pass the edge of
an obstacle

diffraction grating—a surface covered with fine, close-set parallel lines or slits, which disperse white light into colors by reflection or diffraction

diffuse—widely spread or scattered; a rough surface makes a
diffuse reflection, which is just a glow with no detail

disperse—to separate light into component wavelengths

diverge—to leave from a real or apparent common point; a diverging beam becomes steadily wider

double-exposure—a record of two overlapping images on a piece of film

dynamic hologram—reflection hologram made from a material that responds instantly to an ever-changing object beam; the reflected wavefront is phase-conjugated (see optical phase conjugation)

E

electric field—space containing an electric charge at every point

electricity—a flow of electrons in a conductor

electromagnetism—the theory that radiation, such as visible light, consists of an electric field and a magnetic field oscillating in unison, perpendicular to each other and to the direction of propagation, or travel

electron—the subatomic particle that carries the negative electric charge

electron hologram—a hologram made with electron waves rather than visible light

electron microscope—a device that uses electron waves to produce a magnified image with a greater degree of resolution than is possible with visible light

electron waves—a beam of electrons that behaves more like a wave than a stream of particles

e-m—electromagnetic

emit—to release or give off

emulsion—the photosensitive coating on a piece of film

ether—the substance some believed responsible for the transmission of light, now known not to exist

encode/encipher—to apply the rules needed to change a message into a code

F

fiber holoptics—in this book, holography using optical fibers to guide reference and object beams

field—a volume of space having a particular detectable force at every point

film—a piece of plastic or glass coated with a photosensitive emulsion

filter—a device for separating wavelengths by absorbing and transmitting them selectively

first-order—one of a pair of effects, such as an interference fringe or a diffracted wavefront, that occurs immediately on either side of a central, or zero-order, effect

FM radio—frequency-modulation radio; a radio signal whose message exists in variations of carrier wave frequencies (contrast with **AM radio**)

focal plane—area on which a lens or mirror focuses all parallel light rays

focal point—a spot on the axis of a lens or mirror system to which parallel rays converge or from which they appear to diverge

focus—to make an image sharp and clear with an optical system

frequency—the number of cycles per unit of time

Fresnel zone plate—a mechanically drawn zone plate

fringe—an area of constructive or destructive interference

G

Gabor zone plate—a zone plate made from the pattern formed by a spherical wave interfering with a plane wave

grain—a collection of photosensitive molecules in an emulsion

ground state—an atom's preferred, lowest energy level

H

half wavelength—the distance from a wave crest to a neighboring trough

hertz (Hz)—one cycle per second, named after Heinrich Hertz, who demonstrated the existence of radio waves

HeNe—Helium and Neon

hologram—a device that uses the interference of monochromatic object and reference waves to record and reproduce multiple 2-D images of an object for a 3-D view

holograph—(verb) to make a hologram of; not to be confused with the noun holograph, which means a document written in the handwriting of the person who signed it

holographic interferogram—a method of measuring tiny surface displacements with superimposed holographic images

holographic optical element (HOE)—a hologram used as a lens, mirror, or diffraction grating

holographic stereogram—a conventional movie whose frames have been converted to thin vertical holograms; when arranged in a cylinder, an observer sees separate images for an illusion of depth and motion

hyperbola—one of a pair of curves formed by points of constructive interference between two overlapping sets of circular wavefronts

hyperboloid—a 3–D surface formed by a hyperbola spun on its axis

I

image—in this book, what the eye detects (contrast with **view**)

image deblurring—the improvement of an image's focus by holographic or other means

image plane hologram—a hologram of a holographic image, so called because this hologram rests within the image it forms

in phase—a condition in which waves oscillate in unison

incident light—light striking a surface

incoherent—disordered; incoherent light consists of many different wavelengths or phase relationships

induce—to cause an electric or magnetic effect

infrared—long-wave radiation immediately beyond the red end of the visible spectrum; we sense infrared as radiated heat

intensity—a measure of electromagnetic force in a field

interference—the reinforcement (constructive) or cancellation (destructive) of amplitudes when two waves overlap

interferometry—a means of highly accurate measurement using interference fringes

inverse—turned upside down or reversed

ion—an atom or molecule having more or fewer electrons than usual, in other words, an atom or molecule with an electric charge

iris—the structure that expands or contracts to regulate the amount of light entering the eye

J

Jeong, Tung H.—inventor of the 360-degree hologram

L

laser—acronym for "light amplification by stimulated emission of radiation"; a device that produces a concentrated beam of coherent light

latent image—the invisible record of a photographic image before development of the emulsion

Leith, Emmett—co-inventor of the off-axis hologram

lens—a device for redirecting electromagnetic radiation by refraction

light—that portion of the electromagnetic spectrum, from ap-
proximately 380 nanometers to 760 nm, which the human
eye can detect as the colors of the spectrum from violet to red

Lippmann, Gabriel—inventor of a color photographic process
that used an interference pattern similar to that of a reflection
hologram

longitudinal wave—a wave whose direction of oscillation is
parallel to its direction of propagation

M

magnetic field—space around a magnet or electric current containing magnetic force at every point

maser—acronym for "microwave amplification by stimulated
emission of radiation"

master hologram—a hologram used to make another hologram

medium—the substance through which waves travel

microwaves—electromagnetic waves longer than infrared and
shorter than radio waves

milli- —prefix meaning one-thousandth

mirror—a device that redirects radiation by reflection

mm—millimeter(s)

modulate—to superimpose a message wave on a carrier wave

molecule—two or more atoms or ions bound together chemi-
cally

monochromatic—"one color"; a narrow bandwidth of radiation

mw—milliwatt(s)

N

nano- —prefix meaning one-billionth

nm—nanometer(s)

Newton's rings—an interference pattern formed when light is
partially reflected from the surfaces of a film or from stacked
glass surfaces

node—a point of zero amplitude in a standing wave

noise—undesirable effects of light scattered within an emulsion; noise obscures image information

normal—an imaginary line perpendicular to a surface

nucleus—the massive, positively charged portion of an atom
around which electrons orbit

O

object beam—the portion of the laser beam reflected from an object to the holographic film

on-axis hologram—a hologram that produces virtual and real images along a straight line through the center of the interference pattern

opaque—unable to transmit light

optics—the study of light; also, devices that manipulate light

optical fiber—a thin glass strand, or bundle of strands, that serves as a pathway for light

optical phase conjugation—creation of a copy beam of light traveling in the opposite direction with the opposite phase as the original, as if the original beam had been made to travel backward in time

orthoscopic—"normal-looking," said of a holographic image, usually virtual, that looks the same as the original object (contrast with **pseudoscopic**)

oscillate—vibrate, swing back and forth between extremes in a regular cycle

P

parallax—an apparent change in an object's position with respect to its surroundings with a shift in the viewer's line of sight

parallel—the state of being for two lines or planes that are an equal distance apart at all points

pattern recognition—the process of finding a match between different sets of features

perpendicular—forming a 90-degree angle

phase—a stage of a cycle or the relationship between two waves, which is often expressed in degrees—two waves are "in phase" when they have 0° of phase difference and "out of phase" when they have a phase difference to any other degree

phase hologram—a hologram that forms an image when viewing light passes through variations in the density of the recording material; differences in density mean differences in refraction

phenomenon—an observable event

photoelectric effect—the release of electrons from a metal's surface when illuminated by radiation of a certain frequency or higher

photon—a light quantum

pinhole—a small opening, often used with a converging lens, that eliminates laser light scattered by dust and other impurities in its path

Planck's constant—6.63×10^{-34} *joules-seconds*, a quantity that relates a photon's energy with its frequency

plane—a flat surface

plane hologram—one whose diffractive effects are mainly at the surface of the emulsion

point source—a light-emitting body so far away or so small that light rays from it can be considered parallel

Poisson's bright spot—the hole in the center of a circular shadow, formed by monochromatic light diffracted inward from all edges of a round object

polarizer—any material that blocks electromagnetic waves oscillating in all but one plane

population inversion—a condition necessary for lasing action, in which more atoms reside at a level of excitation than remain in the ground state

primary color—one of three wavelengths from which all colors can be generated

prism—a wedge of glass that disperses light into its various wavelengths

propagate—to move or cause to move through a medium or through space

pseudoscopic—"false-looking," said of holographic images, usually real, that exhibit contour reversal (contrast with **orthoscopic**)

pulse—a short, wavelike disturbance

pulsed laser—one that generates coherent light in brief bursts

pupil—the opening in the eye's iris

Q

quantum—an indivisible bundle of energy

quipu—an Incan recordkeeping device consisting of knots in colored strings

R

radar—a method of measuring distances by radio wave echoes

radio waves—radiation from the longest wavelength, lowest frequency end of the electromagnetic spectrum

radiate—to spread out in all directions

rainbow hologram—a kind of image plane hologram viewable in white light; it sacrifices vertical parallax for colored images—also called a white light transmission hologram

rarefy—to make less dense; to allow the particles of a gas to spread farther apart

ray—a line indicating the direction of propagation of light waves or wavefronts; a representation of a single light wave

real image—an image consisting of light focused in space

redundancy—the property of a hologram by which it records image information about a single object point in all parts of its interference pattern that receive light from that point

reference beam—that portion of a laser beam that goes directly to the holographic film; it's the background against which object wave phase differences become information an emulsion can record

reflection—the "rebounding" of light at a surface

reflection hologram—one that reconstructs an image by reflected light, with the reconstructing light source and the viewer on the same side of the hologram

refraction—redirection of light as it crosses the boundary between two transparent media

refractive index—the ratio of the speed of light in a vacuum to its speed in a certain substance

resolving power—the ability of an optical system or recording material to distinguish between details

resonance—the strengthening of certain frequencies in a vibrating system when stimulated by outside forces at related frequencies

retina—the light-sensitive inside surface of the eyeball

reversibility—the ability of light waves to follow the same path from point B to point A as they did from A to B

S

scattering—the formation of visual noise from unwanted reflections within an emulsion

signal-to-noise ratio—the ratio of image information to meaningless and disruptive effects such as scatter

silver halide—any of several photo-sensitive silver compounds

spatial—having to do with space

spatial coherence—a measure of the degree to which light waves in a beam oscillate "in step," or in phase

spectroscope—a device for dispersing light to study its component wavelengths

spectrum—the distribution of wavelengths in light from a given source

specular—like a mirror, not diffuse

speed (film)—a description of the rate at which an emulsion can record a suitable latent image

speed of light—in a vacuum, about 3×10^8 meters per second

spontaneous emission—the release of a quantum when an atom drops by itself from an unstable high energy level to a lower, more stable one

standing wave pattern—the interference pattern formed when two waves of the same frequency and amplitude pass through the same medium in opposite directions

stereogram—a double photograph taken from two positions as far apart as the distance between the eyes, viewed with a device to separate the images for each eye and copy the effect of binocular vision

stimulated emission—the release of two identical quanta when one passes through an excited atom

superimposition—the overlapping of two waves

T

temporal—having to do with time

temporal coherence—a measure of the degree to which light waves are monochromatic, that is, of identical wavelength

three-dimensional (3-D)—having length, width, and depth

360-degree hologram—a single exposure transmission hologram that provides a view from all sides

Townes, Charles—co-inventor of the maser and laser (with Nikolai Basov and Aleksander Prochorov of the USSR, who shared the Nobel Prize with Townes for independent work)

transmission hologram—one that forms an image from the light passing through the holographic emulsion, with the reconstructing light source and the viewer on opposite sides of the hologram

transparent—able to transmit light and images; clear

transverse wave—one whose direction of oscillation is perpendicular to its direction of propagation

trough—the low point of a transverse wave

two-dimensional (2-D)—having length and width, but not depth

U

ultraviolet—short-wave radiation immediately beyond the violet end of the visible spectrum, the "sun-tanning rays"

Upatnieks, Juris—co-inventor of the off-axis hologram

V

vacuum—space emptied of all matter

vibrate—oscillate, move back and forth rapidly

view—in this book, what the brain makes out of visual information (contrast with **image**)

virtual image—one formed by diverging light waves that seem to emerge from a point, but which do not actually exist at that point

volume hologram—one whose diffractive and refractive effects extend throughout an emulsion

W

wave—an oscillating disturbance—the form of vibration or oscillation a particle or quantity of energy takes as it is propagated

wave train—a series of identical waves

wavefront—the two- or three-dimensional shape formed by wave points of identical phase, usually thought of as wave crests

wavefront reconstruction—the reproduction of an image in three dimensions from a recording of wavelength, amplitude, and phase information in the waves of the original image

wavelength—the distance from one point in a wave cycle to the corresponding point of the next cycle

wavelet—a small wave, whose leading edge combines with those of neighboring wavelets to form a wavefront, from Huygens's theory of light propagation

white light—radiation that contains most of the wavelengths in the visible spectrum

X

X-ray—radiation shorter than ultraviolet and longer than cosmic rays

Z

zero-order—an effect, such as an interference fringe, that exists on an axis; when illuminating a hologram, the central, zero-order wavefront consists of light the hologram doesn't diffract or refract into an image

zone plate—a "bull's eye" pattern of concentric opaque and transparent rings so constructed as to act as a converging lens and a diverging lens at the same time

FURTHER READING

Use this reading list as a starting point for further study of holography and related topics.

Asimov, Isaac. *Asimov's Biographical Encyclopedia of Science.* New York: Doubleday and Co., Inc., 2nd rev. ed., 1982.
    Lively capsule biographies of members of Gabor's "Holo-fame" and more than 1,000 others. After style, book's best feature is detailed cross-referencing, which shows how individuals influenced each other. Index.

Engdahl, Sylvia, and Roberson, Rick. *The Sub-Nuclear Zoo.* New York: Atheneum Publishers, 1977.
    Clearly written introduction to the world within the atom. A lot has happened since book was published, so follow with another more recent, such as Sutton's. Index.

Faraday, Michael. *The Chemical History of a Candle: Six Illustrated Lectures with Notes and Experiments.* Chicago: Chicago Review, 1980.
    More than 100 years ago at the Royal Institution in London, Faraday regularly delivered Christmas lectures for young people. This series about the common candle is a classic demonstration of the joys of curiosity.

Haines, George. *The Young Photographer's Handbook.* New York: Arco Publishing, Inc., 1984.
    Nice introduction to photography, with many beautiful examples in color. Index.

Hecht, Jeff, and Teresi, Dick. *Laser, Supertool of the 1980s.* New York: Ticknor & Fields, 1982.
    How lasers came to be, how they work, and how they have changed our lives. Too bad there's no index.

Hellman, Hal. *The Art and Science of Color.* New York: McGraw-Hill Book Co., 1967.
Causes and effects of color, from the measurable to the psychological. Index, reading list.

Kasper, Joseph E., and Feller, Steven A. *The Hologram Book.* Englewood Cliffs, NJ: Prentice-Hall, Inc., 1985
An explanation of holography that goes beyond the topics in this book. Index, reading list.

Klein, H. Arthur. *Holography, with an Introduction to the Optics of Diffraction, Interference, and Phase Differences.* Philadelphia: J. B. Lippincott Co., 1970.
Despite the imposing title, an elegant explanation of the basics. Technical information well-tempered with storyteller's art, such as anecdote about Gabor's holographic pen pal. Index.

Pringle, Laurence. *Radiation: Waves and Particles/Benefits and Risks.* Hillside, NJ: Enslow Publishers, 1983.
Brief but wide-ranging and honest look at ways radiation works for us in medicine, industry, and research—and against us, often with our help. Index, glossary, reading list.

Silverberg, Robert. *Men Who Mastered the Atom.* New York: G.P. Putnam's Sons, 1965
____*Niels Bohr, the Man Who Mapped the Atom.* Macrae Smith Co., 1965.
Engaging accounts of lives and work of scientists who revealed much about atom's structure and forces. Both with index, bibliography.

Tannenbaum, Beulah, and Stillman, Myra. *Isaac Newton: Pioneer of Space Mathematics.* New York: McGraw-Hill Book Co., 1959.
Newton's life—boy, student, and great thinker with his rivals. Fictionalized dialogue kept to a minimum. Index.

Unterseher, Fred, and Hansen, Jeannene, and Schlesinger, Bob. *Holography Handbook: Making Holograms the Easy Way.* Berkeley, CA: Ross Books, 1982.
Useful even if you don't have a laser lab in your basement. Plentiful illustrations reinforce basic concepts of holography. Theory section is weak and might confuse rather than enlighten. Presumably second edition will correct this. Index, glossary, bibliography.

Wenyon, Michael. *Understanding Holography.* New York: Arco Publishing, 1978.
Another description of holographic basics and applications. Index, bibliography.

EVEN FURTHER
READING

Interested readers can learn more about the technical side of holography and the physics behind it from the following books. Holographic art and science are changing so rapidly, however, it's helpful to refer to certain magazines, too.

Laser Focus is a monthly available through most universities. Try the engineering or physics libraries.

holosphere is the quarterly journal of the Museum of Holography, 11 Mercer St., New York, NY 10013. Besides scientific articles, the magazine gives details about holography workshops, traveling exhibitions, and so on. The museum membership entitles you to a subscription.

Bernstein, Jeremy. *Einstein*. New York: Penguin Press, 1976.
Probably no scientist has had more books written about him than Albert Einstein. This one is enjoyable, with a friendly style, and not too technical. Index, reading list.

Cline, Barbara Lovett. *The Questioners: Physicists and the Quantum Theory*. New York: Thomas Y. Crowell Co., 1965.
Planck, Einstein, Bohr, Dirac, and others as scientists and individuals in a lively account of the laying of a new foundation of physics. Index, reading list.

Gribbin, John. *In Search of Schrödinger's Cat: Quantum Physics and Reality*. New York: Bantam Books, Inc., 1984.
Believing that "the best things in science are both beautiful and simple," the author explains quantum theory for nonscientists. Index, bibliography, and science fiction reading list.

Gabor, Dennis. *Inventing the Future.* New York: Alfred Knopf, 1964
——*The Mature Society.* New York: Praeger Publishers, Inc., 1972
——*Innovations: Scientific, Technological, and Social.* Oxford: Oxford University Press, 1970.
Gabor devoted much of his inventive genius to the question of humanity's future. Here he speculates on the threats to survival and the means to prosperity. All have indexes and many references to other books.

Hedgecoe, John. *The Photographer's Handbook, A Complete Reference Manual of Photographic Techniques, Procedures, Equipment and Style.* New York: Alfred A. Knopf, 1980.
Much more technical and complete than Haines, and impossible to page through without stopping. Index, glossary, more than 1,000 drawings and photos—many in color and all fascinating.

Jeong, Tung H. *A Study Guide on Holography.* Lake Forest, IL: INTE-GRAF, 1975.
A concise laboratory manual by the originator of the hyperboloid geometric model, with a hint of the "rigorous mathematics" involved in serious holography.

Kock, Winston E.. *Lasers and Holography: An Introduction to Coherent Optics.* Mineola, NY: Dover Publications, Inc., rev. ed., 1981.
Author used holographic principles to record microwave patterns in 1951 without realizing the connection until later. Compare Kock's setup in his Fig. 15 with this book's Fig. 13–6. Clear, concise explanation of theory. Index, reading list of more technical classics.

Sutton, Christine. *The Particle Connection.* New York: Simon and Schuster, 1984.
Good follow-up to Engdahl/Roberson book, more technical. Reading list, but lacks an index.

Tyndall, John. *Faraday as a Discoverer.* New York: Thomas Y. Crowell Co., 1961.
Originally published in 1868, these lectures describe Faraday's major experiments, including magnetization of light. They also show Faraday as a man highly respected by his peers.

Waldman, Gary. *Introduction to Light: The Physics of Light, Vision, and Color.* Englewood Cliffs, NJ: Prentice-Hall, Inc., 1983.
Well-written college textbook that brings other explanations about light into better mental focus. Index.

INDEX

PICTURE CREDITS

Fig. No.   *Credit/Source*

1–1   Courtesy Juris Upatnieks, Environmental Research Institute of Michigan.
1–2a,b   *Golden Amphora.* Courtesy Dr. Tung H. Jeong, Lake Forest College. (Author's photos.)
1–3   *Lasers and Holography* by Winston E. Kock, 1981 Dover
and   Publications, NY. Used with permission of the publisher.
1–5
1–4a,b   Reprinted with permission from McDonnell Douglas Electronics Company. (Author's photos.)
1–6a,b   Telephone with Lens #1. Courtesy Dr. Tung H. Jeong, Lake Forest College. (Author's photos.)
1–7a,b   Telephone with Lens #2. Courtesy Dr. Tung H. Jeong, Lake Forest College. (Author's photos.)
1–8a,b   Movie Theatre.[1] Dan Schweitzer 1978. Collection of the artist. Photo: Ronald R. Erickson.
1–9   Courtesy of André Gabor.
1–10   Reprinted with permission from McDonnell Douglas Electronics Company.
2–3   Author's photo.
2–4   Author's photo.
2–5a,b   Portrait of a Young Woman. Courtesy of Dr. Tung H. Jeong, Lake Forest College. (Author's photos.)
2–6   Reprinted with permission from *An Introduction to Coherent Optics and Holography* by George W. Stroke, 1969, Academic Press, Inc.
3–1   "The Meeting." Rick Silberman 1979. 8″ × 10″. Collection: Museum of Holography. Photo: Ronald R. Erickson.
3–2   Author's photo.
3–3   Author's photo.
3–4a,b   Author's hologram and photos.
3–5   Hologram courtesy of Museum/School of the Fine Arts Research & Holographic Center. Photo by Terrence Kasper.
3–6   Courtesy of Cameron Knox, Ph.D., TRW Space & Technology Group.

285